Rasta Heart:

A Journey Into One Love

by
Robert Roskind

One Love Press
P.O. Box 2142
Blowing Rock, North Carolina, USA
(828) 295-4610 FAX: (828) 294-6901
email: roskind@boone.net
Website: www.rastaheart.com

Books By Robert Roskind

Miracle in Jamaica Series

Rasta Heart: A Journey Into One Love

The Gathering of the Healers: The Healing of the Nation

The Beauty Path: A Native American Journey Into One Love

Other Books

Memoirs of an Ex-Hippie: Seven Years In The Counterculture

*2012: The Transformation from the Love of Power
to the Power of Love*

In The Spirit Of Marriage

In The Spirit of Business

Building Your Own House

I-dication

This book is I-dicated to the Rastas of Jamaica. Thank you for holding the light so long and so strong.

Acknowledgments

To my wife, Julia, for her insights, wisdom and companionship on this journey;

To Scram for being our guide, our friend, our brother and our co-worker;

To my daughter, Alicia, for opening her heart to everyone and being so much fun;

To my daughter, Julie, for always showing me an example of One Love;

To my editors, Natalie Foreman and JD Dooley, for their suggestions, insights, corrections and encouragement and Jeannie C. Parker for proof reading and polishing the jewel;

To Robert Davie for his support and willingness to keep his heart open;

To Jonathan Gullery for a fiery cover;

To Clive Panton for helping me begin this odyssey;

To all the people in this book, Scram, Renny, Trevor Munroe, Dennis Forsythe, Marcia Henry, Bell, Irman, Bongo Roach, Red, JAH Priest, JAH LandSea, Red, Kevin Pauling, Bookson, George, Wallace and Ray Sterling, Blood, JAH T, and Ras Thomas, who contributed their information and wisdom.

Preface

In this book we are going to go on a journey together, not just a physical journey but a spiritual odyssey as well. We are going to take several trips to Jamaica to meet a few Rastas. I can tell you that we will be changed by this journey. You cannot spend time with these people, either in person or through these pages, and not be profoundly touched and transformed by your association with them. I have seldom, if ever, witnessed a faith or belief system that brings the joy, health, clarity and wisdom that Rastafari does.

Before we begin our journey there are three questions I want to briefly address even though they are answered in full in the book. The three questions are: "What is Rastafari?" "Who is Bob Marley?" and "What is the goal of this book?"

Dr. Vernon Carrington, a Rasta leader and founder of The Twelve Tribes of Israel sect describes Rastafari as follows:

"It is up to each and every one to find the right path in this time. Rastafari is not a faith which can be converted to, in the sense that one can convert to Christianity. There is no one day which someone wakes up and says, 'I think I'll become a Rastafarian.' Rastafari is a way of life which has to be lived.

The feeling of the spirit is like a wave traveling through the soul. A

1

wave which only reveals itself stage after stage. Rastafari is a life, and as in life, you learn as you live. No one person can say, 'This is exactly what the Rastafari doctrine is,' because the beauty of the faith is that it is seen through the eyes of the beholder, not through the eyes of a priest, vicar or pope.

When one declares themselves to any faith, people will always ask them, 'How long have you been a ....?' In the case of Rastafari, people don't realize how complex this question is. How long? When was the exact point of realizing my true life's foundation?...

As you grow, you learn certain things and your eyes open just that little bit wider. It's the same thing with Rastafari. It's not a doctrine which people have to memorize and recite in mantra or a text on which we will be tested. The test is how we live our life, with Rastafari in our hearts... Rasta is a philosophy which reveals itself in stages; a feeling, a vibe, a science, a quote, an ideology, a picture, an outlook, a history, a life... Rastafari is about learning. We realize that life has many mysteries and JAH (God) lets us know as much as we need to know at any given time. This is how we learn...

It is this outlook to which Rastafari becomes more than a doctrine, religion or even faith; it is a way of life which, like life itself, continues to grow in mind, body and spirit... Rasta is not a hair doctrine or a race doctrine, it is a doctrine which it so pure it is open to be embraced by anyone and everyone, regardless of appearance."[1]

Many Rastas live in Jamaica, a tropical paradise, with few worldly possessions and little contact with our commercialized world, the world of Babylon—where nothing is free. They eat mostly organic fruits and vegetables and practice a faith of universal love for all humanity—One Love. On our journey we will experience some of the joy and clarity this lifestyle has awakened in them.

Years ago, Rastas were persecuted by the Jamaican government and society and to some degree they still are. Almost anyone wearing dread-locks (long mats of washed, but uncombed, hair) does so as a testament to their faith. Now that Rastas are becoming respected and are a draw for many tourists, many "wolves" in Jamaica are now wearing real or fake dreads, to exploit this interest. We have bypassed these and sought those who are reaching high, the ones who are expressing One Love.

That JAH wanted Rasta beliefs to be understood and embraced worldwide is clear. He chose Bob Marley as its messenger. It would be hard to imagine a more powerful medium. His music is a global drumming, calling together an international tribe of people to manifest universal love of all humanity.

Consider the following: Over 300 million of his records, tapes and CDs have been sold worldwide. His album, Exodus, was chosen by Time magazine in 1999 as "Album of the Century." The New York Times wrote, "Marley is the most influential artist of the second half of the 20th century" and when they chose one video to epitomize the past century to be preserved in a time capsule, they chose Bob Marley Live at the Rainbow, London, 1977. His song "One Love" was chosen as the "Anthem of the Millennium" by the BBC.

He could draw 180,000 in Milan one night and 100,000 in Dublin the next. On one six-month, twelve-city tour, he performed for more than a million fans. From 1976 until his death in 1981, his concerts were sold out wherever he appeared, especially in Third World countries, where his appearance was seen as a symbol of hope for eventual liberation from tyranny and poverty. He also has a strong following in places such as South and Central America, Germany, Japan, the Netherlands, Europe and the United States.

The Havasupai Indians, who have lived in near isolation for centuries on the floor of the Grand Canyon in the United States, listen to him almost exclusively. In the early 1970s, film director Jo Menell, visited the Havasupais, while making a documentary on Marley. He said, "They have listened to everything Bob ever sang and everybody down there has a small tape recorder and there is always a Bob Marley tape in that. They actually believe that Bob is a prophet and that he is alive and talking to them."[2]

His appearance in New York's Central Park Schaefer Music Festival caused a near riot when he left the stage, a problem that was later repeated at many of his concerts. In the 1970s, on one of his first tours in the U.S., he performed as a warmup act for the then-popular Sly and the Family Stone. After several shows, Sly had him removed from the tour, knowing it was impossible for him to top Marley's commanding performance. To honor Marley, Stevie Wonder, then the most popular star in the Third World, approached Bob about performing with him in Kingston. The benefit concert, on October 11, 1975, was the last time the original Wailers played together (Bob Marley, Peter Tosh and Bunny Livingston). Soon after, Bob replaced Wonder as the Third World's most popular superstar. Wonder's popular song "Master Blaster" is dedicated to Bob.

In 1978 he was awarded the Third World Peace Medal by the United Nations. His song "Zimbabwe" was the rallying song for the freedom fighters in that country as they fought for, and eventually won, their independence from England. As the Third World's first superstar, he was asked to perform in 1980 at the Zimbabwe Independence celebration in front of 40,000 fans, the only foreign entertainer to do so. Bob's song "No Woman No Cry" is still sung as a lullaby by Third World people everywhere.

Though there have been other international mega-stars like Elvis Presley, Michael Jackson, Madonna and Elton John, and even a few, like The Beatles and Bob Dylan, who wrote, and sang, their own songs to carry a message, none compare with the impact of Marley. As Roger Steffens noted in his recent article on Marley on the PBS's February 2001 Website,". . . you don't see thousands of Maori and Tongans and Fijians gathering annually to pay honor to Louis Armstrong; you don't witness phalanxes of youths wandering the world sporting Louis Armstrong t-shirts. In fact, big as the Beatles were, you hardly see any Beatle shirts around anymore, except for those few featuring John Lennon's sorrow-inducing visage. Can you imagine an image of Elvis sewn onto the sleeve of an armed guerrilla? When was the last time you saw a Michael Jackson flag or a Bob Dylan sarong or Madonna rolling papers? All of these exist in Marleyite forms, his iconography well nigh a new universal language, the symbol, as Jack Healey of Amnesty International continues to tell people, of freedom throughout the world."

Though we had not planned it this way, the book is really divided into two parts. In the first part, our trips to Jamaica were centered around discovering the core philosophy, lifestyle and history of the

Rastafarians. In a way this was the theory for One Love, the class work if you will. In the second part, the lab work, explores our attempts to apply this knowledge to real life relationships. During this part of the book various individuals, and an ancient mystery, were introduced into our odyssey so that we could put One Love into practice. In looking back, each of these individuals seem to represent an "archetype" of the various relationships we all struggle with on our journey to One Love.

—Robert Roskind
Blowing Rock, October. 2001

Author's note: All the reasonings in this book are verbatim, taken directly from our video footage. Some of the reasonings can be viewed on www.YouTube.com. Just search under "Robert Roskind."

Suggested artists to listen to while reading this book:

Luciano	Ziggy Marley
Morgan Heritage	Deserie
Abijah	Pato Banton
Burning Spear	Inner Visions
Beres Hammond	Culture
Bushman	Bunny Wailer
Ernie Smith	Prezident Brown
Tony Rebel	Lucky Dube
Midnite	Warrior King
Kymani Marley	Mackie Conscious

---

1. Interview with Dr. Vernon Carrington (The Beloved PROPHET GAD), July 13th,1997 on Jamaican radio station IRIE FM's Running Africa.
2. Malika Lee Whitney and Dermott Hussey, Bob Marley: Reggae King Of The World, (Kingston Publishing Limited, 1984), p.127, quoting an interview with Jo Menell.

Chapter 1

Rafting With Verley

"There's a natural mystic floating through the air. If you listen carefully now, you will hear"
—**Bob Marley**, Lyrics from "Natural Mystic"

Our journey began as a simple family vacation, nothing more. We had no idea it would lead to a series of events that would change all our lives forever. My wife, Julia, our fourteen-year old daughter, Alicia, our thirty-year old daughter, Julie, and I had decided on Jamaica. We had never visited the island but had heard many good stories from friends and relatives. After almost a year's work, I was just finishing up my latest book and was looking forward to a pleasant intrusion into my otherwise hermit-like author's existence. I was also pondering my life's next step.

I searched the Net and discovered a great package deal for flights and rooms at Club Jamaica, a hotel in Ocho Rios. On the beach in the middle of downtown, the facility was relaxed and within walking distance of shopping areas and nightclubs. Our vacation drifted by slowly and pleasantly. Our days were spent laying around the pool, shopping, parasailing, riding jet skis and snorkeling. It was a typical vacation to a Caribbean island.

However, throughout the week we had noticed that several of the waiters at the hotel emanated a kind of calm certainty and kindness. All of us had been impressed by this quality and had remarked about it many times among ourselves. I had even asked two of our waiters about their spiritual

1

Rasta Heart

path, knowing this type of peace is seldom obtainable without one. At first they laughed and avoided the question, telling us that the management did not allow them to discuss politics or religion with the guests. Finally, they confided in us that they were Rastafarians who had cut their hair in order to get their jobs. I had heard of the Rastafarians but only knew the basics, mainly that they were very spiritual, smoked ganja (marijuana) and wore dreadlocks.

For the last day, I made plans for Julia and I to take a ten-hour excursion to visit some sights near Port Antonio, an oceanside town about two hours east. The tour included a stop at the Blue Lagoon, a lush 140-foot deep aqua green grotto, lunch on a secluded beach at Frenchman's Cove and the grand finale, a three-hour rafting trip down the Rio Grande River.

The tour company picked us up at the hotel around eight in the morning. The 15-person mini-bus was filled with young English and Australian tourists. We were the last pickup and the only seats available were the two front seats. The seating allowed Julia and I to quickly become friends with the female tour guide, Perine, and the driver, John, both Jamaicans in their twenties.

As we talked during the tour, Perine and John told us they also were Rastas. As we drove to Port Antonio, Perine and John told us about their faith. I was impressed with how effectively this way of life seemed to be creating joy and peace. Julia and I have been spiritual seekers most of our adult lives, studying both traditional and non-traditional spiritual paths. Our search had produced many benefits. However, I was still impatient with the overall results.

After the swim in the Blue Lagoon and lunch at Frenchman's Cove, our bus drove up the mountains to the rafting area. A few minutes into the trip on the winding roads, Julia got car sick and asked John to pull over so that she could take a breather. After we reboarded, Perine told us not to worry, that once we got up to the rafts she had just what Julia needed.

Fifteen minutes later, we pulled into the small rafting office at Berridale. About twenty captains with their rafts were hanging around the river's edge. Perine told Julia and I to stay behind as she arranged for the other six couples to be assigned raft captains and we waited until they were out of sight around the first bend. Then she told the raft dispatcher that she wanted Verley Valentine as our captain. As we walked out to meet him, Perine handed Julia a small ganja spliff (the equivalent of a large marijuana

Rasta Heart

joint) and some matches.

"Wit' dis and Verley, yah will feel much bettah by de end of de trip. Ya see," she said with an impish grin.

Perine called his name and Verley came strolling out of the nearby bamboo thicket. They greeted each other warmly and chatted in patois, which is a mixture of Pidgin English plus some Rastafarian slang. Officially, English is the language of Jamaica but the island is really bilingual. Patois is more widely spoken, especially in the rural areas or by the poorer citizens. Often interspersed with witty proverbs and off-color idioms to outwit the listener, it is a very musical dialect, with its own unique rhythm and cadence. As one author has described it, Jamaicans talking sound pleasantly like a "child's ball bouncing down the stairs."

Since they were speaking patois, I had no idea what Verley and Perine said to each other but their laughter and smiles needed no translation. Verley had the face of a 50-year old and the trim muscular body of a man half that age. When he first walked out of the bamboo he looked a little serious but once he started to smile and laugh I knew he was a kind, gentle soul. He ushered us to the river's edge where his raft was tied and, like a king, assisted us on to his raft.

We waved goodbye to Perine and pushed off from the bank. Verley started to slowly pole us down the river. As we rounded the first bend I lit up the spliff. Smoking herb is rare for me and much rarer for Julia. Though I had smoked my share in the counterculture years of the 60s and 70s, now I only smoked a few times a year, mostly with friends. Julia, who has a strong reaction to almost any substance, had smoked herb maybe five times in her life. But, hey! We were in Jamaica poling down a drop-dead beautiful river through the majestic jungle-covered Blue Mountains.

The Rio Grande is crystal clear unless it's been raining. You can float for six miles through beautiful tropical rain forests on twenty-foot rafts made of large bamboo poles tied together by wire. There is a low bamboo chair toward the back that can hold two people, maybe three if one is a child. Each raft is guided by its captain, specially trained to take you down the usually slow-moving river.

"Hey, Verley, want a toke?" I asked after awhile.

"No, mon," he said turning toward us with a smile. "I used ta smoke eight spliffs a day but me quit two years ago."

"Why'd you quit?" Julia asked.

Rasta Heart

"I 'ad some stomach problems. I doan't t'ink it was because of de ganja but I quit smokin' and drinkin' alcohol because de doctor said ta. But it alright wit' me if yah smoke it. No problem, mon."

We all lapsed into a comfortable silence as Julia and I inhaled a few hits from our spliff, drifting along, enjoying the quiet and beauty of the surroundings with the ganja deepening the sense of peace. I soon learned Jamaican ganja is much more powerful than the marijuana commonly smoked in the States. The weed has been grown throughout the island since 1845 when it was brought there by indentured laborers from India. Though it was outlawed early on, it is estimated that over 60 percent of Jamaicans, from all social and economic strata, smoke it.

As we floated down the river, Verley gently began to sing a popular Harry Belafonte song from the 1950s, "Jamaica Farewell":

> *Down the way where the nights are gay*
> *And the sun shines daily on the mountain top*
> *I took a trip on a sailing ship*
> *And when I reach Jamaica I made a stop*

> *But I'm sad to say, I'm on my way*
> *Won't be back for many a day*
> *My heart is down, my head is turning around*
> *I had to leave a little girl in Kingston town*

He had a deep clear voice and blended seamlessly with the surroundings, more like hearing a native bird sing than a human. Julia and I quietly joined him and then we all drifted back into a silence broken only by the gentle lapping of the river against the bamboo raft.

"Yeah, mon," Verley said pointing ahead to a teenage boy holding up a coconut on the nearby shore. "Are yah thirsty?"

We drifted over to the bank and the coconut vendor. He and Verley chatted in patois while Julia and I drank the milk of a large coconut through a hole cut in the top. Unlike the coconuts found in most supermarkets, these have a lot of milk. After we finished the milk, Verley borrowed the vendor's machete and with a quick whip-like motion, cut open the coconut exposing the translucent jelly meat. Then he cut two rough spoons from the shell and showed us how to use them to scoop out the jelly. Refreshed, we continued down the river.

After awhile we came to an area where a large rock formation protruded out of the water. The main channel went to the left and a smaller channel went to the right, where it formed a moss-covered narrow canyon between the rock and the steep bank, about ten feet wide and twenty feet tall.

"Dis is Lovers Lane," Verley said, with a suggestive grin. "Errol Flynn named it dis and 'e came 'ere wit' many women. Most captains cayn't go t'rough de lane. But I cayn take ya. When we get in de middle, I turn me back and ya kiss," he said.

Verley poled us through the tunnel and I kissed Julia as we went through.

"Ev'ry day, mon, ya must renew ya love like dis," Verley said, turning back to look at us as we floated into the quiet pool on the other side of the lane. "If ya doan't renew ya love ev'ry day, it will nah stay de same or grow, mon. It will get less. Dat is why ev'ry day ya and yah wife must renew yah love. Ev'ry day me and my wife, we renew our love. We 'ave been married 26 years and we still love each ot'er very much. Ya see, mon needs womon and womon needs mon."

"Why do you say that, Verley?" Julia asked.

"Because in DE BEginnin'," he replied, raising his voice when he said "DE BEginnin'," so that you seem to experience "DE BEginnin'," "dere was mon and womon, as JAH made dem ta be toget'er. And if mon doan't 'ave a womon or if womon doan't 'ave a mon, den dere minds always be restless, nevah at peace, always looking for de ot'er." ("JAH" is the Rasta word for God. It is an abbreviation of Jehovah or Yahweh, the Hebrew word for God.)

Julia and I looked into each other's eyes and smiled. We continued to drift, eager to hear what Verley might come out with next. Around a few more bends, he spotted a man working in a small grove of banana trees. He and Verley conversed in patois until we drifted out of hearing range.

"What was that about?" I asked, curious about his everyday life.

"I buy some young banana suckers from 'im last week and I told 'im I pay 'im dis week," He said matter of factly. "About a month ago, de river flooded and it washed away all me crops and me goats. Now I must start a new garden so I buy de trees from 'im."

"That sounds pretty bad," Julia said. "Is that the first time that the river flooded your land?"

Rasta Heart

"Dis is a new place," Verley continued. "In me old place, ev'ry morning I had to carry my six children on my back ta cross de river ta catch de school bus. And ev'ry afternoon, I 'ave ta carry dem back over when de bus left dem off. If I am working dat day, dey 'ave to wait two or three hours, before I cayn carry dem. It rains a lot and dey doan't like waiting in de rain so we moved ta land me grandmother owns on de ot'er side of de river. I didn't know it floods where I put de garden and de goats."

"You've got six children? Your house must get kinda noisy," I said, knowing they must all live in one or two rooms.

"Nah get noisy, mon. I tell dem dey musin' fight in de house, so dey not fight," he replied, describing some of the best parenting skills I had heard in years.

"Is it tough to support them on your pay?" I asked, thinking how hard it must be.

"Yah, mon. We not get paid much money on dis job. We get twenty five dollars a trip but I give some of it to anot'er raft captain who is too old ta work," he said.

"Does every captain do that?" I asked, impressed with this homemade retirement plan.

"Yah, mon, ev'ry captain get an apprentice when he get old and de young captain 'elp us," he replied. "Dere no ot'er pension plan 'ere on de river."

"Do you work every day?" Julia asked.

"Nah, mon, dis is my first job in ten days. De tourist nah come 'ere much dis time of year," Verley answered.

The average Jamaican earns $3,300.00 a year yet they pay roughly the same prices for their consumer goods as Americans.

"Yah, mon, it's tough," Verley replied, his voice showing no great worry or stress. "But we make it. It's been tougher dis month. De garden flood and dem goats drown and dem were new goats, too. Yah mon. Last month, a neighbor's dogs, dey kill five of me goats. I kept telling de neighbor to tie up 'is dogs because dey keep bot'ering me goats but he just laughed. And den de dogs kill my goats. He doan't even say 'e sorry. De police say I cayn kill 'is dogs and take 'im to court but I doan't do nuttin'."

We lapsed into silence as I pondered his predicament. After we floated awhile longer, he softly sang another Belafonte song.

Rasta Heart

Day-o, day-ay-ay-o
Daylight come and me wan' go home
Day-o, day-ay-ay-o
Daylight come and me wan' go home

Work all night on a drink of rum
Daylight come and me wan' go home
Stack banana till de morning come
Daylight come and me wan' go home
Day-o, day-ay-ay-o
Daylight come and me wan' go home
Day-o, day-ay-ay-o
Daylight come and me wan' go home

Come, Mister tally man, tally me banana
Daylight come and me wan' go home
Come, Mister tally man, tally me banana
Daylight come and me wan' go home
Day-o, day-ay-ay-o
Daylight come and me wan' go home
Day-o, day-ay-ay-o
Daylight come and me wan' go home

"Ya know de ot'er day I was listen' to de radio," Verley continued after he finished singing. "Dere was a news story about a mon who 'ad a large sugar cane field. One night, someone cut 'is cane and stole it and 'e got plenty mad. De next day 'e saw a neighbor walking down de road eatin' sugar cane and he ask de mon, 'Is dat me cane?' De mon say, 'Nah, is not ya cane' but dey got into a fight and dis man 'e kill 'is neighbor because 'e believed 'e stole 'is cane. When de community 'ear dat 'e killed dis mon, dey get so mad dey pull de mon out of 'is 'ouse and kill 'im."

Verley paused as we pondered his story.

"But I nuh 'urt me neighbor even though 'e 'urt me. It's not me way. If dis was dis ot'er mon's way, 'e and 'is neighbor be alive today."

Around the next bend Verley pulled the raft over on a rock bar and started to rummage through some debris that had gathered around a log. His movements were quick and agile, like an eager child scampering on an Easter egg hunt. As he searched, the back end of the raft started to turn down stream with the current and it was clear that soon the journey might continue without our captain.

"Hey, Verley," Julia yelled. "See you at the other end."

"No problem, mon," he said with a knowing grin. Finally he had found what he was looking for and hopped back on the raft at the last possible second. He walked to where we were sitting and put four beautiful seeds, about the size of a silver dollar, into Julia's hands.

"Des are coca seeds. Dey bring luck and love," he said heading back to the front, obviously pleased with his gift and himself.

"Verley, how do you get your raft back up the river?" I asked.

"Yah, mon, I have to drag it up tomorrow. I put a rope over my shoulder and tie it 'ere to de front of de raft," he answered, pointing to a wire loop. "Den I walk in de water or on de bank and drag it back. Some captains dey pay ta bring dere rafts back in a big truck but dat 'urt de raft and it costs five dollars."

"How long does it take to haul back up?" I asked, again impressed by this man's vibrancy and optimistic attitude as I learned more of his everyday reality.

"If de river is quiet, maybe fours hours. If de river is fast, maybe six," he replied.

Around another bend, two young men were sitting on the bank, one with an old acoustic guitar. As he started to play and sing, his business partner waded out to the raft holding a half coconut shell for donations. We dropped in a few dollars.

"Do yah want a Red Stripe beer, mon?" he said pointing to the cooler on the beach, full of Jamaica's national beer.

"No thanks, " I answered, still refreshed from the coconut milk.

"'Ow about a spliff, mon?" he asked, smiling.

"Thanks but we haven't finished this one," I said and we all laughed.

Every now and then we would pass other vendors or farmers along the shore. Verley knew everyone and they shouted in patois for as long as the river would allow the conversation to last. It was comforting to watch their relaxed interchanges.

"How long have you been doing this, Verley?" Julia asked.

"I'm on de river 23 years now," he replied with obvious pride.

"Verley, this river has made you a wise man," I said, contemplating the reality of spending 23 years floating down this beautiful river, working out all your day-to-day problems. Like our waiters and our tour bus guides, I was taken by his confidence and sense of calm.

Then I had an epiphany. It came all at once without my mind traveling down any particular progression of thinking. It came complete and certain. It could have been the ganja, the river, Verley or JAH or all of them together. I turned to Julia and said "I'm going to write a book about the wisdom of the Rastas and Bob Marley."

"Sounds like a great idea," Julia replied, a huge ganja grin on her face, liking the idea.

At the mouth of the river, Verley pulled the raft over at a take-out point located at an old resort. We thanked him profusely, exchanged addresses and gave him a tip along with our masks and snorkel, feeling he deserved much more for the trip. Perine and the bus were waiting for us.

"How was it? You're feeling much bettah, I bet," she said with a knowing grin.

"Yah, mon," Julia said with a wink.

"I knew yah would," Perine replied. "Verley me blood, me cousin. He 'as a Rasta 'eart."

Back in Blowing Rock, our mountain home, I quickly settled back into my day-to-day routine. I was finishing up *Memoirs of an Ex-Hippie*. The book chronicles my adventures traveling in the counterculture of the late sixties and early seventies. During those tumultuous years, I had heard some about the Rastas and had quickly recognized the obvious similarities between the Rastas and the hippies. Both let their hair and beards grow; both strove for a more organic diet and freedom from materialism and both smoked marijuana. Both groups believed "the Establishment" ("Babylon" to the Rastas) to be in need of major healing and awakening. Both groups attempted to interact with it in a limited fashion or to secede from it into communes or rural areas.

Both hippies and Rastas were ridiculed and often met with disdain, condemnation and occasionally, brutality—two back-to-the-land, anti-Establishment, long-haired, bearded, pot-smoking sub-cultures, espousing peace and love, from two very different roots. Many hippies went to Jamaica in the 60s and 70s to check out their "island brothers and sisters." Some stayed.

Rasta Heart

However, unlike our Jamaican counterparts, hippies were not born into poverty and oppression, but rather in affluence and permissiveness. We were "haves" masquerading as "have nots." The vast majority of the flower children have now blended in and rejoined the main culture. Perhaps we have returned to Babylon to irradiate it with a new awareness. The Rastas had no comfortable, seductive nest to return to. Because of this, they continued seeking a purer lifestyle.

Whereas the 60s counterculture began as a social and political protest, Rastafari began as a spiritual movement. Because of this, the Rastas had one other thing that many hippies lacked—a deep belief in God, JAH. Like so many people who have experienced painful lives, either through oppression, traumatic childhoods or events, they found comfort in the Divine.

After we returned home, the magic continued. The day after our return, I was telling the story of my inspiration for the book to two of our friends, Mike and Diana Rubin. I told them I was planning several more trips to the island to meet the Rastas and learn the beliefs behind their serenity. As I talked, Diana's eyes widened with interest.

"I'm from Jamaica. My brother-in-law is Trevor Munroe, " Diana said. "He's a Jamaican senator and a professor at the University of the West Indies. He's been involved in Jamaican politics for over thirty years, mostly fighting for the rights of the people. I know he would be glad to help you."

The next day we were telling John, a neighbor across the street about the book and he said, "My son and his wife just spent a year in rural Jamaica teaching Spanish. They'll be in town in a few weeks and I know they'd love to talk to you. In fact they just had a daughter, whom they named Marley."

Chapter 2

The Book Begins

"Nonviolence is the answer to the crucial moral and political questions of our time: the need for man to overcome oppression and violence without resorting to oppression and violence. Man must evolve for all human conflict a method which rejects revenge, aggression and retaliation. The foundation of such a method is love."
—**Dr. Martin Luther King's** Nobel Prize acceptance speech

In January 2001, three months after our first trip, I returned to Jamaica to begin this book. I decided to spend a week back in Port Antonio. It was off the beaten path and away from the more populated tourist areas. I figured that it would be a good place to meet Rastas. Also, I wanted to spend more time with Verley. A few weeks before returning, I called Trevor Munroe and he agreed to meet with me and have dinner the night I arrived in Kingston. I also called Dennis Forsythe, a Rasta attorney in Kingston who had written a book, *Rastafari: The Healing Of The Nations.* Dennis agreed to join me for breakfast my first morning after arriving. Also, to quickly explain my intentions, Julia had created a beautiful cover for the book.

Shortly before I left, I called the Rio Grande rafting office to set up several trips with Verley. I was looking forward to hearing more from this bush philosopher. When I finally reached his dispatcher, I was surprised to learn that during my stay he and his wife would be in England visiting his parents. This threw me off as I had hoped he would not only be a continuing source of wisdom but perhaps he would lead me to others as well. Plus I was astonished at the thought of Verley in London. Where did he get the money? From his parents? How would he do in a modern city? However, as I got to know more about the Jamaican people, I realized how truly international and well-travelled they really are at almost all economic levels. With Verley off the island, I had no contacts at all for my week in Port Antonio. Later I would see how Verley's absence was another one of those coincidences that guided me through my journey.

Arriving in Kingston, I rented a car and drove to the Hilton Hotel quickly adjusting to driving on the left. As I pulled on the the main highway, a large billboard greeted me with a huge picture of Bob Marley which read: "'Exodus' selected 'Album of the Century' by *Time* magazine and 'One Love' chosen by the BBC as 'Anthem of the Millennium'." Below that in large letters was written "One Love! Jamaica's Message to the World." My radio was already set to IRIE, the local reggae channel, which was playing a lot of Bob Marley in honor of his birthday coming up later that week.

Kingston was a mixture of both the First World and the Third World. Except for passing two large prisons and several windshield-washing hustlers, the drive from the airport to the hotel looked liked a typical depressed American city. However, this route avoided the heavy slum areas such as Trench Town and Dung Hill.

Dinner with the Munroes was a good introduction to the country. Ingrid, Trevor's wife and Kinshasa and David, his daughter and son-in-law, joined us for dinner in the hotel's dining room. Kinshasa is a human resource professional and David is a businessman and lawyer. Trevor is a thin, fit and vibrant man. He had been part of Jamaican politics for more than 30 years. He had always been a people's rights advocate and had machete scars on his back from when he had been attacked during a labor dispute to prove it. I had read a book of his speeches and I was greatly impressed with the clarity of his thinking, as well as his persistent commitment to improving the lives of the Jamaican people. Earlier in his career he had skirted with Communism as a response to the deep injustice and inequities of the Jamaican post-independence society. "We erroneously thought we could beat down Babylon through this ideology," he told me over dinner. However, he was now committed to working within the Jamaican democratic process which he had helped form.

Trevor had also introduced a bill into the Jamaican Parliament to decriminalize marijuana. He said that it was in committee being studied and he thought it would pass into law. (In August 2001, the committee recommended personal use of ganja be made legal. The U.S. vehemently objected, threatening economic sanctions.)

During dinner everyone seemed eager to share their views, not only regarding the Rastas but also about Jamaica itself. I could sense these people truly loved their country, despite all its problems. They felt that Jamaica was always gyrating out of balance in one area, then righting itself before it got out of balance in another. However, they believed that the spiral was heading upwards with conditions slowly improving.

As we spoke about the Rastas, opinions diverged. Everyone at the table agreed that the people of Jamaica had become much more accepting of the Rastas. Before the 70s, Rastas had often been persecuted by the authorities, who viewed them as a threat to tourism, to the island's impressionable youth and to Jamaica's worldwide image. They were arrested and beaten by the police for crimes they didn't commit and given stiff prison sentences even for ganja possession. Their dreadlocks, some taking 20 or more years to grow, were cut off when they were in custody or even when they were stopped at roadblocks. They weren't even allowed to board a plane out of Jamaica with dreads. Their fellow citizens turned on them as Jamaicans told their children Rastas were evil people and they should cross the street if they saw one coming. They were oppressed by the oppressed.

By the 1960s, the Jamaican establishment was becoming more and more alarmed by the growing number of Rastas. With its independence from England in 1962, the political and business leaders of the island were fearful that these highly visible "eccentrics" would send the wrong message to both tourists and potential business investors. They wanted the world to view the new independent Jamaicans as hard-working, clean-cut citizens. The back-to-the-land, ganja-smoking, dreadlocked Rastas did not mesh with this image.

The status of the Rastas improved in the 1970s when prime minister

Rasta Heart

Michael Manley insisted that the government, especially the police and military, treat them with the same respect due any other citizen. However, though their status is greatly improved, harassment of Rasta continues even though they have become a main draw of Jamaica's tourism industry.

There was disagreement among my dinner companions as to exactly how Rastas were currently viewed by their fellow citizens, especially the upper and middle-classes. Trevor and Ingrid felt that the Rastafarians had come to be accepted, perhaps even somewhat respected, as a fringe sect, unusual but peaceful. Ingrid especially held the Rastas in very high regard. From a very young age she had been a political activist and, like her husband, had devoted her life to helping people, especially the downtrodden. After receiving her college degree in the U.S., she returned to Jamaica, something rarely done. She watched two close relatives, including her uncle Mario, leave the fold to become Rastas, a decision viewed as well-intended but naive by other family members.

Kinshasa and David, representing the younger Jamaicans, admired the Rastas. Mario's peace and wisdom was not lost on them. They viewed the Rastas as brave, powerful people who had been willing to stand up to the oppressive establishment and make those in power confront the evil of their colonial and post-independence system, even at the risk of their own freedom or safety. They saw the Rastas' dreadlocks, which made them so quickly and easily identifiable, as a symbol of pride and defiance, both of which they considered highly admirable qualities. Trevor and Ingrid agreed with this conclusion but did not think it was the general consensus.

Dinner ended around eleven with agreements to stay in touch. I had enjoyed the evening immensely. Though they could offer no particular suggestions as to how to contact the Rastas, I left the evening with a clearer concept of their country and the Rastas' place within it.

The following morning, before driving to Port Antonio, I had breakfast with Dennis Forsythe. Dennis is a slim, intense man with piercing eyes and a beautiful smile which he seems to withhold until he has sized you up. I was immediately impressed by his intelligence and I was not surprised to learn he had risen from humble Jamaican beginnings to become a top student and then a respected member of the academic community. He earned a degree in economics and sociology from the London School of Economics, followed by both a Master's degree and a Ph.D from McGill University in Montreal. His teaching career included teaching or lecturing at Sir George Williams University, Howard University and Federal City College. Dennis had been a compatriot of Trevor's during his tenure as a professor at the University of the West Indies. He left the academic fields in 1980 after a series of personal crises. He was now a practicing attorney in Kingston.

Though well-dressed and clean-shaven, he was still very much a Rasta. In many respects he had become a lightning rod for them. He was a spur under the Establishment's saddle that had to be exorcised. He was one of Jamaica's promising stars, a Ph.D and university professor, and now he was discarding many of the values of the aspiring society and embracing the tenets and lifestyle of a vocal and conspicuous spiritual splinter group.

The more we talked over breakfast, the more comfortable we became with each other. After about an hour, I was surprised when Dennis turned to me and asked if I wanted to come to his house and smoke some ganja. At first I thought that this did not really fit with my plans. I had to drive to my hotel in Port Antonio, a three hour drive mostly through winding, narrow mountain roads. Then I thought, "Hey, this is what I came here to do, to be with the Rastas one on one." I looked at Dennis, smiled and said, "Sure!"

I followed Dennis up the hill toward his house. He lived in a well-kept suburb overlooking the city and the ocean. It was a pleasant one-story home that could easily fit in many American subdivisions. He lived there with his wife, who worked in Kingston as a secretary. After changing into shorts, Dennis joined me on his back patio with a bag of ganja. We each rolled a spliff and settled back. As we spoke and as the ganja took effect, a change came over him. All tension drained from his face and he started to radiate an almost joyous glow. He began talking about the beauty of being a Rasta and the power of ganja, something he had discussed at length in his book.

"Ganja realigns all your inner organs as you breathe it in. To breathe deeply is the goal. All my organs have been realigned since I starting smoking ganja. Before I started to smoke, I was very, very sick but no more," he said, sitting perfectly erect and taking a long cheek-hollowing draw on his spliff. As he smoked, his glow intensified. "You must look at yourself when you smoke ganja. You cannot hide."

Rasta Heart

As Bob Marley said, "When ya smoke herb it reveals ya ta yahself. All de wickedness ya do is revealed by de herb. It's yah conscience and gives ya an honest picture of yahself."

"But isn't there a chance that using ganja can reduce ambition and make doers into dreamers?" I said, voicing one of my main concerns about marijuana use.

"Ganja does not reduce ambition, it only changes it," he replied, staring into the sky. "You still are ambitious, but ambitious for other things. For the truth, for love, for joy. These are the things you want now, not so much the cars and the money. But this is a great threat to Babylon because they do not value the truth and the love. Rasta is here to bring about necessary changes. Rasta teaches redemption through sufferation. Through their suffering, they still love and find joy. This is Rastas' greatest gift to the world. And when Bob Marley sings his songs, you feel this love, you feel that he is speaking just to you. That is why he is the great messenger for the Rastas."

Dennis told me that he was presently in a custody battle for his six-year old son that he had with another woman. Though the mother did not have a stable home, she was keeping him from ever seeing his son. Because he had been arrested for one spliff, she was claiming he was a drug addict.

"For one spliff, mon, they try to take my son away. For one spliff! And I am a lawyer with a nice home. But the judges know that I am also a Rasta and they don't like this," he said, deep sadness coming over his face.

"I love my son an I miss him. He does not know the Rasta ways, only the ways of Babylon. Next week is a new hearing and they try to hide this from me. They did not tell me about the hearing. There is little justice in Jamaican courts and I must tell the people this. To take a child from his father for one spliff is not right."

Unfortunately, many Jamaican men have been separated from their children. The Jamaican courts, like most, usually give custody to the mother. Also, Jamaica, though a macho society, is very much a matriarchal society in the African tradition. It is very common for a man, even a happily married man, to have children with several other women. It is also common for women to have children from several different men (80 percent of Jamaican children are born out of wedlock, as are 70 percent of African-American). Because of this "wandering man" syndrome, women are often

16

the head of the household.

It was now about three in the afternoon. Dennis and I had been talking for several hours and it seemed like only an hour. Given that Port Antonio was still three hours away, Dennis suggested that I better leave soon unless I wanted to drive at night. But before I left, I had one other question. "Dennis, why is this belief system working so well? It seems to bring real inner peace and joy."

He thought for a long time and then looked me in the eye, his face still glowing. "The Rasta way is holistic. It is not just somet'ing you do on Sundays. It is for always. It is how you eat, how you take care of your body, how you treat everyone. And the Rastas use ganja to change their consciousness, not alcohol or tranquilizers. Rastas do not use ganja for recreation. Ganja is a spiritual experience." Or as Bob Marley put it, "Why people drink is dey want de feeling I get when I smoke herb. Everybody need ta get high, but some people gettin' high wit' de wrong t'ings."

As we headed through his house, Dennis gave me a pamphlet he had just published, *The Law Against Ganja in Jamaica*. Like Trevor, he was campaigning to get ganja decriminalized, perhaps even legalized, in his country.

Dennis drove with me to the entrance of his subdivision. As he got out of the car, his final words were, "Just turn left and you're on the Port Antonio Road and pay attention. Driving here is crazy."

As I pulled into the traffic, I focused on two thoughts: "Stay left" and "Ya, mon, I can do this!"

Driving in the Jamaican countryside is at best a vision quest, at worst a journey into lunacy. For me, it was more the latter. If you've never been to Jamaica, let me give you a sense of what driving there is like. On our first trip to Jamaica, I was aghast at the driving of our taxi and bus drivers. They repeatedly passed other vehicles on blind curves and at high speeds. Had another car ever been coming in the other direction, we all would have died. They would whip through small towns and villages, seemingly oblivious to the many pedestrians, often young children, walking in the road. After our first day, I became convinced that most Jamaican drivers had some sort of perverse death wish. In fact when one taxi driver let us off, I told him I hoped he wouldn't be insulted if I kissed the ground.

The Jamaican accident rate is 13 times that of the U.S. In fact, when I reserved my rental car, I was told that most credit card companies do not extend their free rental car insurance to rentals in three countries: Israel, Ireland and Jamaica. Except for Ethiopia and India, Jamaica has the highest auto fatality rate in the world and some of the rudest and most reckless drivers. The week I arrived, the country was mourning the loss of two of their key soccer players due to traffic mishaps, including Shorty Malcolm, a very popular player who had just died in a car accident returning to Kingston after a game in Montego Bay. Another player was sidelined that week for accidentally running into, and killing, a pedestrian.

There are several reasons why driving in Jamaica is so crazy. First, Jamaican drivers are mostly young. As we all know, young people, with no sense of their own mortality, are the most reckless drivers. From my observations, it also seemed that a general rule was: the larger the vehicle, the greater the speed and the more reckless the driver. Huge trucks flew down the road, often straddling both lanes.

Also, it seems that everyone drives fast in Jamaica—very fast. Most cars are driven by taxi drivers, both legal and rogue, who make their living according to how many passengers they cart around each day. To them, time, and therefore speed, is of the essence. They pass whenever they want and beep their horns when they pass as if to say, "Look I'm doing something really stupid that might kill both of us and I thought you might want to know." Usually, but unfortunately not always, they zip back in their lane, often within inches of the oncoming traffic.

Then there are the roads—curvy, winding, very narrow and with few shoulders or pulloffs. Often in the mountains, there are steep dropoffs on one side and sheer rock walls on the other. But the madness does not end there. Since few people can afford their own cars, non-vehicular traffic is everywhere. You cannot drive more than one hundred yards in the Jamaican countryside without passing someone walking in the road (and I mean in, not next to, the road). And these are not just normal pedestrians but people with large sacks of coconuts on their heads or with a four-foot fish strapped to their back. Except in the towns, there are few sidewalks and everyone just saunters down the road, unconcerned about the cars racing by at high speed, just inches from their fragile bodies.

Next, you mix in thousands of animals wandering freely on the roads. Not just dogs and cats, but goats, cows, pigs and chickens as well. It's not uncommon to see a goat or cow tethered to a tree with their rump sticking three feet into a main two-lane highway. Often they are just wandering untethered (I guess their owners know how to find them when they want them).

To further complicate matters, the island is dotted with thousands of potholes, ranging from the size of a dinner plate to some stretching across the entire width of the road. All the local drivers have committed to memory the location of each pothole in their driving area and know exactly when to jump into the other lane to avoid it, even if this means forcing the oncoming traffic off the road, which is considered appropriate driving etiquette. Because of this quirk, you must not only watch for potholes in your lane but those in the other lane as well. If you do not see the upcoming pothole or oncoming traffic forces you to hit one, the experience can be anything from a mild thump to a blow so hard as to slam your head against the roof and almost shatter your teeth. Occasionally citizens will fill a pothole on their own initiative and then solicit donations from passing grateful drivers but their efforts hardly make a dent. My bet is there isn't a properly aligned frontend anywhere on the island.

In the final footnote to this absurdity, the island is peppered with signs, like "Speed Kills So Kill Your Speed" or "Drive Left-Stay Alive/Drive Right-Suicide," which constantly remind people of this madness and yet have little to no effect. Wait, there's still more. I almost forgot that using seat belts is considered being a"sissy;" keeping your high beams on at night is considered a statement of power and there is an obsession to immediately close any gap between you and the car in front.

Now I had to make my way through this insanity for three hours over one hundred miles—all while high on some very fine Jamaican ganja. After a while I started to get into it. The ganja actually improved my concentration. I was one with the road, one with the traffic, one with the game. Everything else was blocked out. I was totally focused and immensely enjoying it.

As I drove over the mountains, the DJ on IRIE radio said that in honor of Bob Marley's upcoming birthday he was going to play six Marley songs without interruption. He then proceeded with a selection of his best songs, which put me in a Marley frame of mind.

At the end of the sixth song, the DJ comes back on and in a very slow, deep, melodious voice, says "Ooooh boy, Ooooh boy."

Rasta Heart

And you know just where he's coming from because you're feeling the same way. How can this man create such absolutely beautiful music? And you know thousands of people on this island are feeling just what the DJ is feeling.

I successfully maneuvered through the mountains and turned right on the coast road for my last hour's drive to Port Antonio. The coast road was flat and relatively straight and I knew I had this drive conquered. I was able to relax somewhat and let my mind wander. It felt liberating to leave the city and travel in the beautiful countryside, with the ocean on one side and the verdant Blue Mountains, lofting up to 7,400 feet, on the other.

About a half-hour out of Port Antonio, I started to get hungry so I pulled off at a roadside stand. There was an open air kitchen area along with several picnic benches and tables under a thatched roof. I ordered a Pepsi and a plate of rice and beans. I noticed that the cook had dreadlocks and figured this might be a good time to buy a little ganja.

I approached the cook, a large, young man with a big smile and his dreads under the large yellow, red and green cap or "tam." Many Rastas wear these tams to keep their hair protected from dust and dirt.

"Hey, can I get $20 worth of ganja from you?" I asked, as easily as if I were asking for another Pepsi. I was a little surprised at how relaxed I felt about this.

"Ya, mon," he said without hesitation. "But where will yah put it? Ya might find a police roadblock up de road." He seemed genuinely concerned for my safety, as if he needed to educate me to the dangers.

"I don't know. Should I hide it in my luggage?" I asked.

"Nuh, mon, dey search de car and bags. Yah bettah put it in yah pocket. Dey seldom search dere."

"OK, I'll do that," I responded, feeling grateful for the advice.

I sat down to finish my food and after a few minutes he disappeared and came back with about a fistful of tightly wadded, pungent ganja wrapped in plastic. It was maybe two inches in diameter and three inches long and looked like it had been cut off of a larger log roll. I gave him a twenty dollar bill and stuffed the wad in the front pocket of my shorts. With our business complete and my meal finished, I hopped in my car for the final ten mile drive into Port Antonio.

I drove no more than two or three miles down the road when I was

Rasta Heart

stopped by a roadblock of Jamaican police. They already had several people pulled over and several policemen with clean starched uniforms were searching the cars. I guess the Rasta cook had heard they were out there and maybe that's why he was giving me a warning. I later learned that police roadblocks are very common on the island and their searches very thorough. Few Jamaicans, and none of the Rastas I met, travel with more than a small amount of ganja, knowing that they can usually get some wherever they are going. Not since my hippie days has seeing policemen caused me any anxiety. However, now I was high and I had good cause for anxiety, with an ounce of pot bulging in my front pocket.

Jamaican drug laws for carrying small amounts of marijuana are not particularly harsh as they are for large amounts or trying to smuggle it out of the country. I knew even if I were busted it would probably only mean a quick trip to the local jail and paying a fine and lawyer's fees.

A plump policewomen in an immaculate starched uniform motioned me over to the curb. Before I got out of the car I pressed the wad of ganja as flat as I could and hoped my loose shirt would help cover it. She asked to see my driver's license and rental form. I walked around to the back of the car and got them out of the trunk. As she was looking them over I got out the cover of my book. While she was going over the paperwork, I literally stuck the book cover in her face and started telling her why I was visiting. As I talked, she started reading the back cover which explains about the wisdom of Jamaica and the Rastas and about me writing about my travels on the island.

I could almost hear her thinking: *If we have to put this guy in jail, he's going to write about it in his book, which thousands of potential tourists may read. Describing a night in our jail may not be the best publicity. This could be a real can of worms.*

"Everything looks in order. Go ahead," she finally said, handing me back the book and the paperwork. In an instant I was gone, more convinced than ever that the trip was under blessed winds.

Rastafari

The Rastas had their roots in the 1930s with two black world figures, Marcus Mosiah Garvey and Ethiopian King Haile Selassie I. Garvey was born in rural St. Ann's Bay on the north coast of Jamaica, not far from the small village of Nine Miles, Bob Marley's birthplace. Garvey, descended from Maroons, moved to Kingston in his teens where he worked as a printer and labor organizer. There he matured as a thinker and public orator.

A genius at media manipulation and a fiery speaker with an evangelical style, Garvey, often called "the black Moses," became one of the twentieth century's leading black rights and nationalists advocates. He also became one of the first public thinkers to offer the displaced blacks a positive self-image. A pro-African, he roused his audience and readers with his now famous words, "Africa for the Africans, those at home and those abroad. We should move forward also with One God, One Aim and One Destiny." Garvey understood that blacks needed to be economically strong to gain their rights. He enticed his followers to have pride in their African heritage, as Africa was the cradle of civilization and one of the earliest high cultures.

Decades later, science would prove him right—4.5 million years ago, all humans descended from one woman whom anthropologists called Lucy. She lived in Ethiopia. Because of this, Rastas believe all races and all people are of Ethiopian descent, which makes us all one.

Also, Garvey noted that the Old Testament often refers to Ethiopia as this cradle, even linking it to The Garden of Eden. Genesis 2:13 states, "A river went out of Eden and its name was Gihon and it compasseth the land of Ethiopia." In Psalms it continues, "Princes shall come out of Egypt: Ethiopia shall soon stretch out her hands unto God."

In 1914, with his first wife, Amy Ashwood, Garvey founded the Universal Negro Improvement and Conservation Association (UNIA). At its peak, he claimed the UNIA had over four million members worldwide. At its convention in 1921, he led a parade of over 50,000 followers through the streets of New York, an event that deeply concerned the white politicians and law enforcement agencies. He also started, among countless other ventures, *The Negro World*, a black newspaper, *The Black Man*, a monthly magazine and the Black Star Line, a shipping concern that eventually led to his financial and legal ruin.

With his message of black pride and prophesying that the tormented black race would one day regain its status as God's favorite, Garvey was a threat to the ruling white establishment, which was still committed to keeping blacks economically enslaved and culturally and emotionally diminished. Many Rastas consider him the father of their faith. It was Garvey who eloquently articulated their rising black consciousness. Quoting King Solomon's Song of Songs, "I am black, but comely," Garvey reminded people that Solomon's descendants, which included Jesus, must therefore also have been black. Garvey encouraged his followers to worship God through the lens of their African heritage. He stated, "Whilst our God has no color, yet it is human to see everything through one's own spectacles, and since the white people have seen their God through white spectacles, we have only now started out to see our God through our own spectacles."

Much to the dismay of both his critics and followers, he even met with the Klu Klux Klan regarding possible black repatriation to Africa. White leaders wanted him removed from his public pulpit and soon trumped-up charges were brought against him. In 1923 Garvey was tried and convicted of using the mails to defraud in the sales of stock in his Black Star Line. He spent the next two years in the federal prison in Atlanta before his early release and deportation back to Jamaica.

Though his ministry was shortlived and he died discredited and in poverty in England at the age of 53, in many blacks worldwide he had awakened a sense of racial pride. In 1964, Jamaican prime minister Edward Seaga brought Garvey's remains back to Jamaica and reinterred them in the National Heroes Park. Within fifty years of Garvey's death, all of Africa's fifty countries were once again back in the hands of Africans.

Rastas look to a prediction Garvey made as the genesis of their faith. In 1927, he prophesied "Look to Africa, for the crowning of a Black King; He shall be the Redeemer." This king would lead the blacks from corrupted Babylon and back to their homeland of Zion (Ethiopia/Africa).

In 1930 such a black king was crowned in Africa. A great grandson of Saheka Selassie of Shoa, was made emperor of Ethiopia, Lion of Judah, Elect of God, Light of This World, King of Kings. He was renamed Haile Selassie I. He was reportedly the 225th heir to the throne going back 3,000 years to King Solomon. His was the oldest monarchy on earth. As told in the Old Testament, his ancestors began their reign from the union between the Jewish King Solomon and the black Ethiopian Queen of Sheba.

Many of Jamaica's slum dwellers and rural poor regarded Haile Selassie's internationally publicized coronation as the long awaited fulfill-

Rasta Heart

ment of Garvey's prophesy of redemption and they proclaimed the divinity of Haile Selassie I (which they pronounce "Haile Selassie Eye"). Several popular Jamaican lay people and preachers such as Leonard Howell, H. Archibald Dunkley, Robert Hinds and Joseph Nathaniel Hibbert, began to proclaim his divinity from the pulpits of their churches or on the streets of the Kingston slums. They soon adopted the name "Rastafari" after Haile Selassie's name before his coronation, Ras Tafari: "Ras" meaning "prince" and "Tafari" meaning "To Be Feared or Head Creator."

They became the movement's independent, self-appointed "Elders" with widely varying views. These early leaders also began to flesh out the movement's tenets and beliefs. These early followers believed that they would soon return to their motherland, Ethiopia. However, Garvey, a Roman Catholic, did not believe in the divinity of Haile Selassie I and he described the Rastafarians as crazy fanatics. Rastas, however, continued to revere Garvey nonetheless, remarking that even John the Baptist had doubts about Christ.

Thirty years later, on April 21, 1966, Haile Selassie I finally came to Jamaica. It was reported that the sun broke through the clouds and shone directly on his royal plane as it landed, following a flock of white doves that appeared out of nowhere. He was overwhelmed when over 100,000 Rasta devotees, many dressed in white robes and chanting "Hosanna to the Son of David," showed up at the airport. They began throwing large cigar-sized spliffs at his feet as he got off his plane. He was so moved, and perhaps frightened, by the crowd, he retreated back into his plane until he was eventually brought out by Rasta leader Mortimer Planner (who later became Bob Marley's manager). Contrary to the widely held belief that he was amazed at the existence of the Rastafarians, there is much evidence that Haile Selassie's whole purpose in visiting Jamaica was his desire to meet the Rasta leadership, including Planner and probably Joseph Hibbert. The precise details of this historic meeting cannot be reconstructed, and there exist countless variants in Rasta oral tradition. Before he left Jamaica he told the Rastas they "should not seek to immigrate to Ethiopia until they had liberated the people of Jamaica."

In the crowd on the highway that day was a young woman, Rita Marley, who was told to go there to see the king by her new husband, Bob, who was in the U.S. working as a welder at the time. As Selassie passed Rita, the emperor looked her directly in the eye and waved. On his palm she saw the mark of the crucifix nail, convincing her that Selassie was indeed divine. The Emperor himself did not believe in his own divinity but to the Rastas "even God would not know that He is God."

Chapter 3

Settling into Being Unsettled

"If he be really and seriously seeking to live a good life, the first thing from which he will abstain will always be the use of animal food, because . . . its use is simply immoral, as it involves the performance of an act which is contrary to the moral feeling—killing."

—Leo Tolstoy

A few miles down the road, I drove through the town of Port Antonio. My hotel was five miles or so on the other side of the village. When viewed from a high hill, Port Antonio is beautiful. The town sits on a horseshoe bay, with Navy Island in the middle. Around the turn of the 20th century, poet Ella Wheeler Wilcox described it as the "most exquisite port on earth." The area is sparsely populated with the jungle covered Blue Mountains, famous worldwide for its coffee, rising directly behind the town. This entire area of Jamaica's northeast coast is the least accessible and wettest (though showers usually occur sporadically, often in the morning or at night). The natural beauty of the area makes it a popular destination for serious adventurers and eco-tourists looking to get away from the more crowded Ocho Rios, Montego Bay or Negril.

At street level, Port Antonio is a typical Jamaican village of about 19,000. The downtown shopping district is mostly for locals only, with

Rasta Heart

few tourist shops. The streets are crowded with foot traffic which flows off the sidewalk and into the road. However, some new buildings downtown and a commercial complex called Village of St. George, indicate that the town's prospects may be brightening. There are many hotels, villas and guesthouses in the area. Most tourists venture to the local environs by visiting the beaches, lagoons, waterfalls and caves in the immediate area or by rafting down the Rio Grande.

Port Antonio was discovered as a tourist destination when screen star of the 30s Erroll Flynn arrived in 1946 when his yacht washed ashore in bad weather. Eventually he encouraged others in the social elite and Hollywood stars to visit, and even build, in the area. The town does have its share of fame. Several movies, including *The Mighty Quinn, Lord of the Flies,* Tom Cruise's *Cocktail*, and Robin Williams' *Club Paradise*, were all filmed in the area.

Just before dark I arrived at the Jamaica Palace, where I had arranged to stay the next six nights. We had passed the hotel on our October excursion to the Rio Grande and it looked impressive. It was built in 1989 by Baroness Elisabeth Sieglinde Stephan von Stephan, who also built the nearby Trident Castle. The property sits on a bluff nestled between the mountains and the sea overlooking Turtle Crawle Bay. Built with white marble columns gracing the front, several rambling buildings are set around five acres of tropical gardens with a 114-foot pool built in the shape of Jamaica. Everything is immaculate white—a splash of European royalty surrounded by the lush Jamaican jungle.

I checked into my room, complete with floors and bathtub of pink and white marble, a glass chandelier hanging from the twelve foot ceiling and a tulip-shaped bed—all the comforts of Babylon. While unpacking, I set up my Sony Discman CD player and two small speakers which played Marley's "Natural Mystic" and "Legend" CDs continuously throughout the next week.

After a swim in the pool and dinner of jerk chicken in the restaurant, I settled in my room. Since it was the off season and mid-week, the hotel was empty and I had the whole place to myself. By now the ganja I smoked with Dennis was starting to wear off and I started to think about the next few days and how I was going to go about connecting with the Rastas. I had planned to go rafting on the Rio Grande the next day but I knew Verley

Rasta Heart

was on vacation and the dispatcher wasn't sure there were any Rasta raft captains. I had seen many Rastas, or at least men with dreadlocks or voluminous tams, walking on the road but I didn't feel comfortable just stopping them and asking them to talk with me. To tell you the truth I had no plan, no idea of what I was going to do. As I followed this train of thought I began to wonder if the trip, the entire idea to write this book, was ridiculous. Here I was a bald-headed, white, middle-class American sitting in the neoclassic $14 million dollar resort watching TV while laying on my tulip-shaped bed.

I started to get a little depressed. This was one of the craziest ideas I'd ever come up with. I'd probably spend the next six days laying by the pool, seeing the local attractions and watching TV, just like any other foreign tourist. I started to think maybe I should just admit my mistake and go home.

I had wrestled with these concerns and fears since shortly after deciding to write the book. In fact, several times I had even given up on the idea of writing the book at all. It seemed too crazy, too improbable. I sometimes doubted that I was the proper messenger to carry the message of a black, oppressed, but highly spiritual, people.

Other times, I thought I was perfectly suited. I had been raised by a black nanny in my youth and often felt very at home around African-Americans. When I was in high school I was close friends, and traveled with, R&B singer Otis Redding, who I later learned was Bob Marley's primary musical inspiration. My hippie years had given me an affinity for the Rasta lifestyle.

I decided to smoke some ganja, hoping it would give me a new perspective on my dilemma. I opened the small safe in the closet where I kept my stash and my valuables. The sweet aroma wafted over me. I rolled a large joint and walked out to the deck overlooking the bay. By now it was dark and no one was around except the front desk person on the other side of the hotel. For the first time in 25 years, I got high alone.

In the beginning my mind just wandered from one thought to another, reflecting back upon the last day and wondering about the next few. After awhile, my thoughts started to focus and I became distinctly aware of the gentle, moist night air, the songs of the frogs, the motion of the clouds and the reflection of the moon off the bay. I began to feel the huge forces of nature around me and began to think how small my personality, my ego was in relationship to these forces. Then I began to ponder that I was not this well-defined "self" I had spent years crafting. I was something ephemeral, something much greater than my skin-encapsulated ego. I was part of these powerful forces. The barriers between self and the rest of the world were dissolving.

I was something infinitely small and at the same time something infinitely vast. The usual inner workings of my mind, my everyday thinking and planning, were gone, replaced by the sole awareness that I was not really who I defined myself to be each day, in each relationship, in each thought. The ganja was opening the door to what the Rastas refer to as the "I and I."

My spiritual search had led me, like the Rastas, to believe that we are all much greater than we know. In the past this thought had seemed comforting but now it seemed almost frightening. I felt alone—very, very alone. I felt disconnected from all the people and places by which I defined myself. As this existential loneliness penetrated me, I looked around. The isolation and surrealistic aura of the hotel, the distance from my family and friends, the mystical nature of my mission here, the effect of the ganja, all seemed to crash in on me to the point of near panic. I wanted to be home in my living room, sitting by the fire watching TV with Julia and Alicia. I wanted to be Robert Roskind again, defined and knowable. I wanted the experience to end.

A car drove by on the road below me, radio blaring, people laughing. Other humans. How comforting. Then in a flash a thought came to me that dissolved all sense of aloneness and replaced it with a sense of comfort and warmth. I realized that I am indeed alone. I always have been and I always will be but I share this predicament with billions of other people whether they realize it or not. So in one way I am never alone. I am alone but sharing the experience with every other person on earth. Aloneness was both a truth and an illusion. We are all alone together and we are all together alone. I sat out there for another hour or so feeling fully comfortable in my own company.

The next morning I felt back on purpose but still unsure as to my next move. I called to make reservation for a Rio Grande rafting trip later that

Rasta Heart

day. Then I headed out to breakfast at another local hotel, the Bonnie View—and it does indeed have a "bonnie view." As I was heading out of the lobby to get in my car, the bellhop, Clive, opened the entrance door. Clive was around 30, medium height and thin, with close cropped hair, a moustache and a warm smile. We said "Good morning" to each other. Half way across the parking lot, I had a thought. I turned around and approached him.

"By the way," I said, "I'm down here writing a book on the Rastas. Do you know any?"

"Ya, mon," he said without hesitating. "I know a lot of de Rastas and I cayn take yah ta meet dem."

"I'm not looking for just any Rastas. I'm looking for the ones who really know love," I said.

"Ya, mon, I know dos Rastas. Dem me good friends," he replied, sincerely.

"I cayn take yah tomorrow if yah want."

"Sounds good to me," I said. We arranged to meet at a Rasta restaurant near the hotel.

Now I was feeling much better. Clive seemed to understand what I was seeking but who knows? At least it was a start.

At breakfast, I chatted with the waiter and Gordon, the owner, who was also an old friend of Trevor Munroe. They both held the Rastas in high regard and said that was the general feeling of most of the people in the area. Gordon said that the Rastas, like the Maroons in the area, were considered brave freedom fighters. The Maroons are descendants from escaped slaves who fled to the nearby mountains in the 1600s and were eventually given their freedom by the English, who were unable to subdue them. The waiter, a young Maroon from nearby Moore Town, said about half his friends had become Rastas. They said the Rasta school in the village had burned down but many of the Rasta children were in the public school system and they were having an influence on the other young people.

I spent the day rafting down the Rio Grande with a pleasant, though not particularly wise, raft captain. At the end, I got my car and dropped my captain in town and returned to the hotel.

The next morning I arrived at the restaurant to find Clive already there waiting for me. The restaurant, a cooking shed on a small beach by the bay with three plastic tables under a blue plastic tarp, was run by a local young Rasta who served only organic fruits and vegetable dishes.

"Ital" is the term Rastas use not only to describe their organic diet but their organic life as well. Taking the commandment "Thou Shalt Not Kill" to include all living things, most Rastas are against the killing of animals, even for food. Proper diet is key to living a true Rasta life. They believe that if you eat only whole foods from the earth, you will inevitably exist in a higher, purer state. They understand you cannot divorce the body's effect on the mind and soul. Rastas regard their bodies as holy temples and believe that simply being aware of what you put in it begins to raise consciousness. Most feel that your food should be your medicine and your medicine your food. They base their vegetarian diet on passages from the Old Testament.

In Genesis 1:29, immediately after God created the Earth, we are told what to eat. "And God said, 'Behold I have given every herb bearing seed, which is upon the face of all earth, and every tree that has fruit with seed in it. They will be yours for food. And to all the beasts of the earth and all the birds of the air and all the creatures that move on the ground, everything that has breath of life in it, I give all green plant for food." Many Jewish scholars now agree that the Old Testament supports a vegetarian diet and that everyone followed this from Adam to Noah, a time when the Bible says people lived to be almost 1,000 years old. It is thought that God allowed but did not encourage meat-eating after the flood until the Messianic Era, when everyone would revert back to being vegetarians. This was permitted as God knew man was not yet ready to control his appetites. Accordingly, this permitted meat was called "b'sar ta'avah," "meat of lust."

Ital foods, such as organic fruits, vegetables and their juices, herbs, seeds, nuts and grains, are physically sustaining, mentally and spiritually nourishing, and environmentally conscious. Rastas believe eating Ital connects them to the earth, to "roots." This pure way of eating brings them closer to JAH and His natural creation. To Rastas, Ital is life-energizing, and keeps the body, mind and spirit in perfect balance.

For the most part, Rastas avoid the devitalized inorganic, indigestible foods found everywhere in modern life. They believe that pure, live foods keep your internal systems clean and do not overload the body with poisons and toxins. By eating this way they believe you can avoid most diseases and illnesses. Most Rastas believe that eating meat makes you feel aggressive, guilty and irritable and eating plants make you feel peaceful, like the plant itself.

Clive and I sat at one of the tables, the only patrons this early in the morning. We ordered fruit juices and awaited the arrival of two Rastas, Israel and Elijah. As I looked around, I noticed a sign across the street in red, green and gold Rasta colors. "JAH-Mek-Ya" it read.

As Clive and I talked, I got more of his story. He had worked at the hotel for two years and was supporting his two young children, Michael and Pom-Pom, and his 50 year old mother, Yvonne, who had lost all use of her legs after a botched procedure at a Kingston hospital. His wife was living elsewhere. He had decided to quit because he was being paid only five dollars a day and with the hotel so slow he was receiving few of the usual tips.

After a few minutes our guests arrived. Israel, in his seventies, was tall and thin with a short beard and thick, two-foot-long dreadlocks, white with a slight yellow tinge. His front teeth were missing but that seemed to fit his general persona. He looked both wise and playful, a rare combination for a man that old. Elijah was in his late twenties or early thirties, muscular and with thin, tightly-braided dreads. Elijah seemed rather serious but when he smiled, his warmth came through.

After Clive's introductions, I explained what I was doing and asked if I could record our talk with both my videocam and on my small audio tape recorder. They agreed. I set the equipment on the table, made sure they were both in "record" mode and settled back. Elijah respectfully deferred to the older Israel but as soon as Israel opened his mouth I knew I was in trouble. I couldn't understand a word he said! Though he was very animated and I guess articulate, between his missing teeth, his thick Jamaican accent and his rapidly flowing stream of consciousness, almost every word was unintelligible to me.

Over the next hour I kept politely trying to steer the conversation over to Elijah, who I could understand, but after he said a few words Israel would take over again, his conversation punctuated with his laugh and wild arm gestures.

After awhile I gave up and just settled into watching him, trying to respond appropriately so as not to give away the fact that I was totally lost.

Rasta Heart

His enthusiastic monologue, delivered with grace and humor, was enjoyable to listen to even though I had no idea what he was talking about. His passion for his beliefs was obvious. I just couldn't understand what they were. I kept checking the videocam and tape recorder to be sure they were recording, figuring that maybe I could get Clive to interpret later. They both seemed to be recording perfectly.

After an hour, I politely broke up the meeting. I was discouraged and hoped I could rescue something from the tapes.

When we got back in the car Clive was excited, thinking I had just found what I was looking for.

"Mon, Israel really knows de Rasta ways," he said excitedly. "Yah cayn learn a lot fe ya book from 'im."

"Clive, I hate to tell you this but I didn't understand one word he said," I responded, watching the excitement drain from his face. "Maybe we can go over the tapes together and you can interpret for me," I continued.

"Nuh problem, mon. We do dat later," Clive said, bouncing back with the thought of still salvaging the morning. "Now, we go see me friend Ramscram. 'E's a Rasta too."

When I got to my room later that day, I rewound both the video and audio tapes. Neither unit recorded a syllable of Israel's long oration.

Rastafari

In the early years, the Rastafarian movement remained dominated by independent "Elders" with widely varying views. Not only did no Jamaica-wide "Rastafarian Church" or hierarchy develop, but there was not even agreement on basic doctrine or a canon of Scripture. This "anarchy" was considered a virtue by classical Rastas.

Today Rastafari is not a religion, a human organization, or a philosophy, but an active attempt, by each follower, to discern the will of JAH in their own lives and hearts. They believe this will cannot be known by human effort alone but that "JAH come over I&I." As Bob Marley said, "Rastafari is not a culture. It's a reality."

Most Rastafarians believe you become Rasta through your own spiritual growth. It is a state of mind and soul, a "reality," not a religion. Through this mystical union with JAH you become who you truly are but never were. You do not join as a "member," as you might with a church, mosque or synagogue. They believe that to be truly Rasta means you are in a state of remembering your inner divinity. It is a state of "being born again." That is why every man is a "Rastaman" and every woman is a "Rastalady" but only few "remember" this. As one Rasta, Ras Hu-I puts it: "Rasta is sent to do a job. You see, Rastafari is a reality. Each and every man has Ras Tafari in them, therefore have divinity in them."[1]

Unlike traditional religions that are handed down through the generations, Rastafari is gained and expressed anew by each individual and by each generation. As you will see in this book, many Rastas contradict each other as to what is Rasta. For instance, some think you must have dreads. Some think you should not eat any flesh. Others eat seafood and some even chicken. Some believe Haile Selassie I was God, others don't. By each individual following JAH's guidance in their life, Rasta encompasses all these contradictions. As Bob Marley said, "You change if you change from Babylon to Rasta, but you can't change from Rasta to anything. When the Truth awaken in you, you can't do anything but accept the truth."

Rasta promotes "upful" behavior: tolerance, honesty, integrity and peaceful defiance of oppression. As reggae artist Luciano sings "I live my life as a true example and shine my light with Jesus Christ principles." In spite of their often disheartening life predicament, then and now, Rastas believe in "One Love," which means unconditional love for all. Many believe that only this love can truly transform people and the planet. Bob Marley sings in "Rastaman Chant," "If ya want ta win de revolution, ya must win it wit' Rasta. Ya cayn not win it any o'ter way because if ya win it ot'er way, ya gonna fight again. When ya Rasta, dere no more war."

Many Rastas live by a strict Biblical code based on their interpretation of the Old and New Testament. They are one of the few groups today that attempt to live by the natural law as given in the King James version of the Bible. Many Rastas' lifestyles are similar to God's laws as prescribed through Moses. To them, natural is the only healthy and noble way to live. They also believe that their sufferation is the fulfillment of Biblical prophesy. Again, as Bob Marley says in "Exodus," "We're the generation tried through great tribulation."

Many believe themselves to be descendants from the lost tribes of Israel

Rasta Heart

and hence true Jews. It is not unusual to see a Rasta wearing the Jewish Star of David or adorning their house with this symbol. Their other main symbols are the ganja leaf, representing the Tree of Life, the lion which represents Haile Selassie I, the Lion of Judah, and their dreadlocks, which represent the mane of a lion.

There is a historical basis to their claim of being Jews. The Falashas (the word means "emigrant" or "exile") are a black Jewish sect that has lived in Ethiopia for centuries. Many Rastas link their heritage to these Falashas who also claim, as does Haile Selassie I, to be descendants from Menelik I, the son of Sheba and Jewish King Solomon. Ethiopian Falashas adherence to Jewish traditions is undeniable. They observe the Sabbath, practice circumcision, have synagogue services led by priests (kohanim) of the village, follow certain dietary laws of Judaism, and observe some of the major Jewish festivals. Beginning in 1975, when they were recognized by the Israeli Rabbinate, some 45,000 Falashas fled drought- and war-stricken Ethiopia and emigrated to Israel. This created dismay in some white Israelis, many of whom had seen few, if any, black Jews. The number of Falashas remaining in Ethiopia is uncertain, but estimates peak at a few thousand.

Most Rastas believe the African people are one of God's chosen races. They point to the fact that when Europeans were still living in caves, ancient Egypt was a highly advanced civilization populated by people described by the ancient Greeks as having black skin and woolly hair. In the Bible, Babylon, in present-day Iraq, enslaved the Jews and destroyed their First Temple in Jerusalem. Rastas liken the Afro-Caribs in the West to the Jews, both victims of a "Diaspora" (scattering) from their homelands through slavery and captivity. The Bible says that the "Jews wept in Babylon, remembering Zion (Israel)." So it was with Africans, brutally wrenched from their homeland and enslaved in the West.

But Babylon means much more to Rastas. Babylon is not people but rather a system. It is the sum of the complex institutions, mentality and practices that keep people enslaved economically, spiritually, mentally and politically. The word *Babylon* is also used to describe any person, institution, value, media, thought, or business, that would lead God's children away from Him. A TV commercial, a sexually-oriented pop star, an excessive lifestyle, alcohol, government-restricted travel, anti-ganja laws, racism, the IMF, low self-esteem, are all expressions of the Babylonian system. Therefore we are all Rastas under Babylon's influence. If Bob Marley's music is the drumbeat of Rasta, the "ca-ching, ca-ching" of the cash register is the drumbeat of Babylon.

However, true Rastas do not view themselves as a victim of Babylon. They simply understand how life has evolved under this unconscious system and are devoted to One Love replacing it as Rasta ascends and Babylon falls.

Most Rastas see that people, the "masses," are led astray by a few selfish, and sometimes evil, Babylonian leaders within the governments, businesses and churches. These leaders led the people into war, consumerism, confusion, hatred and greed. Some believe a few devout elders know the time when Babylon will fall. Though some envision returning to Ethiopia as the return to Zion, others feel they have already left Babylon in their minds and are now living in Zion in their hearts. Or as Bob Marley says, "My home is always where I am. My home is what I think about."

Some Rastas believe in the divinity of Jesus. Some Rastas believe Haile Selassie I is a living God. Some believe he is the second coming of Christ. Some believe he is Christ-like, or kin to Christ through his lineage, both coming from the house of David. Some read the Bible, others don't. Some smoke ganja, some don't. Though there are Rastas of all nationalities and races, most see themselves as part of a global extended family that will live on and thrive after Babylon falls.

There are several sacred books that many Rastas read. Most read the Old Testament and many read the New. Some study the *Holy Piby*, the "Black Man's Bible," compiled by Robert Athlyi Rogers of Anguilla from 1913 to 1917. Studied by many early Rasta leaders like Leonard P. Howell, the *Holy Piby* is purportedly the closest thing to the first Bible, which was said to have been written in Amharic, for centuries the official language of Ethiopia and allegedly the original language of humankind. The Holy Piby emphasizes the destruction of white "Babylonia" and the return of the Israelites to Africa, the true Zion. Some Rasta scholars maintain that under the early popes, white church leaders distorted the Amharic Bible in the translating and editing process to make God and His prophets white instead of black.

Another sacred book, *The Kebra Nagast* ("The Glory of the Kings") is considered by some as the lost Ethiopian Bible and is often quoted and studied. This book outlines the history of Solomon's seduction of the Queen of Sheba, the travels of their son, David or Menelik I, the first in his line of Ethiopian kings. It explains how David, believing his father was misusing his sexual energy, took the Ark of the Covenant to Ethiopia, where it is believed to reside today in a small chapel in Axum.

Rastas, like Jews and lions, cannot be herded or easily led. The fact that they are descendants of slaves makes them all the less willing to accept a leader in any form, spiritual or temporal. Many, if not most, followers are just Rastas and belong to no one sect of the faith. Many live alone or with their nuclear families. Some live in small camps in the Jamaican mountains often with one or more Elders.

There are many public or secret sub-sects, including the Nyabinghi Order, Holy Theocratic, Ethiopian Salvation Union, Rastafarian Movement Association, Ethiopian National Congress, Rastafarian Melchizedek Orthodox Church, and The Rastafarian Repatriation Association of Jamaica. Each sect has its own rules and interpretations of the tenets. For instance, the Ethiopian Orthodox sect shuns the use of ganja while the Coptics vigorously trade in it.

The members of the Twelve Tribes of Israel Sect (of which Bob Marley was a member for a while) are usually more educated and worldly Rastas who often are "in Babylon but not of it." They have headquarters all over the world including New Zealand, Sweden, Canada, Africa, Trinidad, New York and Los Angeles. This branch also includes many white members. Founded by Dr. Vernon Carrington (Prophet Gad), they believe in the liberation of all races through the teaching of the Bible, and the acceptance of Jesus Christ. Women in this sect are usually treated as equals.

The Bobo Ashantis live spartan, ascetic lives, many in a Rasta commune above Bull Bay on the southeast coast. They look forward to a time when JAH will lead them back to Ethiopia. They refer to their commune as a "school of redemption" that will help unite all nations in peace and harmony. They do not hold Bob Marley as highly as many other Rastas and have recently begun recording their own music. This sect is somewhat patriarchal and the women usually play a subservient role.

The Ethiopian World Federation (EWF) which, along with the Twelve Tribes, have settlers in Shashamane in Ethiopia (given to the Rastas by

Rasta Heart

Haile Selassie I). There's the Nyabinghi Theocracy Government which has no centralized leader. The Ethiopian Zion Coptic Church, was revitalized partly by white hippie converts in the 1960s. "Coptics," as they are called, incorporate much of classical Rastafarian culture into church life, and their retention of dreadlocks, Nyabingi drumming, and ganja smoking, have helped them gain many converts. This, along with their involvement with the ganja trade, has earned many great wealth, for which they have been criticized (they are supposedly among the largest landholders in Jamaica). Unfortunately, many Westerners believe Rastafarians are hardcore drug dealers due to the news exposure of members of this sect.

Rastas are usually known for their dreadlocks, long mats of hair that are created by washing but never combing, brushing, or cutting. Also, they grow "precepts," which are their matted beards. Their dreads and precepts are grown in observance of the Old Testament command, "They shall not make baldness upon their head, neither shall they shave off the corner of their beard, nor make any cuttings on their flesh" (Leviticus 21:5), a tenet also followed by Orthodox and Hasidic Jews. They believe their dreads, similar to the mane of a lion, are also "high tension wires," connecting them more directly to JAH. Just seeing their dreads flow around their face helps them to remember JAH.

Not all Rastas wear dreadlocks and not all dreads are Rastas. There are many "bald-headed Rastas" (Rastas without dreads). However, for many, their dreadlocks are a covenant with JAH and show a commitment to their faith, a commitment against the customs and social codes of Babylon. Rastas also note that Christ was most likely a "locksman," as there are no references to His cutting or grooming His hair, something that was not done by religious Jews of that period.

Regarding their highly controversial use of ganja (called "herb," "kaya" or "wisdomweed"), which many Rastas smoke in spliffs (joints) or bamboo water pipes called "chillums" or bamboo and goat's horn pipes called "chalices," they refer again to the Old Testament reference that "the leaves of the Tree of Life are for the healing of the nations." It is also noted that ganja was found growing on King Solomon's grave. Perhaps not so surprisingly, many Rastas' dreads look very much like ganja buds.

Ganja was prevalent on the island long before Rastafari began but it seems to have become part of the faith early on. In the early 1940s, Leonard

Rasta Heart

Howell, one of the first Rasta leaders, used it with his followers in their commune at Pinnacle in the hills overlooking Kingston. The commune grew to over 1600 members and was guarded by "Ethiopian Warriors," some of the first dreads. In 1954, it was shut down by police and Howell was arrested for ganja use.

However, most Rastas do not use ganja recreationally but rather use it as a sacrament. They do not seek a fun "head high" but rather a deeper "soul high." With a recreational head high you can smoke pot for years and never get the growth and wisdom that the Rastas do. They often smoke alone to seek guidance and commune directly with JAH. Rastas also "reason together," with or without ganja, by which they mean to discuss JAH, spiritual issues, individual, local and world problems. Reasoning is putting their minds together in "spiritual diagnosis," part theological debate and part prayer meeting, whereby they reason together as opposed to conversing back and forth, which they consider linear, unnatural and unproductive.

In his book, *The Rastafarians*, Samuel E. Barrett, quotes an interview with Ras Sam Clayton, which perhaps best summarizes Rastas' unique perception of ganja:

> "Man basically is God but this unique insight can come only with the use of herb (ganja). When you use herb, you experience yourself as God. With the use of the herb you can exist in this dismal state of reality that now exists in Jamaica. You cannot change man, but you can change yourself by the use of the herb. When you are God you deal or relate to people like a God. In this way you let your light shine, and when each of us lets his light shine we are creating a God-like culture and this is the cosmic unity that we try to achieve in the Rastafarian community." [2]

Many people think Rastas are pro-drugs. In reality, they are the most anti-drug group around. They shun alcohol, nicotine, cocaine, caffeine, sugar, hard drugs, aspirin, sleeping pills, processed foods, fertilizers, pesticides and all other synthetic compounds. They do not consider ganja a drug but a plant, which it is. Some smoke it all during the day while others only on special occasions. They believe that if ganja is not used for a spiritual purpose it will give you relaxation but no wisdom. Or as Julia says, "You must teach yourself to guide your high with JAH."

Many Rasta guide their high by saying a prayer before using ganja. "Glory be to the father and the Maker of Creation. As it was in the beginning, is now and shall ever be, world without end, JAH Rastafari, Eternal God Selassie I." Through this union with JAH, a Rasta becomes who he truly is, a process of self-discovery possible only through intense self-examination and repentance. Ganja is not used frivolously but as a potent tool that fosters vision and clarity. Given that much of their reasoning deals with the plight of oppressed blacks, ganja helps them to forgive and relax. Ganja has become the eternal flame, burning throughout the world. As Bob Marley said, "The more people smoke herb, the more Babylon fall."

Rastas claim their own divinity and then strive to recognize this in everyone they meet. Because of this belief, all life is precious to them. Most are against abortion and all forms of birth control. Many Rastas believe in sexual fidelity between man and woman but others do not.

Though some sects have leaders, Rastafarians are without central leadership, a decision which has strengthened the movement. Unlike most religions, Rastafari has become more decentralized over the years. Some sects have weekly services which include prayers, songs, drumming, eating and usually, ganja smoking. These meetings, which start at dusk and often go until dawn (considered their "tribal time"), are not just spiritual gatherings but a time to discuss individual, local and world issues as well. In addition to Rastafarian prayers, the Bible is often read and studied.

Periodically a "Nyabingi" or "Grounation" will be held, with Rastas from all over the island gathering together for a few days of reasoning, prayer and jubilation. Sometimes these are held on special Rasta days, like the birthday of Haile Selassie I or on April 21st, the anniversary of his visit to the island. Other times they are just spontaneously called. At these large gatherings Rasta men, women and children renew their faith and friendships, discuss sect issues, and celebrate.

Believing JAH to be within each person, they often use the term "I and I" or "InI" instead of I, me, we, him and her or you and they. I and I refers to the unity of the speaker with JAH and with all humanity. This stands in direct contrast to many religions' view of "I, the saved" and "you, the damned or the heathen."

Many Rastas use certain words to be sure their speech is always upful and positive. Dedicate becomes Idicate. Universe become Iniverse and creation becomes Ination. Appreciate becomes apprecilove. Oppressed becomes downpressed. Control becomes Itrol. Continually becomes Itinually. Understand becomes overstand. Another Rasta term is "Irie" which means the temporal and spiritual best, that all is well. Perhaps their most important word is "livity" by which they mean life, the totality of one's being in the world.

Many Rastas adopt a rural lifestyle of simplicity. Since many Jamaican employers will not hire Rastas with dreadlocks, they often work outside the system as crafts people, artists, organic farmers, entertainers or performing various odd jobs as funds are needed. Many shun the rewards of the material commercial world, deciding instead to live a spartan life close to the land. However, now with people all over the world becoming Rastas, they can be found at all economic levels and in all parts of society.

Though Rastas often view the establishment as oppressors, they view each person as an individual, no matter what the color of their skin. Many whites have become Rastas. Indeed, Bob Marley's father was white, a fact that he felt served to remind him that we are all one. As he sings in "War", based on a speech by Haile Selassie I, "...until the color of a man's skin is of no more significance than the color of his eyes. Me say war."

True Rastas exude a confidence that transcends ego. Many believe that their faith and Bob Marley's music will "remove de shackles from de mind of de people." This includes downpressed people recovering from centuries of enslavement and economic and political oppression, as well as middle and upper-class people still caught in Babylon's illusions.

Rastas, greatly underestimated by the outside world, are sophisticated theological and philosophical thinkers. They are a tribe apart, staunchly holding to their tenets and uncompromising in their rejection of the ways of Babylon. Their movement seeks both internal freedom within oneself as well as external freedom from downpression. In all ways, from their diet to their worldview, their world stands in direct opposition to Babylon. Theirs is a way in, not a way out. Into their world all are welcome because all are inherently Rasta. As Bob Marley would say, "de whole Universe is involved in dis revolution."

Over the last 70 years Rastafari has dynamically grown but has not become dogmatic or bureaucratic. It has no central controlling authority or official spokesperson. Though no one knows the true numbers, this movement is spreading across the globe due to its clarity, love and the power of its principal messenger, Bob Marley, and its new messengers like Luciano and Bushman.

1. Tracy Nicholas, *Rastafari: A Way of Life*, (Research Associates School Times Publications,1996), p.34, quoting interview with Ras Hu-I.

2. Leonard E. Barrett, Sr., *The Rastafarians*, (Beacon Press, 1997), p.255, quoting interview with Ras Sam Clayton, Mystic Revelation of Rastafari, summer, 1975.

Chapter 4

Scram

"Is not ev'ry 'eart ready to cherish dis One Love."

—Ramscram

After Clive and I left Israel and Elijah, we drove a mile or so into the town center and pulled directly off the main street into a driveway sandwiched between a colorful dwelling and a small stall selling coconuts, sugar cane, squash, breadfruit, conch shells and bananas. The house was about 10 feet by 30 feet and roughly sided with small split bamboo poles painted red, green, and gold (Rasta colors) and topped with a peaked zinc roof. This was Ramscram's home and shop.

As we pulled in, Scram or Scram-O, as he is most often called (his proper name is Thomas Anderson) came out from his kitchen. Scram is 57 years old with a dark ebony complexion, maybe six foot or so with tightly wadded dreads hanging to his waist. He is trim and muscular, with the build of a well-conditioned athlete. He has a high forehead and the chiseled feature of an Ashanti or Mandingo chieftain. A salt and pepper full beard surrounds his majestic face, the face of a lion.

Though he was dressed in shorts and a sleeveless "DETROIT PISTONS" tee shirt, his whole bearing was one of royalty. Scram moves with the grace and fluid relaxation of someone who is truly at peace with himself and his body. As he approached he was almost intimidating, his power that obvious. But then we shook hands and he smiled and laughed.

That smile! That laugh! They flow over you and caress you with their warmth and genuine care and connection. His smiling eyes revealed intel-

43

ligence and quickness. His entire air was commanding and confident, yet warm and approachable, totally without affectation and yet completely self-assured.

As we stood in his yard, I introduced myself and told him what I was there to do. Cars and trucks were whizzing by in their usual madcap fashion so I suggested that we go to a quiet beach and talk. Clive, Scram and I got in my car and drove five minutes down the road and pulled over in a parking area at a local deserted beach. Clive and I sat on a log, facing Scram, the ocean behind him. I set up my camcorder and portable CD with two small speakers playing Bob Marley's *Legend* quietly in the background.

Clive looked around and found an old plastic five-gallon bucket (these things are everywhere in Jamaica) for Scram to sit on—a simple act of respect and kindness. Scram found a sheet of thin white cardboard and put it on top of the bucket. He sat erect, proud and majestic, in a way that made the funky pail seem like a jewel-studded throne.

"Ramscram, a lot of people in my country, especially college kids, love Bob Marley's music," I started. "Then they start to listen to his message and become interested in his faith. But there is not a lot of information about Rastas available. A lot of people think Rastas are violent drug dealers because the Jamaican drug dealers in the U.S. wear dreads. I want to write a book that tells people what you are really like. Many years ago, I was a hippie, a sort of American Rasta. I met some Rastas on my last trip here and wanted to learn more. That's why I'm here. I want to find the Rastas that practice One Love."

"Ya, Ya. Like dat, like dat. Yah want to be like a messenger for JAH and yah want to be like a messenger along wit' Rasta in yah right mind. Because a real Rasta is 'ard ta find in a tall 'air man (someone with dreadlocks). Yah see. Yah doan't want ta move along wit' de wrong Rasta. Dey still doan't have de love dat real Rasta 'ave," he said, catching my drift as if he had been expecting my arrival.

His voice was melodic, low and powerful, or "MYYtee," a word he would use often. His conversation had a rhythm to it, punctuated with deep belly laughs and graceful body gestures. He was always moving, talking with his voice and his body. He often hesitated, searching for the right word, more use to speaking patois than English. Whenever he saw I understood an important point, he put his fist out to tap my knuckles with his—the Rasta handshake. He was mesmerizing.

"That's what I see in you—that love," I said.

"Ya, exactly. I try to exercise dat special love. Dat love dat sets apart, dat is different from de sex love. Becuz dat de love dat reveals it all. Dat sex activity, dat is partly different dan de true love dat people cayn feel towards all. Ya see, sometimes ya might really feel dat genuine spirit rise wit'in de I. You cayn know dat, Yes, dis spirit, dis feeling, is showing dis true love. Dis feeling flows 'round de wuurld." As he says this, he spreads his arms out and rotates his body in both directions, as if to encompass the entire world. The motion is fluid, natural.

"Even 'eads of government doan't know what true love is. Dey doan't know, doan't know, just doan't know. Because true love 'as a genuine feeling wit'in de spirit of humanity, (Scram rotated both hands by his heart and bounced a little on his bucket) more for giving, more den whenever you're gonna get somet'ing. Ya 'ave to reveal dis system of feeling ta de masses. Ya doan't t'ink about yaself. Wit' dat love, wit' dat feeling, ya felt inside of ya, cayn let ya know dat, yes, dis is de true love. Dat is spiritual love," he said and punctuated his thought with a deep belly laugh. "Ya see a person today and when he comes back tomorrow, ya goin' to look at 'im and say 'I doan't want ya even around.' YaseewhatImean. Dat not love."

"When you were a young child, you knew that didn't you?" I asked.

"Ya, Ya, I knew dat. Whenevertime anyt'ing goes wrong, my tears fell. Whenevertime I 'eard me muddah sing certain songs, I cayn't 'old me tears (he lightly touches his fingertips to his heart). I know that I am spiritual. And I go places and see people and dey need assistance and I cayn't 'elp dem. Dat burning love inside of me dat mean even if dey are sick and I cayn't 'elp dem."

"So when you were a young child, you were already a Rasta?" I asked.

"I born a Rastamon. T'is an inborn t'ing. When ya 'ave dat inborn spirit of love, ya 'ave no fear. Ya 'ave no fear. And to deal wit' it ya doan't just deal wit' special people. Ya want to be with everyone. Ya want to be wit' people dat is sick. Ya want to be wit' animals dat is sick. Ya want to know dat dis animal is going to be around. Ya want to know dat dey will 'ave access to move," he paused, laughed and made another sweeping gesture.

"So dat true love is just a feelin' of joy," he continued, arms outstretched and bobbing around, "and whenevertime de people feel de love, dey're

Rasta Heart

supposed to deal wit' dat real joy and 'appiness. Becuz whenevertime I leave Portland and I go ta Kingston, people say, 'Doan't go to such and such a place' and when I go dere, ev'ryone says, 'We nah go ta school today because we love ya ta death.' Dey cayn see t'rough dere eyes ta know dat I am a person ta be 'eard. People meet me in places and stop me in Kingston, even in de night. So whenevertime ya exert a certain way of love, you doan't 'ave to worry."

"The love protects you," I said.

"Yeah, mon. De love protects ya," he replied, laughing.

"Do most of the Rastas know this?" I asked.

"Not most Rastas because a lot of tall 'air men, dey doan't 'ave de true Rasta 'eart," he said, holding up his two foot long dreads. "Dey have de 'air but nah de 'eart. I know a lot of Rastas dat claim to be Rastas. So we call dem Rascals (big laugh). Ya see, dey try ta imitate Rasta because everyone knew 'ow lucky, prosperous a Rastamon is and dey want to 'ave dis. De 'air is 'ere to grow on everymon because everymon is supposed ta be a true Rasta and de 'air ta represent dis, to show de next person dat dat is a Rastamon but ya could trim off de 'air but de 'eart, de 'eart feelings got to be dere."

"Are there a lot of Rastas on the planet?" I asked.

"Yah, because if it wasn't fe a lot more dan less, I feel dat dere would be a lot more destruction on de planet if many Rastamon were not 'ere. I know we 'ave more religious Rasta people on dis island. Dat is what balance de planet," he replied, holding his arms out to either side and rocking like a scale balancing.

"Are people coming here to meet Rastas?"

"A lot of people come ta find Rasta but when people came to find Rasta and dey see de tall 'air and dey say 'e look like a Rastamon. But 'e is not a Rastamon or else ya would nevah see so many problems on dis island of Jamayca if the people all meet Rastamon. Ya find guys dat appear as Rasta wit' de true love and dey ain't."

"How do you know each other? You know by looking in their eyes?" I asked.

"Yes, we know dem by movin', talkin' and a suggestion of a person will tell ya what's in dere heart and by dere utterance because if ya are good ya speak a lot of good t'ings."

Rasta Heart

"The planet needs to learn this love soon. Do you think that the planet can learn soon enough?"

"Yeah. Yeah.We 'ave a belief. We 'ave a word dat we use, dat we believe when we use dat word dere is a force ta de four corners of de earth. When we call upon JAH, MYTEEE! We know dat t'ings got to work (hearty laugh). Because dere are Rastamon, da true Rastamon, dat doan't look dressed up, and 'e is not official in de eyes of de people, way back on de mountain calling out for JAH! RASTAFARI! and dos words of dat person is very much powerful, as de Rastamon John de Baptist says." He said this loudly, powerfully, JAH! RastafarEYE!, extending both arms fully from his body as if embracing the whole planet.

"And you think that will heal the planet in time?" I asked, visualizing Rastas sitting on mountaintops sending out love to the planet.

"Ya, Ya," he said, with certainty in his voice. "And if de people in de four corners of de earth (throwing his arms straight out in a big gesture) give a listenin' ear to de true Rastamon on dis island of JAHmayca, ya can change ev'rything, even de government."

I could hear Bob in the background singing, "Have no fear for atomic energy because none of dem cayn stopa de times."

"Is that starting to happen?"

"Yeah. Yeah. Yeah. If JAH wasn't working on de government dere would be more problems on dis island (laughs). But JAH doan't give dem much help. Because dey whip RastafarEYE in de beginnING."

"But no more?" I asked, remembering what Trevor had said about Rastas being treated better.

"But nah more and blessed be ta prophets like Muta (big laugh), dat send message all over de earth and ta teach de people." Mutabaruka is a famous black poet and singer living in Kingston where he runs a bookstore called Books About Us. He has a radio show every Wednesday night on IRIE radio, The Cutting Edge, that people all over the island listen to faithfully.

"How about some of the new reggae singers like Bushman and Luciano?"

"Dat's right. An all His prophets doing well. Like Rebel, Sizzla, dos young guys, dey are young prophets. Dey are doing well," he says, sweeping both hands sweep together in a full arc.

Rasta Heart

"They are real Rastas?"

"Yes, dos guys are Rastas. Dey know in dere 'earts. Dos guys are proph-ets, because dey try to carry de message ta de people. Because Sizzla, dat guy, when 'e's teachin' about de fire, it's only a flame of fire cayn burn out de 'eart of de mon dat comes looking like a Rastamon and is not. We need a fire, a spiritual fire, to burn de 'eart of de wicked to keep down de crime," he said laughing and locking both hands together and moving them like he's stirring a big pot.

"And dat is what we are trying ta work on now and ta send special peti-tion dat it end now so dat innocent people will nah be 'urt. De big guys are de ones dat must know Rasta so dey stop de wars. Much of Rasta business is dis same love, same love dey need. No matter where ya go, no matter where ya go around and come around, ya need love, need love, mon. And we need love from de bigger guys. And sometimes even I, in de mountains, 'ave said to MYself dat I am very surprised dat dos well educated guys doan't know. Because dey go ta schools and dey get all de good teach-ing dat dey cayn 'ave dis proper good life, ya know, and yet dey doan't know."

"You knew it when you were a young child?" I asked again.

"I knewww it, I knewww it. Bob Marley knew it. Bob got ev'ry inspi-ration t'ru 'is spirit, ya mon. You feel it burning inside of ya because whenevertime de person wit' de true love speaks (he stopped and smiled contently, listening to Bob sing in the background) it 'as an effect on de 'eart. Ya feel it."

"And that's why he is so popular," I concluded.

"Yeah, 'e is a wonderful guy and a man like dat never dies. 'E is not dead.

"'E's not dead (big laugh). Bob no dead, mon. At no time Bob is dead. A lot of people say Bob is dead but ya not to pronounce 'Bob is dead' 'pon de mon. We must find a different word dan 'Bob is dead.' Because dat mon might be so spiritual ya need another word for dat because 'e is not dead," he said this quietly, breathlessly while his hands freely circled his heart and he laughed loudly.

Julia and I had come to believe that in many ways Bob Marley's songs are like sermons, preached to a very receptive audience, and everyday peo-ple are singing them all over the world. We sat there for a minute listening

Rasta Heart

to Bob sing "Natural Mystic" with the lapping waves in the background.

"Why Jamaica? Why did JAH pick Jamaica?

"If ya look at de muddah country, where Rastamon spring from (Ethiopia), it's like de good God t'rew a stone over (he got up and picked up a stone from the beach) and dat's JAHmayca (he threw his rock with a big sweep of his arms while rotating his legs). Dat where special people are supposed ta be located ta bring a message to the wuuuuurld (big round 'world' sound resonated from his solar plexus). People right now are coming from all over de world to celebrate Bob's birthday. T'ousands dat appreciate 'im dat celebratin'." Bob Marley's birthday, February 6th, was a few days off.

"When you were younger, were your parents Rastas?" I asked.

"Me parents are black people and I know dat dey are Rasta and dey doan't teach me not'ing dat is bad," he replied.

"Do they live here?"

"Mi muddah and mi faddah die," he said, sweeping his arms in a grand gesture, telling you that they have returned to JAH. "I only 'ave four sister and a bruddah and an uncle around."

"Did you raise Irman to be a Rasta?" I continued. Irman was Scram's 37 year old son. I had met him briefly before we drove to the beach.

"Well Irman, my son, supposed be a Rasta because I am a Rastamon 'pon birt' so my son 'as got to be a Rastamon as well. Ya see, like my fad- dah is God and so I represent 'Im. I like a temple (hands on his stomach and big smile) for de Almighteee. 'E live in I. So dey cayn' t find 'Im no more to kill 'Im or dey would 'ave to kill us all," he said, leaning forward and laughing loudly while he clapped his hands.

"Why do you think Bob Marley died so young?" I asked.

"I doan't believe 'e die still," he said with the patience of a kind teacher, "but 'e done his work and ev'ryone appreciate it and ev'ryone dat is born to come, is goin' ta appreciate it. Dat is all we expect, all Rastamon to be alike to show dat love. Because dat is de t'ing dat is holding up all de universe right now. Wit'out de love de 'appiness is not flowing right to and from."

"When did you start learning about Rasta?"

"I was just a little boy (he held his hand about two feet off the sand and looked around for the right explanation). I Rasta from when I knew myself 'walKING. Dos Rasta guys were around and I knew dey were somet'ing good."

"These men knew love?" I asked.

"Yes and I nevah leave dem and dey nevah do me like 'ow you 'ear some mon try to do kids. Dey treat me good all de way and dey told me dat anytime ya 'ear 'Africa, Africa, Africa,' ya know t'ings are comin' ta pass. I start to 'ear dem talk about Rasta business and be careful (his voice is whispering). Dey use ta go in a corner, to 'ide, to talk about Rasta business because when de police 'eard a man walk on de street and say 'One Love,' dey treat ya bad."

"So the police would treat you bad just for that?" I prompted, wanting to hear more.

"Yeah. And dat was supposed to be de true teachin' ta be established t'ru de wuurld. Dey would say 'What are ya? Ya cayn't be talking 'bout One Love. Ya Rastas cayn't talk 'bout One Love.' People afraid of it. Just de word 'One Love' because dey started to speak AGAINST DE WORD (he said this loudly, forcefully, from deep within him)."

I remembered the billboard near the Kingston Airport that said "One Love—Jamaica's message to the World."

"Why did they speak against it?"

"Because dey are very much afraid of it because it is not ev'ry 'eart ready to cherish it. Not ev'ry 'eart ready to cherish dis One Love. But I want people to try it. It's true." He laughed with his whole body and reaches over to me and gives me a light punch knuckles-to-knuckles.

"What do think would be the biggest help for people to know love?" I asked.

"Well de people got ta leave ot'er people's business and mind dere own business. Dat give ya time ta search yahself. When ya cayn deal wit' yahself (hands on his heart) and work wit' yahself on de same side and everyone do dat and den each person will see DERE faults and see what ta mend and den we get along. People getting ta know dat all around de wuurld. We need dese wuurld leaders ta get dat in dere mind as well."

"Do you think these world leaders know it? Does Clinton know it?" I asked.

"(LAUGHS) Yes. Clinton knewww it. I doan't know if 'e tried to hide it or not but 'e knew it and Bush knew as well. Clinton knew it and Bush knew it because all dem guys dey go ta school dat Rastamon doan't go and dey know de true way of life. But dey doan't switch to de true love and ta deal wit' de people wit' dat respect dat you need ta get."

"Do you think Babylon is so strong it just sucked them in?"

"Yeah," he replied and laughed. "Yeah, mon. Babylon try because on dis island, Babylon's systems is dat dey get in dere private councils to say 'Let's charge dem fe stones' (he looked carefully for a stone and picked it up to show me) and we know dat stone is just stone. YaseewhatImean? Dey knew dat when Africans get 'ere, African 'ad to change dere language to English and up to now ya got to pay so much cash to learn what dey say is proper English. Right now and still ya 'ave kids dat cayn't pay dat doan't learn no English yet. If ya seh somet'ing dat dey doan't approve of, dey put ya in jail fe dat (big laugh). Ya see dat's de force of Babylon."

"Is Babylon getting weaker, changing?"

"Yeah, Babylon getting weaker because yah 'ave de ALLMIGHTEEE working on it, weakening dem. Dat's why Rastaman can 'ave access dis day to proclaim his just and his information. We doan't 'ave to 'ide when we say 'One Love' anymore. My uncle, dat take de teachin' of Babylon ta cut 'is 'air ev'ryday and shave up ev'ryday, when I was younger 'e try to hold me between 'is legs ta cut my 'air. And 'e go sideways and 'e go dat way (he pointed both hands to the right) and 'e go dat way (he pointed both hands to the left) an when 'e is finished, a clump of 'air is 'ere (he held his right fingers to his scalp) and a clump of 'air is 'ere (he held his left fingers to his scalp) and 'e know 'e doan't cut my 'air," he said, laughing. His story reminded me of the Roman emperor Domitian, who made all the philosophers in his empire cut their long beards. The penalty for not complying was death or exile.

"Will Babylon one day know they are Rasta too?" I asked.

"Well, ya see, I believe dat Babylon is goin' ta get de right knowledge ta know dat dey are human as well. I believe ev'ryt'ing will change up already and ev'ryt'ing will be free but dey are very much ashamed fe what dey 'ave done ta de people. So dey try ta prolong de t'ing but dey goin' kallup (collapse). Dey is going ta de end of it. Dey are going to run right out and righteousness is going ta overflow dem."

"Will the righteous make them Rasta heart or will it be sufferation?" I asked.

"Well, fe who want it ta change, we are in de time NOW fe dem ta change and ta seh dey are very much sorry fe what dey 'ave done and when dey say dat, de system is going ta change becuz we are supposed ta 'ave like a Christ-like government ta rule wit' de people under One Love and we are heading inta dat right now. We supposed ta walk right in dat and peace apply and knowing dat most of dese t'ings abolish in de name of de AllMIGHTEEE, who is JAH, to prove dat. No destruction is goin' to fall on de earth because right now dey are setting up bombs and whatnot out dere ta pollute de elements but dey are not goin' to work."

"Because JAH is not going to let it happen and Rastafari is sending that love out to keep it away?" I asked, hoping he was right.

"Right, very good," he replied and laughed hard.

"How many Rastas will it take?" I asked.

"Ya know, right now we need de whole wuuurld to follow de system of Rastafari because we love ev'ry one dat 'as breath, ev'ry one dat blow breath (he moved both hands out from his solar plexus), ev'ryone dat 'ave life. We love ev'ryone, EV'RYONE! We just need dem ta change and let us live 'appy together, ya see, because we need ta feel dat loving feelin' as well (hands on stomach, grinning). It's not like when dey alone go inta dere big temple or by demselves where dey cayn enjoy demselves wit' whatever dey want to enjoy demselves wit'. We just want de peace of mind in 'ere," he said, sweeping his hands over his heart. "Because dey really 'elp us not ta know money because dey doan't give me none. Money doan't make me 'appy anyway," he said, finishing with a hearty belly laugh.

"In my country many people have forgotten this," I said.

"Yeah. No love, no love, no love. So no matter where people go and nah matter where dey go 'round, remember that I, JAHmon, known as Ramscram, One Love to all de people," he said pointing to himself with a big Cheshire smile and gently nodding his head. "All de people who 'ave dis One Love, dis genuine feeling fe dere neighbors and yah neighbor is not de one over dere (he points toward Port Antonio) but to de four corners of de earth, dat where yah neighbor is located. Because I felt, no one preached dis to me, I knewww to my belief dat JAHmayca Island is in de center of de wuuurld, most righteous place (arms outstretched and head proudly bobing to and fro as he laughed grandly), where people can be free, where we cayn 'ave just One Love," he said, laughing loudly and we laughed with him.

"Yah know, when I see people should come from ALL OVER DEE

Rasta Heart

WUUURLD (his voice rose, his arms outstretched as his body rotated), come on dis island. I know dat it is special. Ya know, people should 'ave access ta stay anywhere, ta go anywhere. When I see American kids on dis island and English kids came on dis island and people from all over de wuuurld (sweeping his head in a semicircle), my 'eart fills wit' joy and 'appiness and I cayn see de Almightee working on it and setting de doors free right now fe ev'ryone ta be together. Ya see. I love dat."

"True love does not say 'I give to you if you give to me,'" I said.

"Alright, good and it's goin' ta come ta ya 'pon dat. Because if ya look back ta dat person fe recompense, it goin' ta bring a 'atage (hatred) and dey become yah enemy. Dos are de reasons dat t'ings rise up when t'ings are not straight," he replied. "We need love, mon, true love. We got to let dis t'ing motivate (hands churning in the air and on stomach) and let ev'ryt'ing work because anytime de love reach ta de minds of de governing people, de government, dey are de ones dat want ta govern certain t'ings, dey want ta warp de people and dey are hiding de true love, de t'ing dat cayn bring de people's mind to a standstill (he pushed both hands palm down gently toward the ground). Dey are 'iding dis from de people."

"How often do you smoke ganja?"

"Well, ya know, sometimes fe peace of mind, ya know. Yes, everyday I smoke a spliff. It is keeping my mind easy, let ya feel so sympathetic fe de evil dat dey 'ave done. Yes, it makes ya feel sooo sympathetic fe de people dat do evil and know dat dey are looking fe de people dat 'ave dat great love dat dey could learn about it and dey jus' pass dem becuz de oppressors keep people in such a state dat dey want Rastas to look like de worst t'ing (he threw his hands out from his chest) so dey doan't want ta get special attention ta RastafarEYE. Dey want ev'rybody ta seh 'Rasta are no good somet'ing,' because dey doan't want ta be Rasta because dey doan't want ta 'ave de genuine love, ya see. Dat's why dey are afraid of me (laughs)."

"Because most of de time, I believe," Scram continued, "dat when dey go in bed, dey put dere 'ands on de back of de head (Scram intertwines his fingers behind his head, as "Redemption Song" plays in the background), and dey seh, 'What is dat ganja? Why we put so many people in prison and we shoot so many people for de grass dat grow?' It jus' anot'er 'erb dat grow out into de vineyard," he laughed loudly and clapped his hands as he leans back.

Rasta Heart

"Is One Love spreading?"

"YEAH, YEAH mon. It's spreading. I'll give ya one instance in de region it's spreading. It's spreading ta de region ta de white man dat didn't like de big color "B" ta come inta 'is family. Some guys nevah like de color black, de black mon, ta enter 'is family because t'ru 'is teachin' dat 'e gets, 'e didn't like black mon, so 'e came up now wit' de same feelings and when 'e realize dat 'is white daughter 'as a fiancee, a black mon, and right now ya find de muddah and faddah of de white girl, dey gettin' ta love black mon."

"The white father and mother are starting to love the black son-in-law or daughter-in-law," I asked, wanted to be sure I understood him correctly.

"Yeah, Yeah. Dis is 'appening now. Dat is a plain sign ta de wuurld. I know dis. I 'ave seen dis in many people. When ya see dat 'eart open, ya know dat de book soon close," he continued, as he laughed heartily. "Dat is a big t'ing ta show de world. Ya know dat de book soon close because dat is de next 'eart dat is open fe de receiving of de black mon. It is spreading already MASSIVE (the word reverberated as he swept his arms 360 degrees) and dey are going ta change de system. Dey comin' up ta change de system. Because in England de growin' up black boys and white guys toget'er, dey will change de wuurld system. Like Marcus Garvey said, 'Watch it, whenevertime a black womon and white mon 'old 'ands toget'er and walk plain down de street, dere is going ta be a different change on de eart', too.' So when ya see goin' white girl, black mon, black girl, white mon, ya know de Marcus Garvey wurld is come ta pass and we are moved ta victory. It is coming ta pass because it's de people's business, eart' movement, is de people's business."

I felt myself changing as I'm sitting there listening to him. It's as if his words are like a drumbeat, resounding as he speaks. His power and certainty, the rhythm and cadence of his joy and laughter, are like a song that he has claimed and now offers as a gift.

"When I was a child I was raised by a black woman, a nanny, Louise," I said, remembering when I had encountered these black and white issues in my youth. "I loved her like a mother. When my family would go on vacation to Miami Beach, we would have to take her to the police station to be fingerprinted when we arrived. The police wanted to track all the blacks on the beach and to frighten them. I hated to see them do that to her."

"So it is," Scram said. "and ya 'ave yah eyes ta see dat. Dey did nah treat 'er good. Ya saw dis, ya're de spiritual one ta view all dos t'ings ta know dat was wrong. Dat was when life started ta change even fe ya. People need ta learn more and ta get dat love dat is wit'in dem. Ya 'ave ta 'ave dat love fe humans dat ya cayn correspond wit'."

"It seems that this black and white thing is important. The planet needs this settled," I said.

"Very much important. Yeah, mon. It must be settled. It is 'appenin' on de planet, mon. It is changing. Dat why I knew dat dis wicked system of Babylon is changing. Babylon controls all dos system and we about ta get over dem because de people seeing demselves and seeing dat dos movements are not right movement and de right movement is fe people ta 'ave more love fe demselves and we can 'ave t'ings ta share wit' ot'er people. Because de people dat 'ave no love fe demselves, dos are de ones dat are de problem," he said.

I thought about how Louise always told me, "The only problem we have is that people don't love themselves enough."

"Yeah. Give dem love, even if dey doan't want it. Love got ta appear ta dem and dey must produce somet'ing different den what dey are doing," he said. We sat quietly, listening as "Exodus" played in the background.

Bob Marley

Robert Nesta Marley was born on February 6, 1945 in the small village of Rhoden Hall, near Nine Miles (the locals call it "Nine Mile") in rural St. Ann's Parish, the son of a liaison between his black mother, sixteen-year-old Cedella (Ciddy) Booker and his white fifty-year-old father, Captain Norval Sinclair Marley. His father, from a white affluent Kingston family, worked as a land custodian in the area. Denounced and disinherited by his family for his affair with a black woman, but desiring to legitimize his child, Marley married Ciddy before leaving the area to return to Kingston.

For the first five years of his life, Bob lived peacefully in the rural home of his maternal grandfather, Omeriah Malcolm, a man known for his wisdom and strength. It was a near tribal existence, remote and surrounded by family and friends, moving at a slow, deliberate country pace. Bob was

Rasta Heart

his grandfather's goatherder. Though his close relationship with his grandfather was soon to be interrupted, Omeriah served as a father-figure and moral anchor for the rest of Bob's tumultuous life. In 1949, when Bob was five, his father asked that he be sent to Kingston to be adopted by one of his nephews, a well-to-do Kingston businessman. Ciddy refused, fearing she would lose her son but agreed to let him take Bob to the city so he could be better educated, a common practice on the island. It was agreed that Bob would live with relatives of Omeriah and Ciddy.

Captain Marley had no such intent. He placed his child with an elderly women, Miss Grey, and then ceased all communication with both his son and his wife. He hoped that Bob would inherit Mrs. Grey's small estate upon her death. Ciddy had no idea where her son was and she was grief-stricken. Two years later, Bob was spotted in Kingston by a friend of Ciddy and she immediately went to Kingston and brought Bob home. However, to better her economic situation, a year later Ciddy returned to Kingston and settled in the slum area. Bob, who had stayed in the countryside, soon followed. For many years, things did not get better and Bob often had to scavenge at the dump for food. He was to live the remaining of his formative years, from six until twenty-five, in one of the worst slums on the planet.

For most of us, it is hard to imagine the reality of a Kingston slum, both today and 40 years ago. It is an overpopulated, disease-ridden, pressure cooker baking under the intense Tropic of Cancer sun. Typhus, polio, infant mortality, malnutrition, and violence saturate the area as does the smell of urine and cooking fires. Death, often through violence, is an almost everyday occurrence. People are forced to live in shipping crates, fish barrels, oil drums and out in the open. Few have indoor plumbing or electricity. Most use pit latrines and collective yard kitchens. A sense of hopelessness and despair is ever-present. How such beauty as Bob's music could bloom from such a desolate environment is nothing less than miraculous. As Bob said, "Me doan't feel like de ghetto should be my future, like we should always love live (living) in a shit... If ya come from Trench Town, ya doan't stand a chance. Dat's a fact."

As he would have done in any environment, Bob thrived in these brutal and dispirited surroundings but not without it nurturing both the best and worst of his nature. He soon became known as a streetwise fighter, earning him the name of "Tuff Gong" (later to become the name of his record

Rasta Heart

label). To make matters worse, there was considerable political unrest in Jamaica during this pre-independence period, unrest that often presented itself in slum violence and killings. Understandably, the slums of Jamaica have always been a breeding ground for both black pride and anti-white, anti-Establishment sentiments. Both had their impact on Bob. However, his loving nature, and the fact that he was half-white, would keep him from the hatred of whites to which many of his peers would fall prey. He hated the forces that created "downpression" but not the people. As he said in 1977, "Reggae is a music dat 'as plenty fight. But only de music should fight, not de people."

After moving to the Trench Town slum area (named because of the open sewer trench coming down from Old Kingston), he, along with his many playmates, slowly transformed into a "ruddie" or "rude boy," a teenage tough contemptuous of all authority. Though small and fragile looking for his age, he was ferocious in a fight. Many people wonder how someone so poor could be so defiant, so rebellious toward authority. In the Kingston slums, as in slums everywhere, the police have little to no control. The gangs are the controlling authority and Bob was the leader of his gang. He was the "lion in his domain."

Though he was not severely embittered by the violent environment in which he grew, it did leave a lifetime impression. Even as late as a year before his death, he was still able to resort to violence, as he did in an argument with his manager Don Taylor in 1980. His mother reported that Bob beat his sister, Pearl, at her home in Miami after Pearl was rude to him. There were also reports of Bob hitting Rita, his wife, over an argument involving another man.

What are we to make of this personal behavior, so far afield from the values he espoused? Like all of us, when Bob was remembering his divinity, his message of love was clear and true. However, when he was forgetting this, he was vulnerable to his own human insecurities and fears. Like all of us, he was reaching.

Bob Marley quit school as a teenager. When asked about his education in an interview, he said, "Me nah 'ave education. Me 'ave inspiration. If I was educated, I'd be a damn fool." At eighteen, Bob's mother had moved to the U.S. and he was left homeless and hungry, living in the streets or crashing on some friend's floor. The only thing that helped him survive and thrive were his friends and his music, and later his Rastafari faith. He tried welding, mostly to please his mother, but it was music that was his only love. After almost losing one eye in a welding accident and a short stay working in Delaware, where Ciddy had moved, Bob decided to totally devote himself to his music.

Chapter 5

Dinner at Scram's

"No one should question the faith of others, for no human being can judge the ways of God."

—Emperor Haile Selassie I

I dropped Clive and Scram off and returned to my hotel. Clive and I agreed to meet at nine the next morning. I looked forward to a swim in the pool and a quiet evening in my room. I felt both exhilarated and exhausted. I noticed that after spending time with the Rastas, I often felt tired immediately afterwards and felt like I needed to be alone and quiet. I'm not sure why. It may have to do with the hours of strain trying to understand their dialect or just being tired after being exposed to such high energy and vibration levels. Or perhaps it was after just taking in so much, I needed a break. However, after an hour or so rest, I would feel invigorated and couldn't wait until our next meeting.

I had found my connection to the Rastas. More importantly, I sensed that Scram not only understood One Love but his vitality, peace, self-assuredness and exuberance told me that he lived them as well. I have thought much about this. Why is their particular path creating such obvious positive results when so many other paths, many based on the same truths, are not, at least to the same degree? I believe why their faith is working so well has to do with the purity of their outer "setting" and their inner "set."

Rasta Heart

Imagine if you lived in a place where the weather is idyllic, averaging between 80 to 86 degrees all year. Your environment is a tropical paradise with a warm sea lapping (or crashing) against beaches and cliffs, with waterfalls, jungles and clear running streams and rivers everywhere. Though there are signs of the fast-paced commercialized world around, like the cars going down the street or the Burger King in Ocho Rios, for the most part you are separated from that world and its frenzied vibration.

There is organic food on trees everywhere, coconuts, pineapples, breadfruits, ackees, bananas, plantains, plums, so you can eat for free and most everything you eat is healthy, organic Ital food. Imagine that you have very little money and therefore you own or buy very few things. Most of your time, you are outdoors in the JAH-made world, surrounded by trees, creeks, waterfalls, mountains, the moon, the ocean, the sky. Everything expresses JAH's power. You have minimal, but adequate, shelter as you spend most of your day out in the paradise or relating with other people, usually your extended family and friends.

Instead of going to a movie or restaurant, your social activities together might include going to a beautiful beach, mountain top or waterfall for the day, perhaps smoking some ganja together and "reasoning" or playing music or drumming together for hours. Bob Marley's transcendent music is often playing in the air or in your head. Several times a year you might go to a large tribal gathering lasting several days. The pace of life is slow. There is plenty of time.

Now for the "set" (the inner setting). You believe that you, like every other person on earth, are the perfect child of a loving God and there is nothing to fear. You understand that your goal is to remember this truth and to help everyone else remember. And as you travel about your day, you constantly encounter other friends and "strangers" who also know this and each time you recognize each other you hold your fist and head high and sing out, "Rastafari!"

Now imagine this set and setting is your everyday reality, twenty four hours a day, 365 days a year and has been for maybe 20, 30 or 40 years, perhaps your entire life. It is a world full of soft edges. Little from the modern world intrudes to break the spell. It is a reality imbued with clarity, a sense of high mission, warmth of friends and family and universal love for all humankind. THIS IS RASTA!

Rasta Heart

The next morning I met Clive and I went to meet his family. In the middle of the village we pulled down a side street and parked by a river. We hiked ten minutes along the river until we came to Clive's house, set in a compound of five or six other small houses overlooking the river. The house was about twenty feet square with three small rooms and a covered front porch, no electricity or running water. However, they had a phone. Jamaicans by nature are a gregarious, almost tribal, people. Communications with friends and family is vital and necessary to them. Many poor families have phones.

Pom Pom and Michael, Clive's children, greeted us at the porch. They were precocious, slender, and bright-eyed (as most Jamaican children are). We said hello in the front room and then we all went into Clive's mother's adjoining bedroom. The inside was spotlessly clean. His mother, Yvonne, was sitting on the floor next to her bed, which consisted of a mattress on the floor covered by a white cotton bedspread with a floral pattern. Yvonne is about fifty, thin, with a humble but proud demeanor. Her withered legs were folded beneath her. She told me how seven years ago her legs started to tingle. Doctors in Kingston had performed a procedure that had left her paralyzed from the waist down. She had no money to pursue it further.

After a short visit, Clive and I headed back over to Scram's. He was in his kitchen area, a back room with a rough counter and a small homemade wood stove, making some Ital dishes. Scram was totally focused on his cooking, stirring the food in the pans in slow, gentle strokes. His back to us, he started to hum a Marley song. To Rastas, the preparation and cooking of their Ital food is a sacred and meditative experience.

I looked around his house at the few simple possessions he owned. Except for his cooking and eating utensils, Scram probably didn't own more than 40 or 50 things. I could see an electric lamp, a radio, a cigarette lighter, a few gardening tools, a cooler, a machete, a note pad and pencil, and a few articles of clothing. That was it. Not only that, his house would be hard to secure. If someone wanted to break in, they could, so really it didn't even make much sense to own much of anything, especially anything of value. Jamaica has high theft rates and someone would just steal it anyway. His life situation supported his efforts to be unattached to possessions.

In many ways, I could appreciate this lifestyle. As a hippie in the 60s and 70s, I had lived and traveled in a converted school bus for seven years, usually with my best friend, Harley. It had two beds, a stereo tape deck, a sink, a gas cook stove, a wood-heating stove and an overstuffed chair, plus my personal effects. It had no bathroom, electricity or running water. When you live in this tight a space, often with one or two other friends, you just can't buy many things. There is no place to put them. Your life becomes more about what you do outside your home than in it.

Scram put a few items on a plate and walked over to where I was sitting.

"Try dis. I made it special fe ya," he said, smiling, handing me a plate of baked yams, ackee, rice and vegetables, like a waiter at a five-star restaurant.

"This tastes great," I said, amazed at the flavor of such simple foods.

"Yeah, mon. I was a chef fe years at de Dragon Bay Resort," Scram said as he served Clive. "It closed fe a few years and den I set up a small stand on de beach dere and sold food to de tourists dat came to swim. I want to open anot'er stand if I get de money."

"What kind of work do you do now?"

"Well I cayn make a 'ouse, ya know, out of bamboo and out of board as well and in a 'ousing development. I 'ave good eyes for landscaping and I love flowers (big laugh). Farming is me 'obby. Yeah, mon. I 'ave a garden. Ya see Irman, ya tell 'im I said to give ya some fruits dat doan't 'ave no fertilizer. Dat is what we eat and if yah see a little shop like, we put our bananas, our plantain, and our stuff dere whenevertime we 'ave it, when people want organic food for de I. Dat all I eat. All natural food."

"No meat?" I asked.

"Ya see right now sometimes I caught some fish, ya know," he replied. "Becuz sometimes de body go wit' de mind, ya know. But it never tell me ta eat red meat and when I say fish, I space it and I'm getting out of it."

"Do you ever eat bad things?" I pressed.

"Yeah. Yeah. Becuz sometime kids move around wit' other kids and drop dis and drop dat like a sausage," he said laughing again and clapping his hands and pointing at me. "Youuu knewww. Youuu knewww. But nah much bad t'ings. Nah much, ya know. See when I go ta United States and dat mon (his supervisor when he cut sugar cane in the U.S.) ask me 'Do ya eat by de book ev'ryday?' I say 'Yes, sir! I want to reach,'" he finished, laughing.

Rasta Heart

"Where in the U.S. were you?" I asked.

"Belle Glade, Floreeda."

"Did you like it there?" I asked.

"Well, I love de United States, ya know, but I doan't know if I get around well because of da weder. I used ta brave t'ru de weder still because I saw guys say dey not leave out of de camp when it's cold. But I go out and work cuttin' de sugar cane, fast as a bullet. I was dere fe six months. Dat's de only time I leave de island. Dis guys seh ya should run away and hide in de U.S. And I say 'No, I doan't like ta' 'ide.' I like to 'ave conversation wit' people. I doan't like talkin' secret when it's secret. Whenevertime I want to extend my vocals ta ot'er people, I want ta talk and not 'ide it."

Scram finished cleaning up and we headed outside. We agreed that I would pick him up at seven to eat at the Ital restaurant where I met Israel and Elijah.

After dropping Clive off, I headed back to the hotel. As I drove, I passed a converted school bus with a sign that read "Art Bus." The bus had big cut out windows facing the road and I could see art and craft objects inside. I turned my car around and headed back.

Inside the bus was a pretty Jamaican woman named Marcia Henry. She looked to be in her early forties, tall, thin and light skinned. She talked with a raspy voice, like someone just getting over laryngitis. I later learned it was due to an operation she had had on her nose years earlier. She ran the small art stand with her husband, Philip Henry, a well-known Jamaican artist. Their work was on display in the bus; mostly beautiful color landscapes and portraits of Jamaicans, including several Rastas. Soon we fell into a conversation.

"You must expect that this is good for you," she said, talking about my adventure. "I believe that the world view is changing. As it says in the book *Celestine Prophesy* (a hugely popular book by James Redfield), there is a revolution coming and it is a spiritual thing. There are people searching for something other than what they are used to. Some are speaking to a Rasta or reading *Celestine* and are thinking, 'I should try this. There is something more.' Many people here are doing this."

"Is this a safe area?" I asked, curious what it would be like to raise children in this paradise.

"Very little violence. It is very safe here. My girls love it. They miss sometimes the shopping so they visit friends but soon they say, 'I want to get back to my river and my beach.' They go swimming and do other natural activities during the week. They are very physical. Three of them do track at the high school and the little one rides her bicycle, swims, climbs trees. Yesterday they walked in the mountains where their grandparents have land. They said, 'See ya, mom. We are going to pick oranges.' They took a big bag with them."

We chatted awhile about my book. Marcia was warm, very approachable.

"I need to know when the book is coming out. The book will be good because you will need to clarify to the world what the Rastas are about. Because the ones that wear the hair are nowhere near a true Rasta. They call them 'paper lights'," she said.

"How do you feel about the Rastas use of ganja?" I asked.

"I think based on how they use it and view it," she replied. "To them it is a sacred thing, not to be dealt with lightly and there are those who physically cannot deal with it based on their physiology. Just like if you have an allergy to shellfish, stay away from it. If you cannot use it and stay conscious with it, leave it alone. Get your high from something else, natural. Sometimes I think about myself and I say, 'You know, Marcia, you are living a sedentary life. I paint and I go home but I have to go up to the hills because when I go up there I sweat because it is steep."

"That's what I've been wondering. When I go home will it be hard to keep this high?" I said.

"The bush will go with you," Marcia assured me. "There are conscious people all around growing. We are very near the brink but it is good to know there are others like you. Changes are happening slowly but it is picking up speed now."

"Sometimes I think things are moving too slowly but other times I think consciousness could spread like wildfire," I said. "I heard a story told by Dr. Kubler-Ross, the famous researcher of death and dying. When she was first doing research at a large hospital, she noticed after a certain black cleaning woman would go into a room of one of her dying patients, something would happen. The patient would seem calmer, more at peace with dying. One day Dr. Ross confronted the cleaning woman and asked 'What are you doing to my dying patients?'

"She began telling Dr. Ross of her tragic life, how she was born and raised in the worst ghettos of Chicago, raising six children in a cold water flat, often with no money for food or medicine. Then she told of one tragedy after another. Perhaps the saddest event was when her three-year old son died in her arms of pneumonia while she waited for treatment for over three hours in an emergency room at the county hospital. It was such a sad life that Dr. Ross didn't want to hear anymore and as if she could read her mind, the woman said, 'You see, Dr. Ross, death is not a stranger to me anymore. He's like an old acquaintance and I'm not afraid of him anymore. And sometimes I walk into the rooms of these dying patients and they look so scared, I can't help but walk over to them and touch them and say it's not so terrible' ".

"Marcia, I thought a lot about that. It only took her thirty seconds to transfer some of the peace that had taken her years to attain. So if some of us find peace, we can pass it on to others very quickly, maybe just by being with them. Then maybe this awareness can spread very rapidly across the planet."

The sun was setting and I had to get ready to meet Scram. We went out into her yard. It was that gentle time when the day recedes and the evening is beckoning. We hugged and agreed to get together again.

I headed back to the Jamaica Palace. After a swim and shower, I turned on the TV to find a BBC special on mad cow disease. In a short period, over six million cows had to be slaughtered and burned to stop the disease's spread. The BBC, not as squeamish about such matters as U.S. television, showed very visceral images of live cows being killed and their carcasses cremated. That night I decided to try a vegetarian diet.

I drove back to Scram's around seven. He was in his yard wrapping barbed wire around 10 or 15 rusty long pieces of rebar (the metal rods used in concrete).

"I just got dese from de 'ardware store across de street," he said, pointing to a low slung-industrial building, surrounded by a high fence. "Dey are moving so dey say I cayn 'ave all de t'ings dat dey leave behind. I drag dis over 'ere but I bettah secure it or someone will steal it. Once I 'ad a TV and video but someone stole it from me 'ouse. But den I didn't care because I could not pay de electrical bill anyway," he said laughing.

I watched him for awhile, helping when he needed it. He methodically wrapped the rebar and carried the smaller pieces into his shed. Even though the backdrop was rather funky, his graceful unhurried movements lent the scene an air of quiet dignity. After securing the rebar he went upstairs to clean up. His upstairs bedroom is under the peak of the roof, maybe four feet wide, 10 feet long and four feet high. He emerged 15 minutes later looking great in a clean camouflage outfit and a brightly covered turban holding his long dreads.

We drove to the small Ital restaurant where the young Rasta cook greeted Scram and me warmly. He knew Scram well and recognized me from my earlier visit. It was early evening, the air soft and warm. We settled into a table under a thatched canopy—the only patrons. Two men had built a fire on the beach in front of us and they were pulling their nets in with their catch of small fish. It was an everyday scene, peaceful and unpretentious.

Scram and I ordered dinner.

The more time I spent with Scram, the more I became aware of my uncertainty and confusion, in sharp contrast to his conviction and clarity. In Babylon, confusion permeates one's thinking, as it must, given the system itself is based on fear, lies and illusion. Rasta, based on One Love, automatically takes on the power of this Truth and expresses itself in their reasoning, speaking and thinking.

"Dis is an important book," he said. "JAH 'as sent ya ta be a messenger fe Rasta. I know dat. And one day ya and yah wife will live next ta me on de land whenever ya come 'ere."

"What land is that?," I asked, intrigued by the idea.

"Where Irman lives. We are trying ta buy dat land. It is next ta de Palms 'otel so it is expensive but I cayn get it cheap. De liar (lawyer) who owns it said 'e will sell it ta me for 400 Jamaican."

"Jeez, Scram, I can give you that tomorrow. That's only ten dollars in U.S. money," I said, marveling at how cheap land must be here.

"Not four 'undred but four 'undred t'ousand," he said laughing.

"Oh, that's ten thousand dollars. I've got a little extra but I'm not that rich," I said and we both laughed.

Rasta Heart

We talked for several hours, enjoying our meal, enjoying the night. I was in no rush. I dropped Scram off at his house and headed back to the hotel. After spending all day in his world, the contrast of the marble opulence of my hotel room, with its TV, phone, air-conditioning and jacuzzi, was vivid, almost overwhelming. More and more I was beginning to see the wisdom of the Rastas' way of life. Through their faith in JAH, their relationships, their everyday activities, their diets, their ganja, their entire lifestyle, they are creating a very powerful high and protecting it

How do we in the modern world get there? Does it mean that if you really want this state of body, mind and soul you must move to a tropical paradise and live simply? Or can we just move in that general direction by eating better foods, reducing our consumption, spending more time in nature, watching less TV and making people more important than things? Could you really live Rasta in a modern, technological, commercialized world like the U.S.?

Bob Marley

At the time Bob Marley started to record, the Jamaican music scene, mostly made up of "ska" and "rock steady" tunes, was thriving, propelled by a loose coalition of guerrilla, and mostly unscrupulous, record producers such as Sir Coxsone Dodd and Leslie Kong. Bob cut his first songs with Kong. After that he was recording hits for Dodd. Though they were instant hits on the Island, he was paid only a few pounds, a lesson he would never forget. Forming Bob Marley and the Wailers, with friends Peter Tosh (McIntosh) and Bunny Wailer (Neville Livingston), his reputation, and his musical repertoire, grew. When asked why he used the name Wailers, Bob responded, "We call ourselves de Wailers because we started out cryin'."

After cutting his first songs with Kong in 1962, his career continued to grow, though it was not without its setbacks—setbacks that might have crushed a less determined musician. In 1972, he signed with Island Records, run by Chris Blackwell. Blackwell, a white Jamaican from one of the island's more influential families, had an affinity for Rastas, having been helped by some Rasta fishermen after a near-fatal boating accident. His U.K.-based Island Records Ltd. was the hottest independent producer of Jamaican music and a licensing agent and distributor in Britain for leading Jamaican recording artists. He met Bob when the Wailers were stranded and broke in London after a failed tour. Blackwell had been viewing Marley's career from afar and recognized Bob's talent and drive and, more importantly, his charisma. He gave the group 4,000 pounds to return to Jamaica and cut an album and he was blown away at the results. From that point on, the two men's destinies were wed together. From the business side, Blackwell, more than anyone else, was responsible for Bob's meteoric rise to fame.

However, unlike almost all other successful artists, Bob's wealth never changed him. Though he was a multi-millionaire the last few years of his life, until that time he had been penniless. His roots were still in the slums with his "brothers and sisters," the only family he had ever known. As he said, "Me not of de world, y'know. Me live in de world but I'm not of de world."

His only large purchase, other than a used BMW (he said BMW stood for "Bob Marley and The Wailers"), which he later traded for a used Jeep, was to buy the 56 Hope Road home of Blackwell. It was a run-down "great house" on several acres in uptown Kingston, set off the road behind rusty iron gates. Ironically, it was down the street from the home in which his father was raised. This was to be Bob's home, the only one he really ever had since leaving Omeriah's at age five, for the rest of his life. It also became his recording studio and a free-formed Rasta commune for his ever-increasing entourage. The house is now The Bob Marley Museum.

Though he desired few material things (he toured with one duffel bag of clothes), Bob was known for his generosity to others. He formed few boundaries around himself and was available, often to a fault, to everyone, whether it be a reporter, friend or a stranger in need. As soon as he would return to his Hope Road home, crowds would start to gather in his yard, overflowing into the street outside, a street shared by the nearby Prime Minister's residence and the landmark Devon House. Bob made himself available to these crowds, offering not only his presence, but food, advice and money as well. It was estimated that at any one time, he was taking care of over 4,000 people.

Life at Hope Road was anything but serious. It has been described by one biographer as "a non-dogmatic religious hippie commune, with an abundance of food, herb, children, music and casual sex." Music, live Bob

Rasta Heart

Marley music, permeated the air at Hope Road. If the band was not practicing or recording, he would often call a soccer game out in the yard.

Rastafarians were common in the slums of Kingston during his youth, usually hermit-like specters, a pariah to the Jamaican society. An exception to this was Joe Higgs, a Trench Town singer and public figure who befriended Bob. Soon, Mortimer Planno became his Rasta mentor and took him to the Rastas' communes near Kingston. The more Bob learned of the Rastas, the more he felt drawn to them. As he says in the opening shot of his PBS special that aired in February 2001, "When we speak of Rastafari, it touches de 'eart."

Like most Rastas, Bob was apolitical, referring to politics as "de devil's business." Believing that salvation was possible through love and love alone, he said, "Only one government me love, the government of Rastafari." However, given his status in Jamaica, he could not help but get drawn into the tumultuous political elections as the island got its long-awaited independence. Destabilized and demoralized by outside forces, Jamaica's new leaders were never able to deliver the fruits of independence to its people. Due to concerns about his possible support of the socialist-leaning government of Michael Manley (Manley was friends with Fidel Castro), Bob became a target on the radar screen of the CIA of the United States. As noted by former CIA officer Phillip Agee, "The CIA would look upon the radical political content of Reggae music as dangerous because it would help to create a consciousness among poor people, among the great majority of Jamaicans, and of course the climate was created for an attempt on Bob Marley's life."

Such an attempt was made in late 1976. That year Jamaica was embroiled in another violent election campaign, pitting the American and CIA-backed Jamaican Labor Party (JLP) candidate Edward Seaga against the present Manley administration of the People's National Party (PNP). Bob had agreed to perform at the "Smile Jamaica" concert on December 5th at the National Heroes Circle. Sponsored by the Jamaican Ministry of Culture, the concert was supposed to be apolitical.

A few days before the concert, several armed gunmen entered Bob's home on Hope Road, somehow getting past PNP bodyguards. By the time the shooting was over, Don Taylor, Bob's manager, was shot four times. A bullet grazed Rita's head as she ran out of the house with five of her children. Bob's friend Lewis Griffith was shot in the stomach. A bullet grazed Bob's chest right below the heart and lodged in his arm. Miraculously no one was killed and everyone eventually recovered from their injuries. Later Bob said about the incident, "It kinda like dis. Me dere and den dem come through the door and start gun-shootin', blood claat. Dat mean I couldn't move. One time I moved to one side and de gun shot flew over here and den I moved dis way and de gun shots go here. The feelin' I had got was to run hard but God just moves me in time."

Against the better judgment of many of his friends, Bob played at the concert a few days later. Greeting the huge, enthusiastic crowd, he said, "When me decided to do dis yere concert two anna 'alf months ago, me was told dere was no politics. I jus' wanted ta play fe da love of da people." Unable to play his guitar because of his arm injury, he said he would sing only one song, "War" (based on an October 4, 1963 Haile Selassie I speech to the U.N.):

> What life has taught me
> I would like to share with
> Those who want to learn...
> That until the basic human rights
> Are equally guaranteed to all,
> Everywhere is war.

He then went on to play for another hour and a half.

While performing at the One Love Peace Concert on April 22, 1978, Bob once again waded into the cesspool of Jamaican politics. It was election time, again pitting the left-leaning PNP's Manley against the U.S.-backed JLP's Seaga. Rivalry, then and now, between these two main parties is almost like tribal warfare, with both sides using armed gangs in the ghettos to assure votes. For one brief moment during the concert, Bob convinced both leaders to join hands on stage. Manley and Seaga stood briefly, and uncomfortably, together as Bob pleaded for peace between the two opposing parties. His pleas fell on deaf ears. More than 800 people were killed in the weeks ahead. Jamaica's two political parties have been violently clashing ever since, tearing the island apart for their own power.

Health problems began for Bob in 1975 when he injured his toenail in a soccer game. Left untreated, it festered and later both the toenail and nail base had to be surgically removed and skin grafted from his leg to cover it. Eventually the wound turned into a malignant cancer. By 1980 the cancer had spread to his brain and other internal organs. To the dismay of many Rastas, he never consulted Rasta healers. After extensive chemotherapy and alternative cancer treatments at a clinic in Bavaria, Bob Marley passed over just before noon on May 11, 1981.

Hundreds of thousands of people attended his funeral and the 50 mile long procession to his birthplace in Nine Mile. He was 36. Three years earlier, in full health, he had told his mother he would die at 36. As Ian McCann writes in his book, *Bob Marley: In His Own Words*, "Reggae, Jamaica and the world have already had their Bob Marley. One is enough. To ask for two would be sheer greed." In African tribes when a drummer dies, so does his style of drumming. No one can recreate the soul of the original drummer.

He had three great loves: music, women and soccer, probably in that order. At 19, he married his first love, Rita Anderson, an aspiring singer he met in 1966 while he lived in Trench Town. However, monogamy was not part of his lifestyle, as is the case with many Jamaicans and probably most superstars. He had romances with many women, a few of which, including those with Miss Jamaica and Miss World, Cindy Breakspeare, and Jamaican film actress, Esther Anderson, endured for several years. He had between 12 and 17 children, to which he was devoted, including five with Rita (Stephanie, Cedella, Stephen, Sharon and the now famous David or "Ziggy"); Damian or "Jr. Gong" with Cindy; Karen with Janet Bowen in England; Julian with Barbados native Lucy Pounder; Ky-mani with Jamaican Anita Belnavis; Maketa Janesta with Yvette Crichton; Robert "Robbie" with Trench Town-based Lucille Williams and Rohan with Janet Hunt. However, even with all his women and children, Bob was basically a loner, often lonely in the midst of his fans and entourage. As he said, "Me just hang out with I ownself."

Many people feel that Bob misused his sexual energies by having relationships outside his marriage. Others see him as a modern-day King Solomon spreading his seed, something that led to the downfall of the Biblical Jewish king.

Perhaps Bob, rather than a prophet, may have been our tribal drummer,

Rasta Heart

for which greater purity is not always required. In African cultures, the drummer had royal status and was perceived as channeling divine energy. As one drumming researcher, Maureen Warner-Lewis, put it, "The drum is closely linked in learned African philosophy with the Word... The drum is therefore a divine tool of the Supreme Being, a womb or beginning of created life." In African tribes, drummers were considered interpreters of God's words. An ancient African prophet said, "God is dumb until the drum speaks." As Bob Marley himself said "I am not a leader. Messenger. The words of the songs, not the person, is what attracts people."

Marley not only sang, but wrote, his songs as well (he sometimes credited friends with writing certain songs to avoid royalty problems). Not only the songs' presentation but their lyrics and rhythm, all sprang from his remarkable consciousness. Each song had a message. "No Woman, No Cry" was written to comfort widows who had lost their men in Babylon's war. "Exodus" reminds us that JAH's People can leave Babylon and go to the "promised land" in their minds and hearts. In "War," he sings a speech made by Haile Selassie I that reminds the world that there can be no peace without justice. "Get Up, Stand Up" reminds us all to rebel against the forces of greed, hate and intolerance.

Many of his lyrics were based on Bible verses, especially those from Psalms. More amazingly, like Mozart, many of his songs came to him complete and full, needing absolutely no reworking. As his manager, Don Taylor, wrote "It would start with Bob going into the studio and beginning to pick out a rhythm on his guitar. Then Carly and Family Man would come in on the rhythm, and once the rhythm was established Bob would lay the lyrics which would all come from his head. Bob never put his lyrics on tape during my time and I have often wondered how he did it."[1]

---

1. Don Taylor, *Marley and Me*, (Kingston Publishing Limited, 1994), p. 146.

Chapter 6
Journey To Reach Falls

"Peace is the diploma you get in the cemetery."

—Peter Tosh

Around nine in the morning I met Clive at the Esso station in the village and we headed out to pick up Scram. "Let's all drive up to Reach Falls," I suggested to everyone. I had read about them in my travel guide and they sounded appealing.

"Dat's good," said Scram. "Let me roll some spliffs before we go."

He went into the house and came out with a Tefillin bag I had given him the day before. It was now filled with ganja.

A Tefillin is a religious instrument used by Orthodox Jews who "lay Tefillin" (I used to do it as a kid). It is comprised of a set of 1" square leather-bound cases (bayits) with two long 1/4" wide leather straps hanging from them. Inside the bayits are Hebrew prayers hand-written by certified rabbis. One bayit rests on your forehead and the straps wrap around your head. The other bayit sits on your left arm and the straps are wrapped around your arm and hand. By saying prayers as you put it on, the Tefillin leads the wearer into a spiritual state as they remember God and devote their minds, hearts and hands to Him. Or as Luciano sings, "May the words of our mouths and the meditations of our hearts be acceptable in Your sight. O! FARI!" (from Psalm 137).

I had been looking through a catalog of "Everything Jewish" when I spotted these bags. They were deep blue velvet with two golden Lions of Judah embroidered on them. Knowing that the lion was a powerful symbol for the Rastas, I bought several bags to give out as gifts on my trip. They seemed appropriate. They could be used "to-fill-in" with ganja, the instrument that the Rastas use to remember God.

The catalog company representative called me before they shipped the bags to be sure I really wanted six bags. I told him I really did and he asked me what someone in the mountains of North Carolina, not exactly a conclave of Jewish life, might be doing with them. He said that he thought I might be a Hebrew instructor for the local Jewish teenagers. When I told him that I planned to give them to Jamaican Rastas to keep their ganja in, it kind of blew his mind. "Well, I never would have guessed that," he said befuddled but intrigued.

Scram, Clive and I headed to Reach Falls, about a one-hour drive down the coast and then about 30 minutes into the John Crow Mountains. We put on the Legend CD and the three of us relaxed into the ganja, the music and the drive. The ride along the coast is beautiful and dramatic. There are tiny deserted coves on one side and jungle-covered mountains on the other. You drive through small villages with names like San San Beach, Goblin Hill and Fairy Hill. Several quaint hotels, homes and villas (even a golf course) are located in this area and are frequented by the international society set, especially Germans, Italians and English.

About 15 miles out you pass through Boston Beach with its small cove beach, turquoise water and jerk stands. Jerk, a mixture of lime juice or vinegar mixed with island-grown spices, is Jamaica's favorite way of marinading meat, poultry and fish. It is said to have begun in this area when runaway Maroon slaves "jerked" wild pigs, then cooked them over a "barbacoa" (hence the word "barbecue"). The meat is then slowly barbecued over an open pit. Pimento wood is often used as fuel to give it a distinct flavor. It is served right off the grill, usually wrapped in paper. Some jerk can get mouth-searing hot. Jerk stalls, usually small dirt-floor huts with a thatched roof, dot the islands like fast-food restaurants dot the U.S. Some of the best are in Boston Beach.

Farther down, we went through Long Bay, a one-mile-wide bay with blue waves crashing against pristine rose-colored sand. Fishing boats and canoes dotted the the shore of the small fishing village. Surprisingly most of these little local villages often have small hotels or guest houses. Jamaica is famous to travelers from all over the world for its out-of-the-way retreats.

It seemed as if Scram knew everyone along the way. Every time we would pass a Rasta, he would stick his head out the window, hold his fist high, and with a huge smile, shout "Rastafari!" and get the same equally enthusiastic response back. Often he would then tell me a little about the other person, that they were his cousin or they used to work at Dragon Bay Resort together or cut sugar cane together. When we stopped at a local store for a drink (Scram had a beer, willing to occasionally break the Rasta shunning of alcohol), he knew several people sitting around the store. In the several days I spent with Scram, I was amazed at the range of his contacts. He seemed to know almost everyone in Portland parish.

I noticed whenever we passed young women, Scram would yell something to them in patois.

"Scram, what are you saying to all these young girls?" I finally asked.

"Yeah, mon. I greet dem wit' great respect and say 'Hello, my lovely sister. Love and respect,'" he replied. "Dey must always respect demselves and make de young men respect dem too. So I call dem in respect ta remind dem dat dey are to be respected."

"Do you have any children other than Irman?" I asked.

"Yeah, mon," he said wistfully. "Besides Irman, my wife and I 'ave a son and two daughters. When dey were young, we all live toget'er on dis island. Ev'ryday I get dem ready fe school. I brush my girl's hair everyday. I love dat. Dey are all grown and dey live in Pasadena, California. Dere muddah wanted to 'ave more money and so dey go. Now me son and daughter are in jail because dey found ganja in dere car. But dey are all learning too. I miss dem but I cayn nah live dere."

"Would you like to be with a woman again?" I asked, wondering whether living alone got to him sometimes.

"Yeah, mon. If I find a good Rastalady. But ot'erwise dere just be problems like dere was wit' me wife," he replied.

In Manchioneal, a sleepy fishing village, we turned inland off the main road. We drove up into the mountains along a narrow, winding road surrounded by tropical rain forest. Along the way, we passed a few small houses but almost no other signs of life and only one other car. About 30 minutes in, we came to a small stand selling wood carvings. An elderly Rasta man, with two-foot-long white dreads sat on a log carving, along with a younger Rasta and a teenage girl. We pulled over and they greeted Scram like old friends. Their carvings were quite good and I bought one of a Rasta man's head that resembled Scram. It was getting a little late, about 4 o'clock, so I suggested that we continue to the falls.

"Dat was JAH Priest," Scram said as we pulled away. " 'E is a high Rastamon. When ya come back in April I cayn take ya back ta meet 'im."

About 10 more minutes down the road, we pulled into the parking lot of Reach Falls. There was only one other car there. Frank Clarke, the owner, a stocky short-haired man, came from behind the ticket shack and greeted Scram with a big hug. After Scram introduced Clive and me, they chatted in patois for awhile. I paid our $3 fee but he would not take money for Scram.

We headed over to the only other stall, a small thatched roof hut with a few pipes and cups for sale. A Rasta, with thin dreads a foot long, was smoking a large spliff and carving on a bamboo cup behind the stall. He looked to be in his late twenties or early thirties. We wandered over and he and Scram greeted each other warmly.

"Yah, mon, dis 'ere me friend Robert from de U.S. 'E's writing a book on Rastas," Scram said, introducing me. We tapped our knuckles together and he crossed his hands over his heart in a sign of respect.

"Yah, mon, I'm Renny," he said, flashing me a big loving grin that never really left his face.

We chatted awhile and I asked him about the wine bottles filled with an unrecognizable liquid that he sold at his stand.

"Dat's a root tonic. Try some," he said. I took a drink and passed it to Scram and Clive. "Yah, Rastamon, it's good fe de balance de family tree. Dat's natural. You shake it up. It makes you strong, yah mon." The liquid was sweet, a gentle taste, a little musty.

"What do you mean by balancing the family tree?" I asked.

"Yeah, mon. It make ya want to be wit' yah womon," he said with a big laugh.

Renny then took out what looked to be a child's toy. It was a one foot long piece of bamboo about one inch in diameter. You blow in one end and your breath causes a ball with a hook on the top to gently lift up at the other end. You try to hook it on a piece of wire suspended directly above it and then blow again and lower it back into the hole.

"Ya know dis one? Dis one is a game," he said. "Bill bong. Ya blow it and try to hang it up dere. It exercise yah lung and gives yah lung breath." He gently blows in one end, hooks the ball and with the same breath, unhooks it and lowers it back into the hole. To Rastas, smoking ganja involves learning how to breathe deeply and control your breath.

"Dis one is a water bong," he said holding up a chillum pipe made from bamboo. "If ya use ganja and t'ink about foolish t'ings, ya in a foolish way but if you t'ink about righteous t'ings, it is a compass." I bought the pipe. Renny lit the spliff and passed it over to us.

"Yeah, mon. I love ev'rybody in de world," he said with a big grin on his face that told you he really meant it. "Doan't matter yah black or white, you pink or yellow, different color on de outside but same red blood. I seh, my friend, as a Rastamon, my God is a black God but if de white man say dere is a white God, I can nah tell 'im dat is nah. But still one God. In ev'ry nation 'E makes mon and when 'E comes to dat nation, 'E' prove 'Imself to dat nation but dere still one God. To a white man, 'e looks white but it is still de same God. 'E can prove 'imself in every nation. 'E is so powerful and blessful so 'e can prove 'imself in every nation. Dat's 'ow I t'ink, ya know."

"How long have you been up here?" I asked, impressed by Renny's serene nature.

"I 'ave been 'ere fe 32 years, up 'ere. I am forty t'ree (he looked 10 years younger). Yeah. I like it. I be 'appy in me simple way. Yeah, mon. Dat's all I try to do, ya know."

After chatting awhile longer, Scram, Clive and I headed down to the falls. Along the short path down is a crystal-clear river flowing at a fairly good clip, forming a series of jade-colored wading pools and small falls, surrounded by virgin rain forest. At the bottom of the path are the main falls, a cascade of clear water, maybe 100 feet across falling dramatically 30 feet into a swimming hole 100 feet in diameter. Paradise! We put on our bathing suits; Scram pulled his hair up into a ridiculous looking bun and we all headed in.

We played around in the water for awhile, laughing, refreshed and invigorated. We were like three kids on an adventure. You could go under

Rasta Heart

the falls into little caves or sit in natural formed hollows while the powerful falls massaged your shoulders. The water was refreshing and cold. Clive had lived an hour and a half away but had never been to the falls.

After about an hour, we decided to head back, dropping Renny down the road at his house. It was small but well-kept. His wife was gardening in the yard and we said a quick hello. On our way back, we drove a back road to Boston Beach. It wound through the mountains with magnificent vistas and jungle foliage brushing the car as we drove. We were the only car on the road.

As we continued toward home, we would stop and give people a ride. It reminded me of picking up long-haired hitchhikers in my hippie days. Everyone you picked up just melded into whatever was happening in your car. Scram was always very kind to the people we picked up, chatting with them, usually in patois. Picking up people is very common, and greatly appreciated, in rural Jamaica. It's not unusual to see a young school child in uniform, a teenage girl or an elderly women flag you down for a ride. However, most people just walk and friends, neighbors or complete strangers just stop and offer rides. There is also an extensive network of taxis and public buses and private minibuses that link almost every village on the island. Like everything in Jamaica, these buses rarely run on schedule, if one is even posted. Bus stops can be hard to detect. Usually you just look for a group of people standing together on the road. Outside the few urban areas, you can flag down the bus. The buses are often full to overflowing, with people hanging out the doors and all kind of goods stacked on top.

We passed an elderly lady walking in the road and Scram told me to pull over to give her a ride. He opened the door for her, gently telling her "Take yah time. Doan't over work yahself. Where ya going, dear?" She was heading to her church 10 miles down the road. After we dropped her off, we started talking about the book again.

"It is very much important," Scram said, "fe ya ta talk ta de people, ya know. Fe many, many years, I 'ave been 'earing about de reaction of people outside of dis island. Dey give Rasta a bad name, ya know, Babylon. Because I remember one time, long time, I remember ev'ryt'ing dat really 'appened, dey used ta seh is Rasta. If dey 'ear of any movement, like a shop break-in or a mon shot a mon down, dey would 'ave a feelin' dat it was a Rasta. But most of dos guys, dey wear a wig, a Rasta wig."

78

Rasta Heart

"When I was a hippie in the 60s," I said, "they did the same to us. Many people thought hippies were crazy. They hassled us and put us in jail for smoking ganja."

"Yeah. Is de tribulation," he said. "From de first time ya said 'Love,' like ya were reminding dem of somet'ing but de majority of people didn't appreciate dat. Anywhere ya go in de wurld and yah seh 'RASTAFARI,' ya 'ave ta look in tribulation, ya 'ave ta look at jailhouse (laughs). Because even Jehsus tell de people de true way of life. But t'ings are getting bettah fe who feels it, who knows it, mon. Because now if a mon go before de judge fe a little weed, de judge jus' chase dem away, ya know. So dey minds 'ave gotta change ta get t'ings ta de maximum way of life, de mind of de people gotta change." The conversation then wandered to his youth.

"I was born in a village, Bellvue, near Moore Town. We cayn go dere when ya make ya return. We cayn cook on a wood fire wit' yah wife and we cayn 'ave some natural vibes, ya know. We are fortunate now because we 'ave driving roads. When I was young, whenevertime my muddah step off de bus, we got ta go and 'elp 'er ta brings 'er t'ings, over four or five miles (laughs). I 'ad to walk five miles to get ta 'ome because dere were no roads then. We are very much fortunate to be driving on dis road now ta take us all de way in de village," he said.

"How many people lived in the village?" I asked, figuring it must be a very small village if there were no roads to it.

"Bout t'ree t'ousand den but lesser people live in de village now, yaseewhatImean? Because lots of people leave de village and go ta England," Scram said.

"So you lived in a village with three thousand people and the closest road was six miles?" I asked, imagining what a peaceful life that must have been.

"Yah, mon. When de river came down and de boat cayn't go over, de big men dey go down and dey make a raft and dey use dat raft ta take de people over. I was 'appy der. Den if ya 'ave a couple of pounds, ya are a wealthy man but now de cut de pound down ta two dollars and two dollars cayn't buy anyt'ing. Back den, wit' a pound, ya could buy shoes, pants, a belt, socks and 'ave change. Now pound cayn't buy not'ing. Dey been workin' it. It became an expensive island when de dollar changed in '65."

"Is your family still there?" I asked.

Rasta Heart

"I 'ave like four sisters and I 'ave two older brot'ers. Two brot'ers and two sisters in de village, in Bellvue. I 'ave two more sisters someplace in England."

"Do you ever hear from any of them?" I asked.

"Yeah, dey came 'ere when my muddah die, ya know, a year ago. She was living in Bellvue, in de valley. My muddah was a great lady, the greatest woman on eart' ta bring me alive and everyday day I seh 'She won't die. She nah dead.' If she gives love, she nah die and spiritual. Yes. She was a proper lady," he said, wistfully.

It was now dark and we were back on the main highway to Port Antonio. We picked up another man that Scram knew, who was waiting at a bus stop. As he got in, the aroma of white rum filled the car. He seemed to be intoxicated and he and Scram talked in patois. Bob Marley played softly in the background. Strong white rum, "overproof" as it is called, is pervasive on the island, sold in small rum stands everywhere. The man's unhealthy inebriated look once again reminded me of the contrast between Babylon's alcohol and Rasta's ganja. Or as Bob Marley says, "Rum mash up ya insides. Just kill ya, like de system." We dropped him on the edge of the village. Before returning to the hotel, I dropped off Clive and Scram, telling them I would come by the next day to say goodbye before leaving for Kingston to catch my plane home.

The next morning I picked up Clive and we drove over to Scram's. Scram was in his kitchen making us breakfast.

"Ya know, de Rasta 'air is more den 'air," Scram said. "Ev'ry time ya make a move, ev'ry moment a Rasta is reminded of de Love by de locks of 'air. Dey remind ya of JAH, of the RastaMON."

"Here's what I used to look like," I said, showing him a photo of me thirty years ago when I had a full beard and shoulder length hair.

"Ya look more powerful," Scram said examining the picture. "Well, ya see, yah muddah and ya faddah are traveling on de right way. Dey are good. Dey doan't t'ink evil. Dey give ya a good foundation because when parents 'ave negative t'oughts, it goes ta de child. I know de seed. Good tree bring good fruit. Same wit' people as well. But some parents doan't teach dere kids about love."

"Speaking of children, how do Rastas view abortions?" I asked.

"Nah dat, mon. Before ya 'ave yah king and yah queen and ya 'ave yah prince and princess ta be born ta keep dis world goin' farther as de Creator seh, 'World wit'out end.' And ya' find a force dat came in and ta seh 'kill dem' and dat is what is goin' on now and dat is what de spiritual eart' got ta rebel about and ta let kids born so dat we cayn 'ave people enjoying dis eart', world wit'out end. I would really like to see it like dat"

Scram looked out the window. He seemed to be contemplating a "world without end."

"Dat is why Rasta nah 'ave abortion. We nah kill de children. Dey are yah greatest lover. No one love ya like yah child. Life is a big t'ing, a natural life. YaknowwhatImean? Dat child is alive in de womb. Dat is a child and if de mudder kill dat child, she will not get de t'ings dat dat kid cayn give ta 'er. She will not get de love, de attention and she will suffer. Dey kill the biggest love dere is. I know a lady dat 'ad an abortion and now she cry almost ev'ryday fe dat child because she nevah 'ad another child 'cept dat one and she is all alone. Yah spirit sympathize with 'er now."

"What about if someone is really poor and can't support another child?"

"Yah mustin' kill de children. In Babylon, dey doan't overstand dat de children are JAH's greatest gift, dat dey are JAH's children, not yah's ta kill" he said without judgment. "Dat is why dey suffer because de Father give ya dat child ta help ya and ta ease sufferation and ya destroy it. Ya doan't know. Dat child may grow up ta be a lawyer (he pronounced it "liar") or a doctor or own a store and dey build ya a big 'ouse when ya get old. Dat child dat ya kill might be a Rastamon."

"So none of the Rastas have abortions?" I asked.

"None of de good Rastas but imitation Rastas 'ave abortion," he answered. "But fe real Rastas de locks (he holds his long dreadlocks gently between his fingers) reminds us all de time of dis sacred life. People got ta know de enjoyment of de creation is dere fe de people. Dat's why a lot of people want ta leave dere polluted area and ta come ta Jamaica and jus' relax and dey cry when dey are leaving too because people need ta be free and ya cayn feel dis freedom on de island and it is niceness, de rivers, de springs, ta enjoy de sunshine and de cool climate and ev'ryt'ing. Ev'ryt'ing

Rasta Heart

Irie. We jus' want ta know dat de visitors are droppin' into de right people wit' de right love ta feel de right vibe."

"Many people who cannot come here, may just meet them through the book," I said.

"People cayn find people in dis book," he continued. "Dese four guys, dese Germans, dey drive by my shed and dey look at me and dey go up and dey come back and dis guy said, 'I know ya, mon. I saw ya in a book.' Dey could see me picture in it and dey go get de book and bring it ta me. Someone wrote about me in a book and my picture was in it but it was in German language so I doan't know what 'e say about me because I doan't know German. YaseewhatImean."

"I bet they said good things about you."

"I know dey were sayin' good t'ings because de same way ya see me, dey saw me same. 'Ear me now, I meet t'ousands of people and we sit down just like dat and we reason toget'er and I give dem a big surprise because I tell dem about seven days before de Berlin Wall fell. I tell dem dat de 'ands of de people are goin' ta crush dat down. And dey said, 'Scram, it cayn't be like dat because de wall is so thick and it's so tall and it dere for over many years.' I seh, 'De 'ands of de people is goin' ta crush it down' because I know de time when de ALMIGHTEE JAH seh ta drop it. Dey send a piece of Berlin rock ta me, a chip of it. Because dis guy I was speakin' ta, 'e was a Baptist from Germany, 'e t'ought I was a prophet and dere was no one could tell 'im dat I am not a prophet." With this, he breaks out in a big laugh and we join him.

"I think I need to get going soon so I get to Kingston before dark," I said. Scram said he'd catch a ride with me as far as Long Bay.

As I waited for him to get ready, a Rasta woman DJ on IRIE radio, with a very dignified English accent, was speaking.

"Marley remained a steadfast influence," she began. "When he entered the musical genre, Reggae music had not yet been coined. Indeed it was an interesting time when Jamaican music was going through a period of transformation from ska to rock steady and to what is now Reggae music. Now it is Jamaica's most enduring musical form. The growth of Bob Marley and the evolution of his musical style was synonymous with the development of his personal philosophy.

He was guided by the teachings of his Imperial Majesty and quoted the

Rasta Heart

words of Haile Selassie in several of his songs which were later to attain international acclaim. By 1981, the Guardian newspaper described him as the most eloquent ambassador of Reggae and one of the most powerful and conscientious voices of the century. As we observe Bob Marley week, we will take a more in-depth look at Marley on his journey, the first superstar of the Third World and musical man of the millennium."

Scram soon emerged, regal in his immaculate camouflage shirt and long pants, with his locks up under a red, yellow and green turban. We dropped Clive near his home and I thanked him for being such a great guide. We hugged and said goodbye in the Esso station and Scram and I headed toward Kingston.

It was a beautiful day as we drove along the coast road, talking and listening to Bob on the CD player. When we stopped at a gas station about 20 miles down the road, we noticed that the front right tire was low. The attendant put on the spare and said if we could wait a few minutes he would fix it.

Scram and I sat by the car as he fixed the tire. Scram waved to many people as they passed. Sometimes he would yell "Rastafari!" if a Rasta passed. A few people pulled over just to chat with him. A fragile elderly woman, walking very slowly and with a bandaged hand, came by, a pained look on her face. Scram engaged her in conversation, in soft tones punctuated by his powerful laugh. All the while he gently held her bandaged hand. She walked away smiling, seemingly out of her pain.

"Scram, thanks for everything," I said as I let him out in Long Bay. "It's been great. I'm looking forward to seeing you in April with Julia."

"Yah, mon, I see ya in April. I look forward to meetin' yah wife and I get some proper chairs before she comes. Love and respect, mon," he said, crossing both arms across his chest.

"Love and respect," I said, doing the same. I headed off toward Kingston and home. As I looked in the rearview mirror, Scram was heading across the road waving to several friends sitting around a small store.

For the next three hours, I drove along the coastline toward Kingston, passing through many small villages, each with its own run-down but unique personality. In Jamaica, you can never forget the ever-present real-

83

Rasta Heart

ity of poverty. Clean, ram-shackled huts are everywhere, built to make it until the next hurricane. Anything more is a waste. However, this same poverty throws people together. Driving through rural Jamaica is not like driving in the rural U.S., where you seldom see anyone. People are every-where—in the road, by the road, on their porches, working in the fields, in front of the stores, at rum bars, clumped together at bus stops. One middle-aged woman was squatting by the side of the road peeing, her dress unabashedly thrown up on her back. She waved as I drove by. It is a totally unaffected island.

The coast road was flatter and less traveled than the mountain route I had taken a week earlier. Driving took less attention and I was able to reflect on my last several days with Scram, Marcia, Irman, Israel, Elijah, Renny and Clive. Now as I started to get some distance from my experience, I realized once again how powerful it had been. I could see more clearly how JAH was guiding me, from Verley to Clive to Israel to Scram. It was as if they all had a piece of the puzzle, bringing the book together in an incredibly rich and textured tapestry—a tapestry of infinite levels and dimensions.

It was Scram that had the greatest impact on me. He truly brought the entire Rasta reality to life. He was a living, breathing, walking example of Rasta. There was almost no fear or greed warping his being, his persona. Being unfiltered, his light was shining very clearly and very brightly. He made it look easy and in doing so gave you a calm assurance that you could do the same.

In looking back at my time with everyone I had met, I also realized that something "very much powerful" (as Scram would say) was going on inside of me. It was as if I was rejoined with the family I had always been seeking but had never found. It was as if they were on the other side of some invisible fence, the Rasta side, and they were yelling over to me, "Hey, Robert, you're on the wrong side. You're on the Babylonian side. You're supposed to be over here with us on the Rasta side. We've been looking for you like you've been looking for us. Come back. Come home. We're your family." And it's as if they're saying that to everyone.

Arriving in Kingston and checking into the ultra-modern Four Seasons Pegasus Hotel was a culture shock but not an entirely unwelcome one. I was back in Babylon, seduced by its creature-comforts and efficiency. The hotel was complete with gift shops, room service, several restaurants and even a bakery. I indulged.

That night I stood out on the balcony, overlooking the city and the mountains, smoking my last spliff. The city was quiet, not much traffic. The scent of wood smoke, from wood cook fires in the slums, was in the air—an incongruous touch in a modern city. Yet it seemed somehow totally appropriate. This amazing island was part Zion and part Babylon. The Jamaica I had witnessed in Port Antonio was one of the most peaceful places I could imagine. Yet I knew that the Jamaica here in the city, Babylon-influenced Jamaica, was very hard and violent. Just as this island was struggling between Babylon and Zion, I knew this was now my challenge. How do I take this "Zion consciousness" I had been exposed to, internalize it and live it in Babylon? Could it even be done?

Bob Marley

Two decades after his death, Bob Marley's legacy continues to influence not only the world of music but that of politics, religion, philosophy, ethics and economics as well. In 1975, *Time* magazine wrote that in Jamaica "he rivals government as a political force." Feared by many within the governing political structures for his strident cry for ending black oppression, he elevated black pride and civil rights to the level of religion through his Rastafarian beliefs. More importantly, unlike many singers who only appealed to certain cultures, Marley and his message of freedom, rebellion and love had universal appeal.

Watching Bob Marley perform is an almost transcendent experience. He is unpretentious yet powerful, dynamic yet natural. As when you listen to his music, you feel his love and you cannot help but love him in return. His music, lyrics and onstage persona are imbued with transformational power and a unexplainable life-changing quality. Unlike most other performers, Bob does not really project to the audience, almost never directly addressing them or his band. Rather he exudes a distracted kind of magnetism that draws in his audience. He often appears to be in an almost trance-like state, with his eyes closed. He is in his own world and you are welcomed in. In an interview he once said, "It is not de people to I play. I play music."

As Prime Minister Edward Seaga said at Bob's funeral, "Bob Marley was an experience that left an indelible, mystical imprint with each encounter. Such a man cannot be erased from the mind. He is a part of the collective consciousness of the nation."

Unlike many other pop stars, his lyrics and onstage presentation had few sexual undertones. Even the I-Three, his female backup group made up of his wife, Rita, Judy Mowatt and Marcia Griffiths, always dressed conservatively. Moving rhythmically together in traditional ankle-length African dresses and turbans, the I-Three on-stage presence was imbued with power and dignity.

As a performer, Marley was relentless and demanding. He keenly felt the awesome responsibility JAH had bestowed on him. He would think nothing of going over one song for hours until everyone got it right. He often drove group members to near exhaustion.

However, he was much more demanding on himself. He would make himself available for almost any interviewer as he felt that interviews too were part of getting out his Rastafari message. On tour, as soon as he arrived in a city, while the band and I-Threes rested, he would spend all day giving interviews before practicing for hours before the show. After an exhausting performance that night he would again meet with the press until late at night, often going with little or no sleep. The next day he would get up and repeat this for weeks or months on end, with no one to protect or manage him or even really understand him. His commitment was total. As he said, "Me no enjoy success, y'know. Look 'ow slim me is. Me just come to do God's work, me nah really enjoy it."

As Bob's music made the transition from ska and rock steady to Reggae, the musical genre he would come to personify, so did his political and philosophical thinking make the transition from "ruddie" to Rasta. He grew to understand that his goal was not to entertain but to bring people to God and the the message of Rastafari. As he said, "Reggae music is a music created by Rasta people and it carries an eart' force, a people riddim... proud riddim... So you find it cayn't go out, it's like from the beginning of time, creation."

In reality, Bob Marley's music fits no musical genre. Many of his songs sound little like reggae. His music is simply, and beautifully, Bob Marley music. As he would say, "When people say 'reggae,' they expect a type of music. As far as me is concerned I never give it a name. I just play

Rasta Heart

music."

It is the infusion, the intertwining, of the inspirational clarity and love of the Rastafarian belief with his musical genius, that has made his music different from all other. To watch him on stage, with locks flying creating a constant halo around his chiseled beatific face, you cannot help but feel his music is inspired by God. As one writer noted, "It seems he got his spirit and power from God, and used his body as a translator to convey the energy to the people."[1] By the end of his life, he had become so much a part of his faith that he said, "I am not Bob Marley. I am Rasta... I ever was, ever is, and ever will be, Rasta." His transition was complete.

With only his talents and spiritual beliefs, he grew to become a legend. The worldwide fame of Bob Marley was to reach epic proportion before his death. At that time Marley, viewed by his fans as a principled moral authority, was the best-drawing entertainer on the planet. In many ways, his past made him the perfect messenger for Rasta. Being half-white and half-black allowed him to be more easily acceptable to both races. Given that he spent most of his life in poverty gave him the moral high-ground to speak about exploitation and downpression. A singer coming from the middle or upper-class would never ring as true. All the pain, degradation and poverty of his youth prepared him to become a messenger for Rasta. And the fact that he never got lost in his fame or money but remained always himself and with no compromises to Babylon only increased his stature.

Though his lyrics were often angry and defiant, his overall tone was optimistic as he urged his listeners to seek paradise on earth, rather than waiting until the afterlife. Like another black visionary, Dr. Martin Luther King, Jr., he often quoted the Biblical verse from stage, "Righteousness shall cover the Earth like water covers the seas." Or as he would say it, "Rastaman vibration gonna cover de eart' like de water cover de sea."

Two decades after his death, his music still brings us together. Though his life, like a fleeting star, was short and bright, he left behind a monumental body of work. "The reservoir of music is like an encyclopedia," says Judy Mowatt of the I-Three. "When you need to refer to a certain situation or crisis, there will always be a Bob Marley song that will relate to it. Bob was a musical prophet." As he said, "My music will go on forever. Maybe it's a fool seh dat, but when me know facts me cayn seh facts. My music go on forever."

Rasta Heart

By the end of his life, he has become to many around the world an almost messianic figure. He even spoke of a "visitation" one night where he was told he was a prophet. He often was frightened by this responsibility but in the end he was willing to accept it. "By and by," he explained, "JAH show ev'ry mon him hand and JAH has shown I mine." He was, and is, the musical conscience of the planet. This can be plainly seen in many of his songs including "Redemption Song:"

> *Old pirates, yes, they rob I*
> *Sold I to the merchant ships,*
> *Minutes after they took I*
> *From the bottomless pit.*
> *But my hand was made strong*
> *By the hand of the Almighty.*
> *We followed in this generation, triumphantly.*
> *Won't you help to sing these songs of freedom?*
> *Cause all I ever have: redemption songs,*
> *These songs of freedom.*

This was the last song on the last album Marley released before his death.

Chapter 7
Back to Babylon

"No matter what may befall a human being, he can always succeed in overcoming it if he has the strength of faith and prays to God, for inevitably He comes to the assistance of those who believe in Him and those that through their work live an exemplary life."

—Emperor Haile Selassie I

The next day I was back in Babylon, standing in a Walmart, dropping off my film. The bright fluorescent lights, the smell of the greasy fried foods, the glut of consumer goods, the hustle-bustle of the modern day hunter/gatherers, overwhelmed me. I felt disoriented. I looked over at Julia and she knew what I was thinking. We both shrugged our shoulders and said in unison "Babylon!" and busted into laughter.

I had told Julia about the trip and showed her the videos. She was as taken with Scram, and everyone else, as I was. We immediately started to plan for our mid-April trip, eight weeks away.

Then I began to write. Julia started to transcribe the talks I had recorded on my camcorder. She would spend hours in our living room in front of the TV, stopping and starting the video, to be sure she was recording them correctly. One day she turned to me after a long transcribing session and said laughing, "You know I've spent the last six hours transcribing every word of a man sitting on a five-gallon bucket."

We both committed to a more Ital diet and stopped eating meat. Via the book, we were both spending six to eight hours a day in Jamaica, with

Rasta Heart

Scram and friends. And we were loving it.

The more Julia translated everything Scram said, the more his wisdom shone through. I had missed much, either due to my mind wandering or not understanding his dialect. Now we had time to review it word for word. We began to notice that a pattern was emerging. Scram seemed to uncannily overstand exactly what I wanted to know. It was as if he had been waiting for me to come and ask him these questions, as if he knew exactly what he wanted his message to be. Also, Julia added her own insights and wisdom, often hearing things I had missed.

JAH's guidance continued after I left the Island. The day after I returned, I was talking with my cousin Bobby about my trip. Bobby was looking for a house in Jamaica for a vacation home. As we talked, he told me that one of his close business associates was Chris Blackwell. He was also close friends with the lawyer for the Marley family. He promised to introduce us and we planned a trip for later in the summer.

Life returned somewhat to normal at home. Blowing Rock is at the top of the Blue Ridge mountains which look, at a distance, like Jamaica's Blue Mountains, at least during the summer months. There are clear running streams, waterfalls, hiking trails and swimming holes everywhere. The world's oldest mountain, Grandfather Mountain, is 10 miles away. The planet's second oldest river, the New River, begins in our backyard, in a large spring-fed clear pool, set in a grotto of majestic pines and full rhododendrons. It is a natural retreat 50 feet from our back door, always available, always beautiful.

The village itself is quiet and quaint, one main street with shops and restaurants, nearly deserted during much of the winter. Boone, known as a "hippie conclave," is eight miles away, the home of Appalachian State University, which adds culture and youth to the area. Ganja, back-to-the-land living and even dreadlocks abound in the area.

We got a little ganja from some friends and started to smoke occasionally. We wanted to experiment, to see if it would have the same beneficial effects on us as it did for the Rastas. We would smoke with friends or by ourselves on the Blue Ridge Parkway, overlooking the mountains or on a walk through a local wilderness area. When Julia and I smoked together we would get very creative, our hysterical laughing punctuated by insights for the book. We would sit for hours by the fire or in a natural setting, talking

Rasta Heart

and laughing.

Julia and I began to feel a new sense of purpose with its accompanying calm. Having one foot in Babylon and one in Zion, we began to realize how perfectly suited we both were to write this book and then get it out into the world. In all my past endeavors I had sought this sense of purpose in my work. In the 70s and early 80s, I ran a school in California that taught people how to build and remodel their own homes with an eye towards ecologically-sound building practices (solar and wind generated power, composting toilets, etc.). In the 80s and 90s, I produced a TV series and video library on how to do your own remodeling and building projects.

In the 90s I wrote two books, *In The Spirit Of Business* and *In The Spirit Of Marriage*, on how to express unconditional love, One Love, in these areas of our lives. In 2000, I wrote *Psychedelic Odyssey: Memoirs of An Ex-Hippie*, a book, like this one, that attempts to explain a much misunderstood sub-culture. Now, I was glad to have this next assignment. As Bob said, "All me do is beg JAH fe give me work fe do. Because me useless if me don 'ave not'ing ta do. Me 'ave ta 'ave somet'ing ta do. So Him seh, 'All right, I gon give ya way fe doing it' and I do it. So I'm free."

It seemed wherever we turned there was a Jamaican connection. In late March, National Public Radio (NPR) carried a story about how the death rate in the Kingston slums had dropped by 66 percent. Gang members and slum residents had finally and simply decided to try to stop the violence. At the end of the report they played a recording of a meeting of gang members. They were saying things like, "We need ta show de wurld One Love" and "It is Babylon dat make us fight. We nah want ta fight." The next day NPR carried a feature on U.S.-Caribbean trade agreements and ended the report by saying Secretary of State Colin Powell was a big Marley fan.

A new common rhythm tied our family together. Since we returned from Jamaica after our first trip in October, Bob Marley had been singing in the background almost constantly. We listened to him in the morning as we made breakfast and at night as we made dinner. He played in our car on the way to the movies or shopping. Even Alicia had her favorite songs that we played on the way to school (now she's also into other reggae artists like Tony Rebel, Luciano and Bushman).

We started to give his CDs to several friends. A friend in our neighborhood said she had listened to the CD 25 times in the first few days. We gave a copy to another friend to listen to while he washed his car. He called back that night to say he listened to it three times straight and his car had never been so clean.

Then there were times when it seemed that JAH would give me a little helping hand to deepen my faith. I had e-mailed the first chapters to an old friend of mine, Debby, who lived in the next county. The next day when Julia and I returned from a long walk, we had a message from Debby saying that she loved the chapters and to call her back. I dialed her up.

"Is Debby there?" I asked of the man who answered the phone.

"Deb-by?" he repeated.

"Yes, is Debby there?" I said.

"Deb-by?" he repeated again.

"Yes, Debby," I said, trying to be friendly though I was getting a little frustrated.

"Nah, mon, dere is nah Deb-by 'ere," he replied, in classic Jamaican dialect.

"Where are you from? Jamaica?" I asked.

"Yah, mon, I from Montego Bay," he replied.

"Are you a Rasta?" I asked, barely believing this was really happening.

"Nah, mon, I not a Rasta but I 'ave a Rasta 'eart. My older bruddah is a full-dreaded Rastamon in Montego Bay," came his reply.

I was floored. Out of several hundred thousand numbers in that area code, what was my chance of dialing the wrong one and getting a Rasta on the other end? In Miami maybe but not Winston-Salem, North Carolina!

What followed was a half hour phone call between Julia, me and David Grant, a Jamaican living somewhere near Winston-Salem. He had been here six years living with his American wife, his sisters and nieces. As we talked, there was this one magical point where Julia said, "It's not by accident that we are talking together. JAH wants us to link-up." It was like a switch had been flipped. His voice, which had been rather subdued and hesitant, became strong and powerful.

"Yeah, mon. JAH's presence is eversure. JAH renews One Love. JAH will take ya from one Rasta to anot'er. Dey take you ta a 'Binghi service and ta de spring where de water flow from de rock. How good and present it is fe I and I to be present wit' ya. JAH will be yah eversure protector, ever present, everwise. JAH is life everlasting. Wurld wit'out end. One

Rasta Heart

Love, mon."

The weekend before returning to Jamaica for our next trip we made arrangements to meet David in a restaurant at a shopping mall in Winston-Salem, about two hours from our house. Julia, Alicia and I arrived at the agreed upon time but no David. We took a booth and in an hour he still had not arrived. At one point an African-American with full dreads accompanied by his teenage son sat in the table directly across the aisle. At first we thought it might be David but he didn't seem to be looking around for anyone. Finally I went to a pay phone and called him. He said he hadn't been able to get a ride.

When I got back to the table, Julia said that when the other guy and his son got up to go the bathroom, she noticed that they were wearing Bob Marley tee-shirts. I walked across the aisle to their table and showed him my mock-up book cover and told him what we were doing. It turned out this guy, Khebo (Kevin) Pauling, had been a Rasta for twenty-five years and even had a local Reggae band. He was having lunch with his son, Jahman. I asked them to join us when they finished eating. In a few minutes they wandered over to talk.

Khebo was slim, around mid-thirties and bright-eyed. He exuded that same kindness and calm that I had witnessed in the Jamaican Rastas. Jahman was a very sweet kid. He would often put his head on his father's shoulder, not something many teenage boys would do in public.

"So you've been into this for 25 years. How did you get interested? Because of Bob Marley?" I asked

"I used to live in DC for a while and I worked at a local radio station where I heard "I Shot The Sheriff" and I was hooked ever since. Then I moved here to Winston-Salem. We all call it Winstontown like Trench Town. So we all formed a band called Cinnamon Reggae. It was the first reggae band in the area and people really didn't accept the music. After 20 years that band still exists. I have my own group now called Lion Tracks and I also play with a group called Sundown Reggae, all from the Cinnamon era. During that time I was doing pretty bad, feeling oppressed but then I listened to Bob and he opened me to the music and other artists: Peter Tosh, Bunny Wailer. We also had an opportunity to open up some gigs for the Wailer network and also for Burning Spear."

"Is it hard for you to be a Rasta here?" I asked

Rasta Heart

"Well you have to have a presence, you have to have God's heart with you at all times and you have to stay focused and treat everybody as equal. That's when you get it back that way, the love. I am pretty much laid-back and conscious of everything that I do. So you've got to watch what you do. TV has a lot to do with it. A lot of violence and mean-spirited people. So you have to teach. Teach by example. You lead by example. Feel the vibe, feel JAH. Know that He's there guiding you."

"Are you married?"

"Yes. My wife and son, my whole family, are into this also. My son's name is Jahman but Babylon wants to change it to Jamal. Even when he was in the womb, I put headsets on my wife's stomach playing reggae music. At three years old he used to skank around the house. He loves the music. He is 14 and an honor role student. Matter of fact we had a big conversation this morning when we awoke, talking about the universe and he wanted to know about God. What was God and Jesus and where did we come from? Questions he already knew but he wanted to know about the universe as a whole. We are in heaven. That's why Bob said 'You think you are in heaven but you're living in hell.' This is about being honest and humble and spiritual all the time, all the while."

"What do you do in your life to support this?"

"Well, I say that I am a jack-of-all-trades and a master of some. I am an artist by faith and that includes paint and I am a pastry chef creatively and I am into reggae music. I study and read Rastafari music. If I am not studying, I am teaching. And you would know it by the people I keep around me. A lot of things happen in my life that I know I am a Rastaman. I know that JAH is always present and this meeting here today. You see it's through the makings of the Most High that it happens like that and that's the way it is. I meet a lot of Jamaicans and they carry the message but you don't have to be in Jamaica to be Rasta. Rastafarians are worldwide and it is good that the music is there. The music is bringing us together. It's like the Internet connecting up people. I read my Bible and Rastafari is a way of life. I read King James, the *Kebra Nagast* and books dealing with Selassie I, like Barrett's book *The Rastafarians*."

"Do you spend time with other Rastas?"

"Mostly all of my friends, 25 of us, get together in fellowship, a family through our rehearsals Wednesdays, Thursdays and Sundays. I reason with my brethren to get through Babylon. We share each others readings. We come together and whatever the knowledge, we share together. Jahman says he likes this reasoning. We formed a reggae band for the kids to play. He plays base, keyboard and the drums."

"Is it hard wearing dreads in the U.S.?"

"Sometimes. Jesus himself was a Nazarite and there was a vow, the Nazarene Oath, to grow your locks and not cut the corners of your beard. The angels are among us. The ones that are concerned about your well-being in their heart as their own. You can feel love and so can they. We are One Rasta in a conscious state of mind at all times and you treat everyone with respect because we are all God's children. We all exist under JAH rule. In Psalm 68 verse 4 it says, 'He who ride upon heavens called him by his name—JAH.' A lot of books have watered this down but this is still in there and it involves everyone. This passage has withstood the test of time. You find the core of your strength and when you find the truth, it makes you stronger."

"Kevin, thanks for talking with us. We came here to meet a Rasta and we did—just not the one we expected." I said.

"You know, we got to the door and we almost didn't go in. We were going to eat upstairs but then we changed our minds. JAH brought us together. Some things are soon to be revealed. All the while keep it strong. JAH love."

Slavery in Jamaica

To really understand how the Rastafarian movement came to be, we must know a little of Jamaica's past, especially its slave past, as there is a certain continuity from this period to the founding and growth of Rastafari. Around 700 AD, Jamaica was settled by Arawak Indians, an AmerIndian group. They called the island Xaymaca and their legacy included such things as tobacco and the hammock. They were an egalitarian and communal society, where private ownership and materialism were unknown concepts. Christopher Columbus, who traded slaves earlier in his career, claimed the island for Spain when he landed there while exploring in 1494. He remained a year before being rescued. Within a few decades of his landing, the entire Arawak population of between 6,000 to 60,000 was wiped out. If they didn't die from mistreatment by their Spanish conquerors, or from European diseases, they often killed their own children or committed suicide rather than submit to slavery.

Soon the black slave trade entered the scene. Blacks were stolen from Africa to work lands stolen from the Arawak. The immensity of the slave trade that developed during this era is almost impossible to comprehend. It involved three continents, Africa, Europe and America and lasted for 400 years. It is estimated that over 15 million Africans landed in the Western Hemisphere (1 million in Jamaica and the fiercest remained there). However, for every one captured, one was killed in the slave hunt and 25 to 35 percent died during the ocean crossing. These dead were left chained together with the living. Nothing on this scale had ever been undertaken before in human history.[1] The "civilized" powers of the world, mostly the Spanish, English, French, Dutch and Americans, decided that the African was a heathen, a sub-human and, quoting Scripture, determined that God had created them to be slaves for the Christian world. They depicted Africa as "The Dark Continent," devoid of history and culture, populated by barbarians and savages that deserved servitude. They systematically destroyed all religious, cultural and artistic expressions of Africa in their own countries.

By 1517, the Spaniards began importing slaves to the island. Spain never really developed Jamaica and in 1655 the English invaded and successfully captured it making it part of its empire. However, before leaving, the Spanish freed their slaves and encouraged them to harass their new English captors. These freed slaves, cimarrones (wild runaways) or Maroons, as they were called, fled into the mountains, many of them fleeing to the very remote Portland Parish area near Port Antonio and Cockpit Country to the west. There they lived a tribal existence in well-guarded compounds.

The English developed Jamaica as a slave colony. Slaves were often sent there and then on to the American colonies. The Africans that remained in Jamaica were usually "the property" of absentee English landlords who owned large sugar or banana plantations and hundreds, maybe thousands, of slaves, usually controlled by brutal overseers or "bushas." This system allowed the wealthy slave owners to distance themselves from the brutality of slavery. Though they often built ostentatious mansions, called "great houses," the plantation owners spent most of their time in England. When they did live on the island, they lived a life of indolence and overindulgence, made possible by slaves catering to their every whim. After landing in Jamaica, the average lifespan of a field slave, who worked 18 to 20 hours a day, was seven years.

Africans captured and made into slaves were neither docile nor passive victims as they have often been portrayed. Often unbroken, they resisted and struggled with all their might. It took two to three years to "break in" these fierce African warriors, mostly from the Ashanti, Cormorante, Mandingo, Ebo and Yoruba tribes.

Plantation owners lived in constant fear of slave rebellion and chose to discourage revolt by using violence to keep the slaves terrorized. For every slave born, six died, due to abuse, brutal hard work, disease or malnutrition. By 1700 there were 7000 English and 40,000 Celtic settlers and slaves. By 1800, there were 20,000 English but over 300,000 slaves—15 slaves for every free man—a ratio that assured rebellion.

By the early 1800s anti-slavery sentiment was growing around the world. The American and French Revolutions provided hope for all those seeking freedom. In 1831, during the last and largest slave revolt in Jamaica, slaves burned plantations and killed many planters and overseers. Finally, the English Parliament made slavery illegal on August 1, 1834, 31 years before the U.S. emancipated their slaves. Adding insult to centuries of injury, the English Parliament awarded the slaveholders compensation for their freed slaves. The slaves received nothing for the years of backbreaking work.

Jamaica's long nightmare of slavery was officially over but oppression by colonial rulers would, and does, continue in a more "civilized" form. The Jamaican unemployment rate is very high and the wages very low. Many people are "jobless in Eden." Fifty percent of Jamaica's land is presently owned by less than one percent of the population. Though 450 years of colonial rules is over, in many ways, Jamaica is still a small island whose internal political and economic systems are controlled by large foreign powers, most notably the U.S. and the U.K. In post-independent Jamaica, the people have responsibility without real power, exploitation without redress. It is freedom from this form of slavery that is now part of the Rastas' struggle.

Chapter 8
Return To Paradise

i am the man
you love to hate
sitting in the slums of
ghost town, trench town
back o' wall
no clothes
to hide my nakedness
filth and mosquitoes smelling
bitin 400 years of black flesh
scarred by whips and sticks
i am the man
　　　　　—"I Am The Man" by **Mutabaruka**

On April 14, 2001, Julia and I returned to Jamaica for an eight day stay in Port Antonio. Julia was even more excited about going than I was, looking forward to meeting all the people whose words she had spent weeks transcribing. We arrived in Montego Bay mid-morning and loaded everything into our rental car, including two extra boxes for Clive and his family.

"My bet is no matter what we think the next eight days will be like, they won't be," I said as we pulled out of the airport.

Driving along the coastal route listening to Bob Marley, we settled in to

Rasta Heart

the four hour drive to Port Antonio. We stopped in Falmouth where some Rastas had carts set up selling organic fruits and vegetables and cold coconuts. We chatted awhile, once again pleased at how easily you can fall into a deep spiritual conversation with these people.

After stopping for lunch outside of Ocho Rios at a small restaurant overlooking the ocean, we arrived in Port Antonio a little before dark. Though Scram wasn't expecting to see us until the next day, we decided to stop by his shop since it was on the way to our hotel. We pulled in the drive and as we headed toward the house, Scram appeared in the door. When he saw us, a huge grin flashed across his face as he strode across his yard to embrace Julia. He was as happy to see us as we were to see him. We all hugged and laughed. He ushered us in to his shop where he had proudly set up four "proper chairs" and a table with a hard cardboard top. He served us some fresh juice and we settled in together like three old friends at a private banquet. It was great to be back in his presence.

Plywood from shipping crates covered the walls, on one of which Scram had painted in red, "ONE LOVE, Let's Try." Also he had turned the front room of his house, which is only a few feet from the main road with all its foot traffic, into a small store. He had stocked it with a mixture of Rasta and Babylon treats including organic fruits and vegetables, soft drinks, Red Stripe Beer, white rum, cigarettes, cigarette papers, and a few snacks. You could also get a good Ital meal or borrow his bike for a small fee. Small shops like this are everywhere in Jamaica. It is one of the few viable ways to make money on an island where almost everyone walks and therefore needs to shop close to home.

As we lit up some spliffs and settled back, Scram lovingly prepared a delicious Ital meal for us. After dinner, he moved the tables and chairs outside where it was cooler. The evening was pleasant and the road traffic had died down. Every so often someone would stop in to buy or sell something. People with stalks of bananas or a string of small snappers or a burlap bag of coconuts, would try to hawk their stuff. Customers would get a beer, a Ting soft drink, a single cigarette or even just buy one or two rolling papers for just a few cents. This is a very poor area of a very poor country.

Listening to Bob Marley on the portable CD player, Julia and I gave Scram a few presents we had brought including a CD set consisting of a portable CD player with a headset, along with CDs by Bob Marley, Slim

Rasta Heart

Smith, Bushman, Luciano, Dennis Brown, Sizzla and Tony Rebel.

By now it was getting late and Julia and I had been traveling since three that morning. With plans to go to Reach Falls the next morning, we headed to our hotel. The San San Tropez is a small, quaint hotel. Its seven rooms wrap around a tropical courtyard and its pool area is canopied by a huge shade tree under which you can dine.

Surprisingly, the hotel includes a great Italian restaurant. Each night the restaurant serves both tourists and local patrons. The atmosphere is very relaxed, almost like you are all dining together in someone's home. It is run by two young Italians, Nino and Fabio, and their Jamaican partner, Lisa. The heart vibes in this place are very strong. Before going to bed, we ordered a little dessert from the restaurant and went for a swim under the moonlight.

The next morning we stopped for breakfast at the Jamaica Palace, where I had stayed on my previous visit. The manager was eating in the dining room and we joined him for a few minutes at his table and brought him up to date on the book's progress. Hans, a middle-aged man, was sitting nearby, overheard our conversation and joined in.

"I'm from Germany and I've lived here eight years," he started. He was chainsmoking and looked unhealthy. "I can tell you that these Rastas are lazy bums. Every time I go downtown they beg from me. I can take you down there now and show you 500 beggars. They do not want to work. Always stoned. These Rastas are not what you think they are."

"Boy, that guy sure was bitter," I said as we drove away. "I couldn't get away from him fast enough. Let's ask Scram about what he said."

We picked up Scram and Clive and headed out for Reach Falls, again following the route we had taken a couple of months earlier. With Bob Marley singing in the background and everyone smoking a spliff, we settled into an easy conversation.

"Julia and I were talking with this German guy who's been living here for eight years. He says Rastas don't work and every time he goes in downtown Port Antonio, a lot of dreads come up and beg from him."

"A beggar is de most kind person in de world," Scram said, laughing. "You 'ave ta give it ta 'im ot'erwise 'e cayn't get it. A hustler is much different from a beggar. A hustler is tryin' always ta get money from yah pocket. De wurld try ta seh dat a Rastamon is a beggar but a Rasta is not a beggar. A Rasta doan't want a job. Dey want livity, love. But Babylon want ta 'ide it. Dey want people ta work like everybody else. Dis mon does not know how ta associate wit' Rasta, wit' de true love. Ya feel de person."

"He was very negative, very angry," I said. "He seemed like a very sick, unhappy man."

"'E did not find a Rasta ta take 'im around. 'E found a dread but not a Rasta. Some people 'ere will tell ya to watch out fe Rasta but den when dey get sick de find a Rastamon ta cure dem. Dey try ta put it ta de Rasta. A Rasta is a true vine of love. Rasta is de true vine of livity."

"Scram where are the Rastaladies?" Julia asked.

"Ya will find some Rastas wit' one lady and anot'er wit' lots of ladies. Ya will find Rastamon dat does not 'ave any sex. 'E is clean ta de bone. From de beginnin', womon 'ave de biggest task becuz if ya try ta do de womon's work, even in de 'ouse, ya would know dat is one of de 'ardest work dat ya ever face. Dey are de 'eadquarters. De womon is always de 'eadquarters. If ya build a 'ouse and ya didn't consider at anytime dat a lady is supposed ta be in dat 'ouse, de 'ouse is unfinished. If a lady doan't come inta de 'ouse, move around, set up 'er life and 'er order inside, de 'ouse is unfinished. So every mon who nevah pass t'ru dat philosophy, 'is 'eart unfinished. Me 'eart unfinished too," he said, and cracked up laughing.

"So your heart's not finished," I said.

"Me 'eart just need ta be repaired," he said, still laughing. "But I doan't wan' ta 'ave my woman live in poverty."

"Scram, I think the reason so many marriages break up," I said, "is that we don't understand their true function. As I see it, like all relationships, marriage is just a learning vehicle to teach and learn One Love. So you choose a partner to learn to love unconditional, which usually takes a lifetime. This helps you love everyone as they are, without conditions. I think everyone deserves a good mated relationship."

"Well, now, when ya 'ave some cash, den all de ladies wan' ta be wit' ya," Scram said. "I chose de wrong queen. She fooled me."

"There's your barrier, your fear. We were meant to be mated and happily so. But our fears block JAH's gift. Our fears that we won't ever find a truly loving mate, that we're unworthy, that the other person is too imperfect, that we're too old or too fat or too poor, all these fears block His gift to each of His children."

Rasta Heart

"Scram, you know how I've been putting those rocks in your yard?" Julia said. She had outlined a large garden with white stones in the shape of Africa. "I'm doing that as a gift to you as a king who knows One Love. You've known it all your life and you've given that to me and I want to give back to you the honor and respect. And everytime you walk by those rocks, you will know how much I honor and respect you for reminding me of One Love. I told this to about eight of your friends so that your dwelling is now blessed by a woman that loves you dearly."

"My vision now sees dis person comin' up, dis genuine person and dat person not goin' ta even know dey are de person, ya'earme? But dat person gwanna be so genuine and so nice."

In Boston Beach we headed up a less-traveled back road rather than the road from Manchioneal. As we headed up the mountain, Scram started talking about ganja.

"Ya 'ave weed out dere more powerful den ganja, ya know, because ya 'ave anot'er one called 'shame-me-darlin' or 'touch-me-not.' Anywhere we stop, we see a plant dat ya drink. Ya know why I say more powerful?

"Ya see people catch gonorrhea and dey root up dat weed and boil it wit dat root and drink it. Dey don't go ta doctormon (he laughs). Dat why it is like a leading plant. Ya doan't get high but it's good fe disease and colds. Pull over. It's anywhere."

"Wait till we get to a straightaway," Julia said.

"A straightaway? You've got to be kidding. There hasn't been a straight-away since we left the main road," I said and we all laughed.

Finally I found a place that was relatively safe to pull over. We all got out and Scram showed us a small plant with an open flower growing by the side of the road. Scram gently touched it and it closed.

"Ya see when ya touch it, it closes its leaves. If ya 'ave cold in yah joints dis warm dem up."

"Scram, I have high blood pressure," I said as we drove on. "What's good for that? Someone said coconuts."

"Yeah mon, but ya must use de younger one dat doan't 'ave much meat. Even de back of it good for boiling."

"Babylon does not keep us healthy," I said. Julia and I had bad coughs that started a week before the trip and continued until a week after we returned.

103

Rasta Heart

"No. Becuz of de pollution ya 'ave ta drink certain roots ta clean up yah system every time. Of course ya 'ave ta work wit' Babylon too. We associate wit' dem but we doan't work wit' dem, ya know. We doan't mind about dem."

We rode a little further and started talking about the book.

"You know, Scram," I said, "after the book is out, we want to put together a road show, a multi-media presentation with video of Bob Marley playing and all of us on stage talking about Rasta and answering questions. We could go all over, wherever there are Rasta communities like Washington, London, Philly, Miami or just about anywhere."

"We were talking about bringing the show into the ghettos," Julia said. "This would really be great for young blacks to see. They could see powerful blacks who have lived in poverty and kept their vibes positive."

"No seh, mon, no seh!" Scram said enthusiastically. "I am ready ta do dat, mon. So it tis. Yah doing a great work. Me ready fe dat, ready fe all dos t'ings."

As we turned the next corner, a little store appeared on the left, a small one not much bigger than Scram's, maybe 20 feet square. About 15 people were milling around, mostly boys from adolescence to mid-twenties. A shiny red pickup truck, loaded with sugar cane and coconuts, was parked in front on the road. Two sets of huge speakers, about seven feet high and five feet across, were set up, one near the store and the other directly across the road, next to a small cemetery.

Several of the older guys were wiring the speakers into DJ equipment, with mixers and a turntable. Wooden boxes held hundreds of 45 records, all in alphabetical order. Most of the younger kids were watching, a few from a perch in a large shade tree. Everyone seemed to be thoroughly enjoying themselves, lots of laughing and kidding.

This was Easter Saturday. In Jamaica the entire Easter weekend and Easter Monday are holidays and celebrations are everywhere. People travel all over the island to visit friends and relatives and every little community, such as this one, has some type of party. A middle-aged man, Mr. Brown, the owner of the pickup, had been hired by the store owner to bring his sound system, essentially a mobile disco, up for the day and night. The store owner sells more stuff and the community gets a free party.

These sound systems are everywhere. They are uniquely Jamaican and provide a main source of entertainment. Evolving from Kingston in the mid-1940s, they are set up by stores or bars and the shop owners act as the promoters. Sometimes the area is fenced in, referred to as a "dancehall" and a small cover is charged. The systems can be quite large, as this one was, blasting a deafening bass with 30,000 watt speakers. It was these gatherings and DJs like Coxsone Dodd and Prince Buster who first started playing Bob Marley's early tunes and eventually launched his career.

We parked and wandered over to the store. The speakers weren't hooked up yet so the scene was festive but quiet. Behind the store a couple of teen-age boys were cooking some jerk chicken and pork over a 55-gallon drum cut in half.

Scram greeted the middle-aged women behind the counter. In this area, Scram knows just about everyone. They chatted awhile in patois while I ordered apple juices for Julia and I, a Red Strip for Clive and a white rum for Scram. Scram took a sip of rum and started spitting it around the floor.

"Something the matter with the rum, Scram?" I asked as he circled behind us still spraying.

"No, mon, dis is a Maroon rum blessing fe protection and t'anks," he said. "I do dis all de times. Ya see, it bring us luck on our trip."

We stayed around for about an hour just watching the scene. Everyone was in a festive mood and it was contagious. After awhile they got the speakers working, drowning out almost all conversation. Scram started dancing, moving fluidly like a man half his age. He was really hamming it up. The music was so loud I couldn't take it for long, so we continued on to the falls.

"So how many hours a day do you have to work to make ends meet?" I asked Scram as we got back on the road.

"Ya mean I in person. Well me tell ya. Whenevertime I am hungry, some time I plant fruit and let it bear. Ya see, when you 'ave de faith ya cayn wait. Ya know how long I 'ad to wait ta 'ave dis program dat you are revealing today? I have been planting dis program for a long time."

"Yeah, I really love your garden," Julia said.

"When did you see his garden?" I asked.

"I'm talking about the garden he's planting with us in it," Julia said.

"Dat's right, t'anks. Long time I been watering it and right now I'm coming ta a point where I'm eating de fruit because you're 'ere. You is a garden ya know. I am eating de fruit of ya now, mon, because I cherish it fe a long time. So ya a garden dat I've been watering a long time."

We arrived at Reach Falls late in the day, passing JAH Priest's empty stall on the way. On this holiday there were 20 or 30 cars lining the entrance, many from as far away as Kingston. By now it was almost four and many people were leaving. In addition to Renny's craft stand, there were two additional stands run by several woman. One was selling roasted corn and the other selling seafood stew. Renny was at his stand, as mellow as ever. We wandered over and I introduced Julia.

We chatted awhile and bought a water pipe from him. By now, Scram had befriended four women, Monica, Angela, Roberta, and Nadisha, who were standing nearby around the trunk of their car.

"Hello, Princess," they said to Julia as we approached.

"We drove by all of you this morning in Port Antonio and blew our horn," Monica said. "You two were talking to Scram near the road. We were driving over from Kingston."

"So it is. Dese people, Robbie and Julia, dey are writing a book on de Rastas and we are making some good relationships now dat people cayn know dat it's not what ya heard but what ya know," Scram says.

"Yeah, that's good. It's not what you hear but what you see with your eyes," Angela says, "but when ya see it makes a difference and then you believe it."

We talked with them awhile and showed them the book. They were soft, gentle women, all in their twenties, very kind, very dignified. By then we were getting hot and the falls would be closing soon, so we headed down. We stopped and bought our tickets from Mr. Clarke and our usual round of drinks.

About 20 or so people were down at the falls, mostly families and young couples. We swam and talked under the falls for around an hour. Invigorated and clean, we headed back up the path toward the parking lot. As we did, Scram pointed out a heart-shaped pool a short distance above the falls.

"Dat is a special place," Scram said to Julia.

"What does that heart mean?" Julia asked.

"Dat's a real symbol, ya know, because ya see dat water going t'ru de

Rasta Heart

'eart-shaped rock formation. It's like everyt'ing going t'ru de 'eart to be purified, even human livity. Everyt'ing go t'ru de 'eart and de mind ta get de true love. It 'ave ta go t'ru da heart as well ta get anyt'ing natural and ta get everyt'ing purified. Den we know 'ow ta deal wit' ot'er people."

"Scram, in your letter to us, you wrote 'everyt'ing is everyt'ing' at the end. What did you mean?" Julia asked.

"When I say 'everyt'ing is everyt'ing', it's like everyt'ing is so natural ta de eyes of people but dere is just one problem dat de people just cayn't be in de Oneness, ya know. Because we need dat because dat where de love supposed ta be located, in de Oneness, not everyone t'inking different t'ings. Like when we speaking de One Love system dat what we 'eading ta and dat is what we want de people ta know and dat is what we mean. Ev'ryt'ing is supposed ta be de one right way. We are looking forward ta all de people ta subdue demselves and consider dere own mind ta freedom because right now world leaders dey 'olding up everyt'ing because dey knew what de love is but dey doan't want ta establish it dat way, de true way. Dey want ta be over everyt'ing like de big embassy. If ya doan't go t'ru de embassy, ya cayn nah go ta de United States. So dos are big gates ta de city fe de people and we need ta get all dese t'ings rectified and if de people doan't 'ave love, we'll never get t'ru de door."

By now it was getting late and only a few people were hanging around in the parking lot. The four of us wandered over. The food stalls selling corn and seafood stew were still open. Clive and Scram got some corn, while Julia and I tried the stew. It was delicious. Renny was still there and we walked over. Julia started talking to him about the roots tonic I got from him on my last visit. He had sold out for the day.

"In de full moon ya look fe de root," Renny said. "Ya wash it off and ya chop it up and put in de fire but ya must dig it up in de full moon because den it 'as de power in it. De strength, de medicine come inta de root. In de new moon, de plant is weak. Yah body work wit' de full moon, so ya get strong and ya get power from it."

"Babylon does not work with the moon," Julia said. "Even though the year breaks down perfectly into 13 moon cycles of 28 days each, just like a woman's cycle, Babylon makes it confusing instead of natural. Julius Caesar changed the calendar to be 12 months, some with 30 days, some with 31. We gave up the natural calendar."

Rasta Heart

"Yes, mon, in life de natural t'ings are bettah, ya know, and One Love and one life. We are flesh and blood. It doesn't matter de color."

"When I was here before, you said that ganja was a compass," I said.

"Yeah, mon, dat is real. Ya know what I'm telling ya. It is like a compass dat leads me. When I get up, I burn my spliff and if life is 'ard I try ta go over de 'ardness, ya know, no matter de 'ardness of life, I try ta find myself somewhere."

"I find that it reveals itself gently to you," Julia said. "So you let go of things. I've been saying a prayer before I smoke asking JAH to guide me."

"Sometimes I seh dat in my mind," Renny said. Julia starts singing softly "With JAH standing by my side, then why should I be afraid," a song by Tony Rebel. Renny starts to sing along with her.

"What I do to guide my high," Julia said, "is sit and allow myself to remember my JAH Mind. To me it's a natural right to know JAH in my meditation. As I take a slow deliberate inhale of ganja, I start to smile and marvel at an herb that could make me feel so good about myself and others with just one breath. Then I hold it as if I don't want to let my JAHSELF go. Then I exhale with JAH in my voice like a reverent sigh. Soon I start to feel the expansion, the warmth and fullness as my heart opens to allow thanks and praise to come up naturally. I feel JAH in my structure, my very soul. It's like letting myself feel big, letting JAH have control, like being on a roller coaster. It feels as if I pick the love of JAH over my fear of approval. One is full of joy. The other full of confusion. I've learned to protect the high if someone or some situation changes the vibe. Listening to an artist I trust is coming from the heart like Luciano and Bushman really uplifts me. I feel like my high is a gift to be enjoyed every minute of my life and to know that each visit to JAH makes a difference. If I'm feeling depressed and think a high is not possible, I just remember that depression is when my mind is merely ignorant of the spirit and relying on it's own misunderstanding. I just guide my high to my heart and let it feel the love that's always there."

As Bushman sings "When I was down and out and I was blue... He fills me up and lets me overflow with JOY."

"Sometimes when I dance and I 'ear a good tune," Renny said, "when I feel good, I pray in my 'eart cause dat is de spirit, de 'eart beat ya cayn feel so ya 'ave ta pray. Yeah, mon, dat is full. Dat is power. Ya 'ave ta give praise. Dat's 'ow I do it. It comes natural ta meditate, dat true. Ya want ta shout praises ta JAH. Dat is natural. Yeah, mon, respect de vibes. I cayn see dat ya are in de power. Dis is where I live. When ya come back, I be 'ere wit' some roots tonic. Respect, 'ave a nice time and be 'appy and be good. JAH protect ya every time. JAH LOVE. Niiiice."

By now everyone was packing up their stalls. We offered Renny a ride home and waited while he put his cups, pipes and bamboo games under his counter. As we headed out, relaxed from the swim, we lit a spliff and put on a Bob Marley CD. There was nowhere else I wanted to be at that moment but in that car, on that road, with those people.

"Ya, mon, niiice, very niiice," Renny said, looking from the back seat like he felt the same. "JAH protect ya. Niiice," he said as he got out of the car at his house.

"In Babylon, there is not much time to think about JAH," I said. "All day long Babylon sends its message through all the media, powerfully and relentlessly. Many people live 24 hours a day in that world. They turn on the TV, go to work, listen to radio to and from work, come home, shop, turn on the TV until they fall asleep. The only time they are in JAH's world is when they go from their car to their house."

"Dere t'oughts are supposed ta come in ya mind," Scram said, "dey just not supposed ta stay. Dey just come and go. Ya just view it and if its not right, ya just let it go. YaseewhatImean? De force of Babylon is also very strong on dis island. Dey try ta take away de freedom of dis country and de leaders know dat dey are doing dis. But right now de vibes are changing. Ev'ryt'ing is everyt'ing."

"Scram, where's your mother?" Julia asked, interested in what type of childhood formed such a man.

"My mother died a year before last," he said wistfully. "Me kind of miss 'er but glad ta know she did nah suffer in 'er bed before she died. Some people suffer wit' bed soars. But, ya know, de old people doan't go t'ru de t'ings dat de young people goin' t'ru now. Dos days a women did not 'ave baby until dey were 21, strong. But today dey are wishy-washy. Dey were very much strong den. It is a sign, ya know, of Babylon getting weaker. Babylon is on it's way of falling now. Dey even want ta say dey are sorry. Dat's what is givin' dem a hangover. Dere are still many 't'ings dat Babylon 'as ta teach de people before dey fall."

"What do they want to say they're sorry for?" I asked.

"Dey won't say dey are sorry fe makin' ganja illegal," Scram continued laughing. "Dey beat Rasta. Put dem in jail for a likkel bit of weed, fe a likkel spliff of weed. Dey put ya in jail wit' a mon dat kill anot'er mon. Dey put 'im dere wit' some sort of t'ief. Dey put in dere wit' lot of mess fe one likkel spliff. YaseewhatI mean? So right now Babylon find demselves guilty and dey know dat if dey retreat so sudden, de whole world is gonna ta come down on dem. Dat is what dey say dey no more want Rasta in jail wit' ONE LOVE business. In Kingston, Rasta can walk around wit' a spliff and no one boder dem. When ya go ta Nine Mile to Bob's grave, ya got a big ganja plant. Ya mon, when dat weed grow, anot'er small one is planted because wherever Bob go, de weed got ta be dere (big laugh)."

"What do you want to do tomorrow?" I asked Scram as we neared Port Antonio.

"Tomorrow I take ya to Nanny Falls and Moore Town," Scram said. "It is a very special place. I was raised in Bellvue not far away. Moore Town is de 'ome of Nanny and de Windward Maroons. Some people call dem de Blue Mountain Maroons. She was a great leader. Everyone in de town is Maroon and dey run de town demselves. I take ya up ta meet de Colonel. 'E is a friend of mine."

I was looking forward to going to Moore Town. The more I read and heard about the Maroons, the more I began to feel there was some deep connection between them and the Rastas. We dropped Scram and Clive off and arrived back at our hotel in the early evening and ate a great Italian meal in the dining room. It was Lisa's birthday and we were invited to join the festivities. We finished the evening with a swim.

Nanny & the Maroons

When Nanny, a small wiry woman with piercing eyes, arrived in Jamaica, slave rebellion was already in full swing and towns of runaway slaves, called "Rebel Towns" or "Negro Towns," were all over the island. The Maroon villages, well organized and defended, were the strongest of these. The first Maroons were slaves who escaped from the Spanish or were freed by them when the British captured Jamaica. This was in pre-plantation days when most slaves lived semi-free and hunted wild boar and rounded up stray cattle in the bush, thus leaving the Maroons well-equipped to live in the jungle.

The history and life of Nanny, also affectionately known as Queen Nanny, Grandy Nanny or Granny Nanny, will always remain somewhat of a mystery. Nanny is an Anglicized term for the Ashanti "nana," a term of respect given to chiefs, spiritual leaders, and especially elderly women. "Ni" means "first mother" in Ashanti. "Grandy" refers to "possessing female ancestor spirits." Nanny's life was documented by her enemy, the English, who had only one or two actual encounters with her. Her story was written by the enemy's pen. Also, we are talking about events that occurred over 265 years ago in a remote part of Jamaica where few people could read or write.

Some accounts say she was never a slave but a queen in Africa before coming to Jamaica to free her people. It is said that she used her spiritual powers to magically hide on a ship and that the crew was shocked to see her and her entourage disembark. Others say she was born in Africa and brought to Jamaica as a slave and soon escaped from a plantation. It is agreed she was from the Ashanti (or Asante) tribe, one of the most powerful tribes in West Africa.

Other Africans escaped British rule and many joined the original Maroons. Even free Africans left their jobs and lives to join. Some of these people were of Arawak Indian blood. Soon, all were called Maroons. Both the English and the Spanish offered them freedom if they would fight on their side but they chose complete independence even though it made them hunted fugitives. Of the more than 250,000 slaves in Jamaica, it was estimated that only between 1,000 and 2,000 were Maroons at any one time.

Though many African tribes were represented within the Maroons, all recorded leaders came from one particular group, the Koromantee. These people came from the Gold Coast, now Ghana. However, in reality they were from the Ashanti, Akan, Twi and Fanti tribes, many of which were enemies in Africa, and were brought to an area called Koromantee in the Gold Coast before being sent as slaves to the New World. Their language is still spoken by some Maroons.

The Koromantee rose to leadership within these newly formed tribes.

Rasta Heart

They were known as fierce warriors with a strong penchant for survival, resistance and freedom. Nanny, like all other African women, had been treated with respect in her country where women were honored, for without their gift of children, the tribe would die out. On slave plantations a woman's life was cruel and degrading. She was considered breeding stock and often raped by her master. Her husband and children were often sold, never to be seen again. Within the Maroon culture, women were the most stable element and formed the core of their society.

For Nanny, her people's life in Jamaica as slaves was untenable. Soon after arriving, Nanny and her five brothers—it is not certain they were her actual brothers—Cudjoe, Accompong, Johnny, Cuffy and Quao, fled into the remote areas of the island. Nanny and Quao headed to the eastern "windward" areas of Portland Parish in the Blue Mountains near Port Antonio. Cudjoe, Accompong, Johnny, and Cuffy settled in the western "leeward" side in the Cockpit Country in St. James Parish and built a village called Cudjoe Town. Accompong went to St. Elizabeth where the town of Accompong is named after him.

Their destinies became tied to this island as this Ashanti "family" soon became leaders of the Maroons. Some accounts say Nanny also had a sister, Grandy Sekesu, who became a slave. As Grandy Nanny is considered the Mother of all Maroons, Grandy Sekesu is considered the Mother of all slaves who were kept in bondage until emancipation in 1834. The Maroons call these relatives "niegas."

By 1720, Nanny was in full control of the Blue Mountain Rebel town which was renamed Nanny Town (near present day Moore Town). Situated on a high ridge overlooking the Stony River, the town was well protected. Only one small trail, easily defended, led to the village. Warriors kept guard constantly against intrusion by British soldiers or planters. Organized like the Ashanti society, 600 acres were cleared for agriculture. From there they raided plantations, often setting the slaves free and stealing weapons and supplies.

The Maroons mastered the art of mountain guerrilla fighting and used an extensive spy network to warn of any British attacks. They built smokeless fires and could camouflage themselves using large "cocoon" leaves so as to be nearly invisible to their enemies. They waited until the English soldiers were in their ambush and then attacked, often with no Maroon casualties.

Rasta Heart

Maroons used an Abeng, a revered cow's horn with a hole at the tip and a blow hole in the side. It could transmit complex messages (even individual names could be blown), thereby allowing the Maroons to communicate through the dense jungle for many miles. The British had no comparable communication system. In fact, it was the Abeng that may have given the Maroons the greatest tactical advantage over their oppressors.

Nanny was the Windward Maroons' spiritual and military leader during the First Maroon War from 1720 to 1738. What is said about her is steeped in more legend than history. Before the Haitian slave revolt and the Jamaican emancipation in 1834 and the American emancipation in 1865, Nanny led her people to freedom. They were the first enslaved Africans to win their freedom in the Western hemisphere after hundreds of years of slavery. She was a great healer and extremely powerful obeah woman, a person with supernatural powers. Both the Maroons and the British believed she used these powers to both defeat the British and keep her own warriors obedient. Stories of her supernatural powers spread throughout the island. As an obeah woman, Queen Nanny had strong ties to her African ancestry, the source from which her power was derived. She helped her tribe retain traditional African religions and customs.

She knew the best moment to wage war and used her powers to weaken the English psychologically and make her own warriors invincible. Legend has it that she kept a large cauldron next to a steep precipice at the foot of Nanny Town, where water boiled constantly with no fire under it. The British soldiers, shocked at the sight, were said to have gotten sleepy when they peered over its edge and would fall over the cliff. It was also told that when her tribe was almost defeated and near starvation, Nanny, after praying all day and night, had a vision and was told never to give up the fight for freedom. She was told to plant the pumpkin seeds which she had been given by her ancestors. The next day the whole hill was covered with ripe pumpkins. In time, this area came to be known as Pumpkin Hill, located six miles from Port Antonio.

In 1734, Captain Stoddard of the British army shelled Nanny Town with cannon fire and took control of the village, proclaiming it a great victory. However, this "victory" only made the situation worse for the settlers as the Windward Maroons, now forced to live in the jungle, raided nearby farms and plantations. Maroon tactics kept the British confused and fearful. The Maroons were vastly outgunned and outnumbered, with often 500 half-starved Maroons fighting against 5,000 of the best-provisioned and best-armed soldiers of the British Empire. After decades of struggle and losing thousands of soldiers, the British tired of fighting the Maroons. By the end, the British had lost thousands of men during the war while the Maroons confirmed losses totaled less than 100.

Before the English asked for peace, the island was in a state of chaos and marshal law had been declared. In open contempt of British authority, the Maroons controlled the main highways and had taken over several plantations near Port Antonio. Increasing numbers of slaves were fleeing to the Maroon villages. An island-wide slave rebellion was feared. Investors refused to invest in the island's commercial ventures, settlers were fleeing the rebellious areas and the Maroon War was costing England lives, money and prestige. Indeed, it was thought that if peace was not attained soon, the British might need to vacate the island. The fact that the well-trained British army had yet to win a single meaningful battle against this ragtag group of dedicated guerrilla fighters was a source of constant embarrassment to the arrogant British.

The situation is best summed up by the memoirs of Phillip Thicknesse, a lieutenant in the militia who fought against the Maroons. In his memoirs he stated, "Such who are unacquainted with that island will be surprised when they are told, that all the regular troops in Europe, could not have conquered the wild Negroes, by force of arms; and if Mr. Trelawny (The governor of Jamaica) had not wisely given them what they contended for, LIBERTY, they would in all probability have been, at this day, masters of the whole country."

In 1737, the British sued for peace. Reportedly, Nanny refused to sign a peace treaty. Her Windward Maroons had lived in the area for 83 years and perhaps she felt no treaty was needed to assure their continuance. She believed in total freedom and sought to unify all freedom fighters in Jamaica. She took an oath on Pumpkin Hill to fight the British to the end.

Before the treaties were signed, 300 Maroon men, women and children, led by Nanny, set out on The Great Trek, one of the longest marches in Jamaican history, to meet with the Leeward Maroons in Cockpit Country. They marched from Portland to St. James, over high mountains and wild forests and under constant harassment by British soldiers. When they reached St. James, Cudjoe refused to unite with Nanny's Maroons. It is believed that Nanny wanted this unity to fight the British. Cudjoe wanted peace with the British. It was reported that he would be willing to fight even against Nanny and the Windward Maroons after he signed the treaty. Nanny's people had to journey back the long way they came.

The Leeward and Windward treaties (there *were* differences), signed in 1739, guaranteed, among other benefits, tax-free lands in different parts of the island where succeeding generations have since lived continuously. This treaty, signed in blood by all parties making the signers "blood brothers," also gave the Maroons the rights of free people if they agreed to three main conditions: not to fight against the British, to help capture runaway slaves and to help the Government put down future rebellions or invasions. In essence, the British would use the freedom-loving Maroons to keep other Africans enslaved. The Maroons transformed from a symbol of freedom for their enslaved countrymen, into a symbol of suppression. To this day many Jamaicans still resent the Maroon descendants for this.

Cudjoe, who by now was 60 and had been fighting the British for 48 years, signed the peace treaty. Though Nanny would not sign the treaty, her brother Quao eventually did sign a treaty on behalf of the Windward Maroons in either Charles Town or Crawford Town, both in Portland Parish.

After the treaty was signed, the Maroons did help the British in enslaving their fellow Africans. To the Maroons, their fellow African slaves had often been their enemy, assisting the British in capturing Maroon villages. It is even written that the Maroons themselves had slaves from the time of the treaty until the Emancipation in 1834 (it was reported that 66 of Moore Town's population of 560 were slaves at the time of emancipation). It is also recorded that in 1865 Maroons captured Paul Bogle, the leader of the Morant Bay Rebellion and one of Jamaica's National Heroes, and turned him over to the English who immediately hanged him. This may serve to remind us that nobility, bravery, ignorance and betrayal favor no color.

Soon after the treaties were signed, the Windward Maroons split into two groups. One went closer to Crawford Town with Quao, their chief. Nanny and her people settled on 500 acres at Cottawood for which Nanny had bargained. Some believe Nanny died during the 1750s. Others believe she never died. Many of Nanny's direct descendants live there today.

Rasta Heart

The treaties did not bring peace to the island or a cessation of the war with the Maroons. The British, well-versed in treaties compared to the Maroons, slanted the treaty highly in their favor. In years to come, they also broke many of their agreements. The British had lost the war but won peace. What they could not win on the battlefield they won at the negotiating table. Slave rebellions raged through the island in the years to come and the tension never ceased. A second Maroon war broke out in 1793, which ended in 1795 with many of the Maroons being either hanged or deported, even though the British promised they would do neither.

Today the Maroons are struggling to keep their culture alive through songs, dance, drumming and recording their history. To them, Nanny is regarded as a Priestess and Queen Mother. She is often called "Mother of Us All" and her direct descendants are called "yoyos." To many of the present-day Maroons, Queen Nanny is more than just a heroine, she is an everyday presence. The Maroons still love, respect and revere her as if she is a living spiritual leader.

Nanny of the Maroons is the only female among Jamaica's national heroes. For over 50 years, Nanny, described as a military genius, led more than 800 free Africans. However, she was much more than just a military leader. Nanny was also a wise woman of the village, who passed down legends and encouraged the continuation of customs, music and songs that had come with her people from Africa. Some say she was a messiah to the Maroons who came to free her tribe held in bondage.

Colonel Colin Lloyd George Harris has written much about Nanny and the Maroons. Colonel Harris was village leader of the Moore Town Maroons for thirty years and for many years also served as the principal of its school. The author of a number of books and articles on the Jamaican Maroon heritage, he is also a poet whose work has appeared in the *Jamaica Gleaner* and a number of other publications. Col. Harris writes:

> "Often in interviews the question has been asked of me, 'What does it mean to you to be a Maroon today?' When it is considered that Grandy Nanny, Kojo, Accompong and others of our leaders prevailed against the forces of a kingdom that ruled more than a quarter of all the lands on earth, then the pride of their Maroon posterity can be understood and appreciated. Yet these physical vic-

tories gave rise to other victories of deep moral, psychological and spiritual significance which increased that pride and its concomitant thankfulness a hundredfold. If the Maroons had been defeated, meaningful black resistance to the indignity and cruelty of African slavery would have ended—at least for a season—and so even today the cries of the tortured might still have been heard on the plantations, in the dungeons and from myriad village squares across the world. The knowledge that the Mother of my fathers, from her base in little Jamaica, burst asunder the prison bars of black bondage means more to me than life itself. It is like a sacrament taken daily as I kneel in humility at the feet of Nyankopon (The Creator) in the peaceful evening hour. Nyame adom (Thank God), I would not change my Maroon heritage for occupancy of the White House nor the grandeur of the British throne.

"It is most important to understand that these people brought language, culture and extra-sensory attributes from Mother Africa some five centuries ago which survived the vicissitudes of existence in what was once a 'strange land'—an inhospitable environment—and they are dedicated to the preservation of all that is best in their past. And though extremely poor in terms of dollars and cents, they refuse to be mendicants or ciphers in a ruthless political game. Thus our vast potential for the greater good of humanity awaits the coming day when some wise, decent gentleman or lady will join us in developing our assets to his or her benefit and ours."[1]

Like the Rastas that would emerge centuries later, the Maroons stood apart from the Jamaican population—respected, proud, confident and free from Babylon's oppression. They fought Babylon for their physical freedom just as Rastas now fight for their economic, mental, emotional and spiritual freedom. Both groups called to us from the other side, "Come, join us. Your freedom is here, with us. You leave only your bondage in Babylon."

Chapter 9
Journey To Nanny Falls

"I learned that courage was not the absence of fear, but the triumph over it. The brave man is not he who does not feel afraid, but he who conquers that fear."
—Nelson Mandela

On Easter morning, Julia, Scram, Clive, his Rasta friend Shakey and I headed out toward Moore Town and Nanny Falls. Scram, Shakey and Clive are all Maroons and Clive lived for awhile in Moore Town as a child. Scram was raised in Bellvue, a few miles away. Though Moore Town is only 10 miles from Port Antonio, it took us two hours to drive. The journey begins in the John Crow Mountains and passes through the Blue Mountains. The potholes in this area of the parish make the roads around Port Antonio look like interstate highways. Every few hundred yards we had to stop to let everyone out of the back seat so the car bottom wouldn't scrape. Often they would walk a hundred yards to get past a series of deep potholes.

We stopped at a few places to get a drink or for Scram to say hello to old friends. Once, as everyone piled back in the car, a well-dressed woman was walking down the road, probably on the way to Easter services. As we got in, she said something to us in patois. By the look on the woman's face and the tone of her voice, it sounded like an insult. Many Christian Jamaicans think Rastas are almost devil worshipers.

As he closed the car door, Scram looked over at her, and politely and proudly said, "No, darlin', I wouldn't be doing dat."

Rasta Heart

"What did she say?" Julia asked.

"Well, now, she's just mixed up. She said Rastas going ta hell," he said. "But no matter. Pull over up dere. All dese places are de battlefields fe de fighting wit' de English and de Maroons. Like Buffalo Soldiers, fightin' fe survival."

We pulled over to view a large valley below us covered in banana plants with the Rio Grande River at the bottom. In the distance were the cloud-covered peaks of the Blue Mountains, rising to over 7000 feet. Women were washing their clothes by hand in the river and laying them out to dry on large hot boulders—a roots laundromat. As we stood there, a young Jamaican rode by on a dilapidated bicycle. He was talking on a cell phone.

"Dis is Pumpkin Hill where Nanny made pumpkins grow in one day," Scram said. "Nanny was an obeah woman, someone who held the sacred secrets from Africa and could work magic. She 'ad many powers. Dis is a special place fe Rastas. It was a strong place. It is a little weak now but it is only resting. Many Rastas are Maroons. Clive, Shakey and I are Maroons. Nanny never knew slavery. She was totally free natural womon. Respect to mama. Dis is eastern Portland Parish. I want ta build some cottages 'ere so people cayn visit and stay. But if someone's wallet is empty and dey 'ave no money, if dey stay wit' me, I sleep on de floor and dey stay on de bed. Ya cayn stay wit' Scram fe life," he says and busts out in a big laugh.

As we drove into Moore Town, we stopped at a well-built concrete block home surrounded by a beautiful stucco fence with a wrought iron gate in front, a contrast to the more modest homes we had passed on the way. Scram knocked on the door but no one was at home.

"Mother Roberts is a 'ealer lady," he said. "De only 'ealer in Moore Town at de moment. Dis lady is a Maroon lady like Nanny." Mother Roberts is a local faith healer who performs in the Deliverance Tabernacle, where people gather from all over on Mondays for revivalist music, dancing and healings. On Wednesdays she has private healings.

We continued into the town, passing a large cemetery.

"See dat church over dere," Scram said, pointing to a large stone church next to the cemetery. "Dat de building dat de white man leave. Dat so 'e cayn come back," he said with a big laugh.

We continued into the town center. The town is in a narrow valley, maybe a quarter-mile wide and a mile long. The valley floor is fairly open and level with the Wildcane River rushing through the middle. On either side are low steep hills dotted with homes, mostly small and simple. There are more homes in the open valley floor, as well as a large playing field and a small post office, the Moore Town Primary and High School, a town administration and health clinic building, a small bar, a store and a community hall. At the far end is an all-age school. Seven churches dot the village, testifying to the strength of their Christian faith.

About 1,000 people live in Moore Town. Ten years ago 3,000 people lived there. Until recently, there was African drumming ringing throughout the valley every night. At the southern end of the village is a restored church and "Bump Grave," supposedly where Nanny is buried, though many locals believe her remains are in old Nanny Town nearby. The grave is under a raised flat area about forty feet square and topped by a flagpole flying both the Maroon and Jamaican flags. A laid stone obelisk stands at one end with a plaque that reads:

> Nanny of the Maroons/National Hero of Jamaica
> Beneath this place known as Bump Grave
> lies the body of Nanny,
> indomitable and skilled chieftainess of the
> Windward Maroons who founded this town.

We pulled over near the grave and wandered over to where a few people were hanging around, most of whom Scram seemed to know. The village teenagers were playing cricket in the field, an odd but appropriate touch given the island's English heritage.

After talking with the villagers for awhile, we walked up the hill to Colonel Sterling's house, an attractive one-story concrete block structure next to the all-age school. Moore Town is governed semi-autonomously by a colonel, a major and a captain and a council of 24 elected members, from teenagers to senior citizens. It was then headed by Colonel Wallace Sterling.

Scram knocked on the door and Colonel Sterling came out to speak with us. Dressed in Bermuda shorts and a sleeveless tee-shirt, he looked to be in his early thirties, trim, fit and with close cut hair and a moustache. He spoke in a dignified manner, with a crisp English accent. At first he was reserved, as if he didn't really welcome this intrusion, but then, the Maroons are known to be reserved, often secretive, cautiously guarding their isolation. He loosened up as we talked but I think he was always wondering, *Just exactly what are the people going to do with my information?*

"Dis is a very important person," Scram said as he gestured toward the Colonel. Scram leaned forward, bowing his head toward Colonel Sterling with a big smile on his face. "Dis is a young Colonel ta revive de system of de Maroon business. We want de entire wuurld ta know it is a ONE LOVE t'ing. 'E is very young so dat is why I work in de midst of 'im ta big 'im up because 'e is young. We want de book ta tell about Nanny and dis One Love because we want de good news ta get around a fast way ta get de t'ing done cuz' we all need upliftment in dis place."

With Scram's introduction completed, I showed Colonel Sterling the mock-up of the book and requested permission to ask him some questions and record his answers. He agreed.

"Someone told me that the Maroons were never slaves. Is that true?" Colonel Sterling smiled like a patient teacher. He was starting to relax.

"I have never seen anything with so much controversy than the story of the Maroons. But if you look at it from an objective point of view, the fact is that many of our foreparents weren't born into slavery. What happened is that you have generation after generation who never spent a day on a plantation in this part of the world but then from time to time there were other slaves who left the plantation to join those who were fighting up in the mountains."

"Some people believe Africans came to Jamaica before Christopher Columbus," I said.

"In days gone by you listened to what you were told and you were not permitted to ask too many questions. Now I can ask my mother anything, but when my mother was very young she did not have that opportunity to ask her mother, her grandmother and her great-grandmother those kinds of questions. I don't want to put my neck on the block to say that our foreparents actually came to this part of the world before Chris Columbus because to me there is no historical evidence. It is quite possible because, at least from where they lived in Africa, they could just go out on a boat and drift across the ocean and end up on this side of the island. It is possible that in our region people came here before Columbus and they did not make a big show of it."

"The history books all say that the Maroons helped capture other runaway slaves for the British," I said. "Is that true?"

"Yeah, that is always a controversy. I could show you documents that were signed by our foreparents and the British. What is written in those documents is that runaway slaves should be returned to their master and the Maroons would be compensated for their trouble of doing so. Now this is what is written in the document but let us look at it from a pragmatic point of view. Of what interest would our foreparents have to return a slave to the plantation? As a matter of fact, I do not call a slave that leaves the plantation a runaway slave. If the children leave their parents' house without their parents' consent, I consider that a runaway child because the child belongs to the parents but the slave did not belong to the plantation owners. They were taken from their homes in Africa and brought here to work forcefully. So when they left the plantation, they took unto themselves the freedom that was theirs. But the history books were written by the planter class, the colonizers, so they look at things from their perspective. I don't blame them because if I were in their position it is the same thing I probably would have ended up doing. The truth that is known about our foreparents, is the true history that could not be written. The English have hidden in their history books the deeds of our foreparents. The signed document was a fraud because the first thing it says is that Maroons sued for peace. Now all our foreparents fighting in the Blue Mountains and the Cockpit Country, were free. They did not go down to the plantations, to the great houses, to the parliament building, or to the assembly, to ask for anything. It was the British that came to them for peace and it should state that the British sued for peace."

"The Maroons were a big threat to the British. They represented freedom on the island when almost everyone here was a slave," I said.

"When you get down to the situation of writing the things on the document, the English wrote that the Maroons sued for peace, implying they were the losers," he said. "They were saying, 'We have subdued these people,' and that was not true."

"And because we are big-hearted in our victory, we will give them some land," I said.

Rasta Heart

"The British had to hold their dignity," Julia said.

"That is the whole policy of the British," he said. "When they reported back to England about this island they had to say that this little group of Maroons, which they consider wild and uncivilized people, were giving them such a hard time. It was an unpleasant reminder of when the barbarians overthrew the British."

"So Maroon is not their real name?" I asked.

"No. No. Not Maroon," he said. "If you constantly apply a term to a given situation, whether it is true or not, the lie becomes true in the end. When the document was signed, the term Maroon was used. That is not to say our foreparents called themselves like that. The term they used to describe themselves was 'Yank Yoo Yoo' (pronounced yan-koo-koo), which means a free people, an independent people, a people that are self-reliant."

"So basically the English rewrote history to suit their own needs," I said.

"Well, I guess the world has been like that from the beginning," he said.

"How do Maroons view their history today?" I asked.

"It is very important. We are reluctant to trust an outsider because we have been living in a situation for over a hundred years where our survival depends on relying upon ourselves. You just have to just carry on because we might say 'Chamo, Chamo,' which means you say some and you leave some. All Maroons consider themselves to be blood relatives, whether you are actually so or not, but this is a general concept. We still say we are the children of Grandy Nanny. Whether we are her biological child or not, we are still a part of her in the fact that we are her descendants. To say Granny Nanny yoyo or Granny Nanny peekeeboo, means children, descendants."

"Colonel, tell us about Nanny. It was amazing that a woman in the 1700s could become a leader and also a great military fighter and have so much power," Julia said.

"That may have been unusual for Europeans but not for Africans. Africans have great respect for their women," he replied.

"Did she have many children? Did she have a husband?" I asked.

"That was information that was important to her and those involved (we all laughed). What is revealed about her is what is important for you to know. She was a priestess. She was the queen. She was the mother. She was this great military leader and she prepared her people to go into battle. She did not at all times go into battle but she would prepare the soldiers before they went. That must be understood. She sat down as a military leader and laid down the strategies and the tactics to be applied. Once all these warriors follow these instructions, things would be OK. To deviate from them might bring disaster. Nanny prepared them for battle. She trained them. She put the protection with them when they were going out and sometimes she needed to stay by the fire to see that the fire was burning while they were out fighting."

"Keep the fire burning, the eternal flame?" Julia said.

"Right (reverently closing his eyes). They did not always go out and just fight like that, ya know. They were prepared in a metaphysical way to go into battle."

"In their minds, they would get themselves in tune with their JAH power," Julia said.

"Right," Colonel Sterling said, in a subtle way to let us know "chamo chamo." It was getting rather late and Nanny Falls was still a half-hour walk away, so we said our thanks and that we would visit again on our next trip. Julia and I drove farther up the dirt road while Clive, Scram and Shakey walked next to the car. A couple of the Rastas we met in the village joined us.

As the six of us wandered up, Shakey spotted some star apples growing in a tree. Without a word he broke off from the pack and easily scampered 12 or 15 feet up the tree to pick some for everyone. He dropped them down to Clive and they came over with their arms full and we all stopped for a quick feast. The Jamaican star apple is an amazing fruit. It is about the size of a grapefruit but the moist, sweet inside is like a fig in the shape of a star with five seeds. After a delicious break, we continued.

"Dat de area where I started ta build de cabins, " Scram said when we got to the concrete stairs leading down to the falls. The frames of two small cabins were rotting in a cleared area now overgrown with brush. "It is very important dat people cayn come 'ere ta Nanny's 'ome. Dis is a very powerful place."

"I can really feel her power, Scram," Julia said. "It's like she's really here with me. I've been feeling it since we entered the valley."

Rasta Heart

Nanny Falls is darker and more intense than Reach Fall. It is in a deep grotto surrounded by rock walls, maybe 150 feet in diameter and 50 feet high. The 25 feet wide falls plummets to the pool below with a powerful force. It gets little sunlight except when the sun is almost directly overhead. We changed into our bathing suits and headed in.

After an hour we wandered back. A Rasta who had waited by our car had picked some more star apples, coconuts and plantain and had laid everything out on mats he had woven from palm fronds. It was a gourmet lunch Rasta style. Refreshed and relaxed, we headed back to Port Antonio. On the way, we passed several women walking back from church.

"Robbie, pull over 'ere," Scram said. "Dos are my cousins."

We pulled over and Scram introduced us and they started talking in patois. The conversation was very animated and seemed to swing from laughter to serious discussion.

"What was that all about?" I asked as we pulled away.

"My cousin, she tell me dat my Aunitie just died in Bellvue. She was de last of 'er generation, de last of me mother's generation. Dere will be a hole digging service dis Thursday and de funeral on next Sunday."

After awhile, I remembered that I had made a copy of Bob Marley's famous concert at the Rainbow Theater in London, considered one of his best. I could play it on my small screen on our videocam.

"Hey, guys, when was the last time you saw Bob Marley perform?" I asked everyone in the backseat.

"Maybe ten years ago on TV," Scram said.

"Same for me," Shakey replied.

"I've never seen him. Only heard him," Clive said.

"Would you guys like to watch him?" I said handing them the camcorder with Bob on the screen.

Shakey really got into it, jumping around like a little kid with his eyes all lit up. "Mon, look at 'im do dat," he would say, imitating Bob's almost spastic movements in the backseat. "Oh, mon, I cayn't believe dis. I could watch 'im all day."

Even as they got out of the car for the potholes, they would saunter down the road, Shakey holding the camcorder high and everyone bouncing to the music.

We dropped them off and were heading home in the dark when we saw someone hitchhiking, obviously drunk. It was Hans, the German guy we encountered at the hotel who was so down on Rastas. He looked like a pathetic figure, lonely and lost.

"What ya say, Julia, let's give Hans a little loving," I said slowing down.

"Let's. He could sure use some," she replied, laughing.

"Me brethren!" I yelled enthusiastically at him as we pulled over. "Where ya going?"

I got out and helped him into the car and we drove on talking to him like he was our oldest and dearest friend. By the time we got to his hotel, he was smiling and laughing and so were we.

Ganja

No plant has had a more checkered and interesting past than ganja, perhaps because no plant has been more important in human history. The Sumerian/Babylonian word for cannabis hemp, K(a)N(a)B(a), is one of the oldest root words. As early as 8000 B.C., hemp was used to weave fabric. Its utilization as a medicine dates to 2700 B.C., when written records show its use in the pharmacopoeia of Shen Nung, one of the fathers of Chinese medicine. In 550 B.C., the Persian prophet Zoroaster, placed hemp at the top of his list of 10,000 medicinal plants in his sacred text, *The Zend-Avesta*.

In 800 A.D., Islamic prophet Mohammed, while forbidding the use of alcohol in the Koran, permitted the use of cannabis. However, early Christianity was not so easy on the herb. In 1430, Joan of Arc was accused of using the "witch herb" to hear voices. Fifty years later, Pope Innocent VIII labeled cannabis as an unholy sacrament of the Satanic Mass and banned the drug. However, 150 years later, mostly due to the use of hemp in paper, fabric and rope manufacturing, the Western world took a more favorable look at the drug when Queen Elizabeth I ordered all landowners to grow at least 60 acres of hemp and King Phillip of Spain ordered it grown throughout his empire, from Argentina to Spain.

From 1000 B.C. to 1833, cannabis hemp was our planet's largest agricultural crop and most important industry. The majority of the world's fiber, fabric, lighting oil, paper, incense and medicines came from hemp. Hemp fabric is longer lasting, more absorbent, more durable, warmer and softer than cotton cloth. Until the 19th century, 90 percent of all ships' sails were made of hemp fiber, as was much of a ship's rope, rigging, oakum, nets and even the seamen's clothing. A ship's maps, logs, charts, and even Bibles, were all made from hemp paper, which lasts 50 to 100 times longer than papyrus and is a hundred times cheaper and easier to make. Until 1883, 75 to 90 percent of all paper in the world was made from hemp.

Ganja history in the U.S. dates back to 1619 when the Jamestown Colony of Virginia passed the first ganja laws. Ironically, these laws did not prohibit its use but rather mandated that all farmers grow hemp. Massachusetts and Connecticut soon followed with similar laws. Some colonies even allowed citizens to pay taxes with hemp. Though some of the colonists may have been using the plant for "medicinal purposes," it was mostly grown for fabric, rope and paper. The first two drafts of the Declaration of Independence were written on hemp paper. By 1850, there were 8,327 hemp plantations, a minimum of 2,000 acres, in the U.S.

By the mid 1800s, ganja's "other" beneficial uses continued to emerge. From 1842 until the 1890s, various ganja and hashish extracts were the first, second or third most prescribed medicines in the United States and produced by such companies as Eli Lilly, Squibb and Parke-Davis. At the Centennial Exposition in Philadelphia in 1876 celebrating America's 100th birthday, fairgoers were encouraged to visit the Turkish Hashish Exposition to "enhance their fair experience" with a few hits of hash. By 1883, hashish smoking parlors were opened in almost every major American city. The New York City police estimated that there were 500 such parlors in that city alone. Even Queen Victoria (whose name was lent to the prudish "Victorian Era"), was getting stoned to alleviate menstrual cramps. By 1895, ganja was fully endorsed by the powers-that-be when the Indian Hemp Drug Commission concluded that it had no addictive properties, some medicinal uses and a number of positive emotional and social benefits.

In the 1970s, there were three large field studies of ganja in Greece, Costa Rica and Jamaica. These studies, which evaluated the impact of ganja on users in their natural environments, were supplemented by clinical examinations and laboratory experiments. The data from these studies, published in numerous books and scholarly journals, covered matters such as ganja's effects on the brain, lungs, immune and reproductive systems; its impact on personality, development, and motivational states; and its addictive potential. Although these studies did not answer all remaining questions about ganja's toxicity, they generally supported the idea that ganja was a relatively safe drug, not totally free from potential harm, but unlikely to create serious harm for most individual users or society.

In March 1999, the *Institute of Medicine Report* (IOM) stated that there is "no clear alternative for people suffering from chronic conditions that might be relieved by smoking marijuana, such as pain or AIDS wasting... Few marijuana users develop dependence and if there are withdrawal symptoms, they are mild and short-lived."

Thousands of additional studies have been conducted and together they reaffirm ganja's substantial margin of safety. In over 10,000 studies worldwide, only a dozen have found negative effects from ganja and these studies could not be replicated. There are no studies that show marijuana to be a "gateway" substance but rather its illegal status often puts users in contact with unscrupulous dealers who offer them addicting drugs.

For centuries, ganja has been used to treat fatigue, coughing, rheumatism, asthma, delirium tantrums, migraine headaches, glaucoma, nausea, tumors, epilepsy, infection, stress, arthritis and the cramps and depression associated with menstruation—all without any recorded negative side effects. If there were any, centuries of use would have revealed them. Also, cannabis is the best natural expectorant to clear the lungs of smog, dust and the phlegm associated with tobacco use, all while raising your consciousness and promoting a state of well-being and self-assertiveness.

In 2001, the BBC reported:

"There is scientific evidence to suggest that cannabis may be useful in treating a wide range of conditions. For instance, cannabis appears to be able to help reduce the side effects of chemotherapy treatment given to cancer patients... Cannabis is an antiemetic, a drug that relieves nausea and allows patients to eat and live normally. Extracts also seem to benefit patients suffering from multiple sclerosis, stopping muscle spasms, and reducing tremors... There is evidence that cannabis may stimulate the appetites of AIDS patients. It may also help relieve the pain of menstrual cramps and childbirth. Campaigners claim the drug is useful in treating depression and other mood disorders. Cannabis has been shown to prevent seizures in epileptic patients when given in combination with prescription drugs. The drug can also help in the treatment of patients suffering from glaucoma, a common cause of blindness, by reducing fluid pressure in the eye. Claims have also been made for its use in treating asthma, strokes, Parkinson's Disease, Alzheimer's Disease, alcoholism and insomnia."

However, this remarkable plant's value goes much further than what it can do to heal the human body and mind. Of the over 3 million edible plants, hemp seed has the most nutritious vegetable oil known, complete and high in protein. It can help feed the planet with a crop that grows anywhere without use of fertilizers and chemicals. If its use as a fabric was encouraged, it could replace cotton, the growing of which accounts for almost 50 percent of agricultural chemicals that are polluting our planet. Hemp provides four times as much pulp, with at least four to seven times less pollution than paper made from trees. By switching back to hemp paper, we could save our forests and greatly reduce global warming and other problems created by deforestation.

Research indicates that 10 to 20 percent of all pharmaceutical prescription medicines could be eliminated by using ganja, potentially saving hundreds of billions of dollars annually and decreasing the amount of poisons we take into our body through these "better" medicines. Add to this the amount of over-the-counter medicines that could be reduced and ganja's benefits mount even higher.

Cannabis hemp is the only annually renewable plant able to replace fossil fuels and thereby reduce their unhealthy and dangerous effects. It is the only resource that can make every country energy independent. It is the planet's number one biomass resource, capable of producing ten tons per acre in four months. This can then be used for everything from fuel for vehicles and heating to making plastics. In fact, Henry Ford once made a partially hemp-fabricated car he "grew from the soil." Finally, ganja makes hard physical work much easier, lessening the burden of the toiling masses while offering them relaxation without an alcohol induced hangover.

Given the above, it is easy to understand why the plant (it is not a drug), was made illegal by Babylon. Cannabis hemp would be free to anyone who had a few square feet to grow it. It threatens many industries including energy, pharmaceuticals, cotton, pulp paper, prisons and police, tobacco, alcohol, psycho-therapy and drug rehab, as well as the illegal drug trade. This is why the 4,000 "Families Against Marijuana" type organizations in the U.S. get half their funding from drug and pharmacists groups and most of the other half from alcohol and tobacco companies.

Chapter 10
JAH T

"Because of the progress mankind has achieved and because of the difficulties that are at times part and parcel of progress and   prosperity, we find ourselves at the crossroad where we might make the world safe for our future generations or we might perish together."
—Emperor Haile Selassie I

The day after visiting Nanny Falls, we spent the morning around the hotel. We ordered lunch and our waiter, Ronald, set a table under a beautiful shade tree while we swam in the pool. After a half hour or so, he had the table decorated with white linen and flowers and a beautiful meal laid out. We had noticed Ronald earlier. He was in his early twenties, handsome and fit, and definitely a Rasta heart.

After lunch we headed over to Scram's. We settled around the table in the front room and hung out as various friends and customers came through. Bell was also there. Bell is a Rasta friend of Scram's, sweet and quiet. He was in his late thirties, short and slim with gray precepts and dreads. He seemed older and wise with a hint of sadness in his thoughtful eyes. Scram had him watch the store when he was out with us. As soon as we arrived, Bell served us some beautifully prepared foods. We didn't have the heart to tell him we had just eaten.

Julia began coughing, which we both had been doing a lot of since we arrived.

" 'Ere is some good root tonic fe yah cough. It is sweetsop. It 'as a spice I get from my 'ouse. No furtilizer up by my 'ouse. Irman brought it by fe you. 'E knows 'ow I like to get it done so I just ask 'im ta do it. It coming up, it coming up, yeah," Scram said as Julia coughs.

"So you go to Moore Town," Irman said, after arriving by bike. "Lots of pot 'oles. It is a nice place. I love it up dere. Scramo did a lot up der, ya know. Ya know, de place up by Dragon Bay, ya see 'ow clean it is. Scram he clean up de places, mon. Dat land was owned by a good friend, a lawyer."

"'Is name was Alfred. I take good care of 'im until 'e die," Scramo said. "I took care of Alfred in 1964 and I stayed by 'im. I worked as a gardener. 'E was not originated den," he said pointing to Irman and we all laughed. "I was der wit' 'is daughter and 'is son. I would push dem on the swing and got to 'old dem and walk wit' dem."

A friend of Scram's, Dwight, came in. He was very thin and looked very poor. His skin was black but his features were Indian. Many of Jamaica's early immigrants were from India, mostly Hindus from Northern India. They now make up one of Jamaica's largest ethnic group. After slavery, they were brought over as indentured laborers and lived a life of such appalling semi-slavery that the Indian government forbade migration to Jamaica in 1917. Many Indians, after completing their forced service, moved to Kingston, where many prospered as merchants. They also introduced ganja, the plant and the word, to the island.

Dwight joined us at the table and we offered him some of our food. At first he declined but we insisted, telling him we could never eat it all. Finally, he accepted with much appreciation.

"I leave Portland and I go ta St. Thomas fe a few years fe work because my parents were poor," Scram continued. "I go and I leave school ta look fe some work and I work as a small boy. I do shepherd work wit' dis white man from England, Captain John Rose. 'Is father used ta be Major Rose in England. Big guy. So I used ta work wit' 'is son up by de property by Green Castle in St. Thomas. Shepherd de cows, sheep and keep de foul, swan and de likkel ducks. Dey 'ad a big 'ouse."

"Was that the first time you saw how the rich lived?" I asked

"Ya, mon. Dis guy was nice, as an English guy. 'E 'ad a good 'eart because I and my cousin, we got de same job at almost de same time. 'E 'ad about 75 'ead of sheep and we bring it up ta about 275. 'E give me one sheep and one layer hen and a duck and my cousin de same as well.

Rasta Heart

I saddle de 'orse in de morning fe 'im and when 'e is not riding around, I ride around on de 'orse and look fe de sheep all over de place. I was about 15 or 16 and it was like picking up stones on de ground. What make me so comfortable was my uncle was living in de area in St Thomas. I was living in de big 'ouse in a room dey 'ad fe me because dey 'ave maids living in de big house wit' electricity, plumbing, everyt'ing. It was a good life and on de weekend, dey pay us a likkle money but dos days de money you make was good but today you cayn't buy a cigarette with it (big laugh)."

"I would get a pound a week. It's de same now, one pound go fe two dollar. It was twelve shilling fe one pound. Dey step it down massive but dey did not bring wages up. I work fe dis Chinaman fe one pound and two-pence a week and I save de two-pense fe me because I 'ave ta share it up and I 'ave ta go ta de movie and 'ave ta save some. All dese movie guys came dere. Lots of people would go ta de movie, an indoor t'eater wit' fans. Ya 'ave lots of people goin' down de street, crowded. Sometime ya could go ta t'ree movies in one night. It used ta be nice and fun ta do. Once Peter O'Toole was in front of de t'eater ta 'ave a drink. (O'Toole was in Port Antonio while filming *Club Paradise* with Robin Williams)."

"When I work fe dis Englishmon, dey try ta test me wit' money because one time dey ask me ta wash de kitchen floor and close by, where dey knew I could see it, dey put a big pile of money ta see if I would steal it. I wipe de floor down and den I make sure I call de maid and call de boss ta say, 'Ya see de money is still dere' (laughs). Den I sell de sheep. I sell back everyt'ing ta John Rose because I was so 'appy ta return ta Portland and I needed de cash. I wanted ta return ta my mother because I 'eard she was pregnant. I was 'omesick and I wanted ta be wit' my new brot'er dat was born. It was de same period of time dat I met my cousin and 'e said I should come down ta Port Antonio when 'e leave 'is job wit' a lawyer and I should come down ta get 'is job, right 'ere in town in a big 'ouse and I 'ad my own room."

"Does the lawyer still live near here?" I asked.

"Nah, de lawyer, a black guy, die and everyt'ing just goin' down. It pass over ta 'is little son, de one I used ta swing. Dis son went ta England an when 'e come back, my wife and I noticed one of 'is legs started to get swollen. So we got some seawater and island roots dat we 'ad and it healed. But den 'e go back ta England fe about t'ree months and come back. 'Is leg swell big again. 'E doan't act so collected. Well, now 'is father is dead. 'Is 'ead is not so right. 'E is mad at everybody but me. So we take care of 'im. When my kids come to see 'im, dey 'ave ta clean 'im because 'e doan't know ta clean 'imself. 'Is mind gone completely now but whenever time 'e sees me, 'e settles down. We are very good friends even up until now and 'is mother gave me some land by Dragon Bay before she die and ev'ry year I pay de taxes on dat land so de government cayn't take it away."

Scram and I went into the kitchen to clean up our dishes and Irman joined Julia. Bell walked over and gave us fresh squeezed pineapple juice.

"Bell, what's your history?" I asked.

"I used to swim and was on the gymnastics team," he said. "I travelled with the Olympic team a lot. I don't travel with it any more because I have a business but it isn't prosperous. I am doing a little farming. I lived in London and in Canada for many years and worked with computers."

"What kind of farming do you do?" Julia asked.

"I grow plantain and cocoa and I sell it I right here," he says pointing out the door to the stand. "I used to take it on a truck. I have a guest house I am fixing up."

"So you decided rather than go Babylon's way, you'd come back here and live as a Rasta?" I asked.

"I get tired of that because everything is money, money, money. It's too much hustling and bustling. I can't take that no more. If I don't get work for today, I know I can eat because I work my farm, ya know. So I just come here for awhile. I came about five years ago. It's much better for me down here, away from Babylon. But Babylon could be anybody. Babylon need you to work and you get your pay. You just go to the store and you are in Babylon. Babylon is the people who are robbing the poor. They are the Babylonians. The people that just look for themselves alone. That means they would do anything to survive. Babylon is just for himself and his immediate family. They don't look for anyone else to help. If anyone else should come, they underpay. That is Babylon to me. Takers which do not give back in the system. But if you read the Bible, it will tell you the right thing to do. But anyone can be Babylon. You don't have to work in the system to be Babylon. Your mind could just be Babylon," he said pointing both forefingers to his temple.

"So just like Rasta is a state of mind, Babylon is also a state of mind?"

Rasta Heart

I said.

"Ya, mon, Babylon is a state of mind."

Scram wandered in with a plate of sliced oranges and mangoes and joined us at the table.

"Yeah. So dat is ta show dat Rasta is in every living person," Scram said with a big laugh. "Only de teaching of Babylon is showin' people ta do away wit' Rasta but ta do away wit' Rasta is ta do away wit' demselves, ya see. Everyone is Rasta because has an inborn love dat flow t'ru de 'eart of everyone who want ta cherish dat feeling. Dey are de ones dat are true Rastafari, praise JAH ALMIGHTY."

"Praise JAH, ALMIGHTY JAH," Julia said.

"Babylon is a system, ya know," Scram said slowly, deliberately, loudly. "Ya cayn 'ave de 'eads of government and dey might not be Babylon. Dey might send money or food from dere office ta a person in de government 'ere and den dat person mess it up. Ya cayn see where Babylon start from because de Prime Minister sometimes 'is 'eart is so smooth and so good becuz 'e send down ta dis office and 'e say, 'Share it up. Share it all, fe all de people, fe many people.' But when it get 'ere, dey say, 'Give it ta over dere and give a little ta over dere and doan't give any ta over dere.' And dat is where de small people meet de pinch and de small people cry out and seh, 'Eads of government now got ta change.' But it was sent from de 'eads of government so de masses cayn be fed and dey go right dere and mess it up. 'E send it, 'eads of government send it, down ta de office and dos people are supposed ta distribute dat ta everyone, ta let everyone be fed and it right dere. Dat where Babylon start from but it doan't always start from de 'eads of government but it start just down below 'is foot. Like when Moses went up Mt. Sinai and everybody got crazy and build up dis golden calf again, 'eading back ta de same system dey just fled from."

"Scram, I'm still not sure where I see a woman's place in all this," Julia said.

"So it is. Rasta is an inborn love dat welcome ev'ryone," Scram says, slowly thoughtfully. "A womon, she is most 'onorable ta ev'ry mon and a womon is not someting dat mon should joke about. Because I feel dat ev'ry womon is a Rasta wit'in 'erself and if ya call yaself a Rastamon, ya 'ave respect fe ev'ry womon, not one womon. So both mon and womon should look 'pon demselves as greatest people 'an disrespect should nevah come inta de mix."

"As a Rasta, ya want ta protect people," he continued. "Ya see dese girls come 'ere, ta Dragon Bay, a lot of girls from New York, from Pennsylvania, from Boston, Chicago, Ireland, France, ya could name places all over Europe. Girls come in my presence, come in my vision and I tek care of dem. Ya see I speak of myself and dey are out dere ta ask and ta speak of me. Dey burn fire in de night, on de beach and I make sure dey are OK. Dey want ta go inta town, I got ta be dere. Dey go dere and I stood by de bar while dey drink what dey want ta drink and I just tek care of dem and de presence of dese people is very much nice and important ta me."

"And I trust that in you. You've always shown me honesty and true genuine feeling," Julia said.

"Yes, inborn because if ya see somet'ing you doan't like about me, ya tell me because ya are goin' ta be my teacher (laughs). Everyday ya goin' ta be my teacher because I doan't seh I am so old and someone is not dere ta tell me somet'ing. Someone got ta tell me somet'ing new I nevah 'eard before, ya know."

"Yes and I want the ladies to trust that is so and that women are respected," Julia said.

"Well, let me say that we have to warn the ladies of wolf in sheep's clothing," Scram said. "Den when dos ladies come and she sit beside Scramo and I will guide 'er all de way t'ru. We want ta 'ave a good vibe about dis t'ing. We want de ladies ta jump and shout and know dey all are Rastawomon. Becuz according ta 'ow most people speak about Rasta and Rastawomon is de wrong t'ing. Because Rasta is de love, ta break down all barriers. We want de ladies ta know dat dey are Rastawomon no matter 'ow shiny dere 'air is."

A fisherman appeared at the door and asked Scram if he wanted to buy his catch. Scram stopped his discourse but didn't answer. Not wanting to break his train of thought, he closed his eyes and slowly turned his head from side to side to tell the man "no" before he even asked his question. The fisherman respectfully disappeared and Scram opened his eyes and continued.

"We doan't want dese ladies ta 'ave de feeling of being left out due ta what another sub-Rastaman 'as done. Maybe it is because dey like de women ta an extent. Maybe Bob Marley did de t'ings like 'e did ta get

Rasta Heart

de praise of a lots of women but dat is not ta seh dat is de right tradition of Rastaman but JAH know best, ya know. Ta de beauty of a womon, ya will find Rastaman 'imself (laughs) wanting ta reach over ta touch 'er but we 'ave ta 'ave our vision de right and proper way because everyt'ing dat brings life, we got ta really nourish dat."

"I think that there are so many wolves here," I said, "and if you are a woman traveling alone or with just other women, you'll get propositioned all the time. It can really make you uncomfortable."

"Scram, we've decided to leave tomorrow," I said. "We are going to Negril for a couple of days. We want to check out a hotel for our June trip. So we're going to leave tomorrow around lunch."

"Dat is good," Scram said. "I want ya ta meet JAH T. 'E is a good Rastamon and 'e just came back in town. We cayn see 'im in de mornin'."

The next morning we picked up Scram and went to find JAH T (also called Tony). JAH T played in a reggae group and had been living in Ocho Rios until recently. We picked up JAH T at a store on the main road in Port Antonio. He was thin, medium height and in his late 40s with salt and pepper precepts and long braided dreads wrapped like a turban around his head. He spoke slowly, thoughtfully, his speech reflecting intelligence and education. He seemed humble, quiet and kind.

We decided to go to Folly Beach, a local park in Port Antonio where it was quiet and private. We settled around a table in a small open-air restaurant overlooking the bay, with a beach out front. JAH T and I ordered some lunch, Scram lit up a spliff and Julia went for a swim.

"How long have you been Rasta?" I asked.

"Since 1972," JAH T answered.

"What happened that made you become a Rasta?"

"Well, I'm 47 right now. There were opportunities my parents 'ad in store fe me. They sent me to school to take care of the business. My mother died and there was a conflict of the will in those times. After I get the inspiration to be a Ras there was an opportunity to go to Dallas, Texas. I resented it because I wanted to know more about Rasta so I went into the hills with my friends. My brother married an American woman and separated and after a few years 'e sent fe me cause 'e saw the potential of me as a youth. I resented that opportunity. I was more curious about Rasta. It was a very 'ard time to be a Rasta. They said we kidnapped children and killed them. They called us all sorts of degrading names because they did not know about us. From a Biblical point of view, they did not understand 'ow a man with tall 'air could 'ave a religious background. They could not understand 'ow that was so. God must 'ave a purpose to 'ave this 'air grow on our face. So we let it grow but it was a lot of tribulation and 'ardship to be a Ras."

"What did your parents think?" I asked.

"They could not understand what was going on. They took it to 'eart and feel sorry about the thing. Then all races started to accept it. Even the Chinese Jamaicans accepted us and then they started to pay attention. What drew the people's attention was the hair, the women weaving their hair so it becomes a style, braids and things. So that makes it a little easier to accept Rasta. It becomes like a style."

"So did you meet Rastas that you were drawn to?" I asked, wondering if he had had the same experience as a youth as Scram.

"I left my parents 'ouse and lived in a Rasta 'ome and smoke ganja where I get my inspiration. We started reading the Bible and playing the harps and we camped out but the policemen came and took us down. We usually preached in the market place and walked with a sign that said, 'King of Kings.' People were very curious to understand. There was police brutality just for carrying a sign. They would carry us to the station and give us karate in the neck just like that (he does a hard karate chop to his neck)."

"When did that stop?" I asked.

"I wouldn't say it has stopped altogether but there is a positive look now because we don't get that police brutality but they still resent us. What 'appens now to my son. We usually take a beating and call it love."

It is clear that discrimination and police brutality toward Rastas still continues. In a letter to the *Jamaica Gleaner* in August of 2001, the writer, a Rasta from St. Andrew named Dilpi Champegnie, writes, "We are the the first to lose our jobs and the last to be employed. We have been murdered, beaten, taken to the mad-house and prison, because of our religious convictions, an indigenous religion which is still not legally recognized."

Rasta Heart

"JAH T, what is a Rasta to you?" I asked, knowing this would prime the pump.

"We accept people not because of their locks," JAH T began as we settled back. "We accept them as close brethren because of the way they treat people. Very nice, very humble, sympathetic and we say, 'Yes, this is a Ras.' But what if I'm thinking of you as a Ras but ya are not seeing yaself as a Ras. You know where ya are coming from because you were born wit' dat loving touch but you do not accept Rasta as your way of life but you accept love as the foundation but you did not say that you accept the way of life."

"So what you are saying is that if you express One Love, you are a Rasta at heart but until you live the lifestyle, the diet, the dreads and precepts, the belief in Haile Selassie, you are not yet fully a Rasta?" I asked.

"Yes. And we accept your love because that is what Bob Marley is saying. We need One Love regardless of what color, class or creed. Rasta is something you 'ave to know. It is like studying fe medicine. You 'ave to know medicine in order to prescribe medicine. You 'ave ta know love. Rastas appear in their own form in order to identify themselves. I call Rasta my way of life, my natural freedom. You live more loving. You see more reasons to share love because you practically take 'old of life, like the tree, the birds. Because what you were grasping fe was the free togetherness of Rasta, the warm welcome of Rasta, the heart vibes of Rasta. That's why the Bob Marley syndrome establish that you cayn be a part of me. I accept Bob Marley as a prophet and an elder one. It's the reason why JAH send Bob Marley that way. If Bob Marley was pure black, 'e would not be accepted or the ot'er way around. 'Alf and 'alf. Black and white. That's why 'e was sent by JAH because of what 'e did. 'E sang fe you and fe me."

"And when you have Rasta, there will be no more war," Julia said, returning from her swim

"Yes. 'e said we need peace, we need love and we do not need any more war. I believe that. If we cayn accept what Bob said, we will accept the truth and the togetherness 'e wanted us to express because there is no need fe us to war when I really look at it . We are created by the same force or the same source."

"We can stop that Cain and Able thing," Julia said.

"Yeah. We doan't need that. It does not work because all we are doing is sinking, causing war, this one against that one. We need to share. You come to my home and I treat you like a king and visa versa. We 'ave dialogues together. We cayn 'elp each other together. We cayn learn from each other. We cayn build a great empire unto that force that cause us to be. I cayn't see people predicting God to come in war, in crime. I believe we 'ave to come together as one to prove that we need to see Him. The more war, the further we are prepared fe de coming of JAH. So when we say 'Rasta,' that is not war. Some people predict war, an eye for an eye. It does not make sense because if I 'ate you fe what your ancestor did, you are not guilty of that. You were not the one that did it. We've just got to stop the war right now. We need love in order to reach that destiny, to see what is behind the curtain. Only love can bring us there. Love is the vehicle. The whole thing is based on love, the fullness. There is no other way. The fullness is just love."

"So to you, Rasta, is this love?" I asked.

"Rasta is more like a state of mind, the function of the mind because there are a lot of religions around. Ours is a natural way of thinking. People complicate things because they cayn not see the natural 'eaven. 'Eaven is a 'appiness. It makes no sense to look to the sky in the future fe 'eaven. We 'ave ta live toget'er 'appily first before we cayn think of being in 'eaven. I believe we 'ave to love each other and communicate together and share that 'appiness. So if I try to do it and you do not do it or visa versa, it does not work until we all sing the same song."

"What are your feelings about Haile Selassie?" I asked.

"Whenevertime I 'ear a strong argument towards 'im I get dos bumps on my skin because the story 'as never been told about 'im. There are many great works he did that 'ave been 'idden. I believe according to the Bible we 'ave not seen the ALMIGHTY in the flesh as we would want to but according to Revelations, certain individuals we emphasis that 'e is Haile Selassie, King of Kings and the Lord of Lords because in my world, 'e is not an unseen God to me. God could be a title to a one that fulfill that prophesy to return. I believe that the main objective right now is fe us to see God, to show that togetherness in one full harmony. I believe that Haile Selassie fulfilled the message of the Christ according to the revelations. We are 'ere ta establish 'is name by calling ourself Rastafari. We are not denying it. We are calling ourself by the same name."

Rasta Heart

"Did he live a Christlike life?" I asked.

"My answer to that is once as a lamb to the slaughter, now as a conquering lion of the Tribe of Judah," he replied. "If you are coming to conquer, you are coming in a different form. We are reaching a point where basic love will do but it will not do if the enemy does not decide to love too."

Haile Selassie did indeed have a powerful divine destiny, offering the Rastas an image of a proud black king so that they could claim their power and play their special role in bringing One Love to the planet. In this way he could have indeed been "the opener of the scroll and its seven seals."

"What did most of the Rastas think about Bob Marley?" I asked.

"Well to be perfectly 'onest with you, some still did not think that was the way to go. You still 'ave some Rastas that resent reggae music. They prefer the traditional Nyabingi drumming and chanting. That's the original Rasta."

"Do they see Bob Marley as destructive?" I asked.

"No, they don't see 'im as destructive. The message 'e sent they see as very important because of what it did to the outside world. But even today they do not accept 'im as that glorified prophet."

"Maybe he was was a glorified drummer and perfection is not required of a tribal drummer," I said.

"There is no real total perfection right now today. There is not total perfection in anyone. So when someone makes a mistake, you just move along and try to get over it. Even in Nyabingi, there is no one that is perfect. So right now we try to accept Bob as a real prophet because of 'is work, because 'e really did prophetic work. So whether they want to accept 'im or not, the day will come when they will 'ave to because even the Bobo Ashantis are going out on the road with their music. So they understand what Bob did but they did not understand before because they prefer a natural vibe. They don't like cars, trucks, CDs. All Rastafari organizations profess that they are very strict. Even the Nyabingi say they are very strict. But you cayn not be too strict or you will not discover what you are supposed to do because it will prevent you from exploring. It will keep you confined to just one page so you never get to understand what's on the other page in later days. You got to be on the move in order to understand and to establish whatsoever you are doing. So they are realizing and some are still in primitive stages and taking time to get out of it. They got to get out of it because you 'ave to accept inventions whether we want to or not. Otherwise how could His Majesty come on a plane to Jamaica? So we 'ave to accept the knowledge of man because these things are in us."

"There are many sects. Do most Rastas accept each others' choice of these different tribes?" I asked.

"Yeah. It's left to what you desire. If you want to be a Bobo, it's up to you. If you want to be a Nyabingi, it's fine. The main objective is that we all sing the same song. We all praise the praises. It's like the twelve tribes. You 'ave Ruben, Benjamin, Joseph. When Christ walked, 'e did not walk with an organization. 'E walked freely so 'E could meet everyone. 'E didn't especially establish an organization. What 'E established was love fe everyone, all nations and that is what I'm trying to do now. If I confine myself to an organization, I will not go to anot'er organization and I will think what they are saying or doing is wrong and they could be right. So it's better to leave yourself free to accept each one. That's my opinion. It's better fe me. When I belong to an organization, they can say 'Don't go there. Don't do that.' So I left myself available to do the work whatever way. The main objective is to deal with the basic love. That way it doesn't matter what nation, what race, what tribe or what. Love is the only answer for all situations. When we cayn get that, the tribal thing will be no more around. We'll all be one people doing their own thing. Because this tribal thing, it really creates segregation and separations because we think because we are this tribe we are the first. The Nyabingi say they are the first. The Bobo Dread say they are the first. The Christian say they are the first. The Roman Catholic say they are the first."

"Are the Rastas in Jamaica getting closer or farther apart?" I asked.

"Well, I wouldn't say they are coming together in their physical movement but in the concept they are. Ordinary Rasta will support a stage show but Nyabingis will not. The Genesis to Revelation has completed itself. 2000 is 'ere. I believe earth to be heaven and 'eaven to be earth and you make it what you want it ta be. It's what we make it to be. If we make it hell, we get to enjoy hell. If we make to be 'eaven, it will be 'eaven. This is a place designed fe man. The first Rasta was a priest in Kingston and the coronation of Haile Selassie in 1930 convinced 'im totally that was the Christ on earth. 'E 'ad de vision and passed it on to the church and they accepted it. It would be very hard fe Rastafari to function without the belief in Haile Selassie because 'e is the very foundation."

"So this preacher was like the three kings seeing the light in the sky and announced the Christ is here?" Julia said.

"Yes," JAH T said.

"So to you, being Rasta is more than expressing One Love?" I asked.

"That could be a part but that is not the ideal to be Rasta. It 'as been said in the Bible, whenevertime you start to accept Christ, there is tribulation and things you 'ave to go through like Christ did. So unless you accept and carry de cross, unless you carry de locks, people will not know that you are Rasta. If you are dealing with just love, no one is going to know you are Rasta."

"What would you call a person who had the love but not the locks or belief in the divinity of Haile Selassie?" I asked.

"'E is just an ordinary man defending love but 'e did not commit 'imself to be a Rasta. Rasta must take a vow to be 'oly, to grow the locks as said in the Bible and make a Nazarene vow," JAH T said.

"Could you eat meat and still be a Rasta?" I asked.

"You could but many Rasta don't deal with the meat eating but it is very difficult to place food on a religion," JAH T said. He had ordered fish for his lunch. "What I believe, those chemically grown foods, those are the most detrimental. If you raise a chicken naturally, it's ok. But I don't believe man's destiny lies in what 'e eats. It is good to eat natural food but it does not determine man's eternal destiny because you 'ave many people that do not eat meat and they are very violent."

It was now around noon, and we wanted to head out to Negril. We thanked JAH T and dropped him off at his house.

"Scram, it's been quite a week," I said, as we dropped him off at his shop. "We'll be back in June with our daughter."

"So it is. I wan' dat I should meet 'er and I know dat dere will be much love dere." We hugged and headed out, feeling closer to Scram than ever.

Ganja

One must ask why alcohol, which in the U.S. alone accounts for over 100,000 deaths annually and 40-50 percent of all murders and highway deaths, is legal while marijuana, which has a zero death rate in 10,000 years, is illegal? The laws regulating both legal and illegal drugs are seldom passed with the best interests of the society in mind. Their development has been influenced not only by well-meaning, though often misguided, intentions but also by financial interests, moral viewpoints and political expediency. Usually behind the passing of every anti-drug law is a well-organized, effective lobby determined to convince lawmakers that a certain drug is a menace to public safety, health and morality, whether they believe this themselves or not. Economic issues become intense in the passage of drug laws.

Politics come powerfully into play in the passing or elimination of any drug laws. In the U.S., President Nixon stated publicly that he would never legalize marijuana no matter what the National Commission on Drug Abuse, in charge of studying the problem at the time, recommended. Clinton, who many people hoped would decriminalize pot, actually increased enforcement when he realized it was politically prudent. Even when a president is in favor of legalizing cannabis, he is helpless against the massive anti-marijuana lobby. President Jimmy Carter, feeling that penalties against drug possession should not be more damaging than drug use itself, stated in his address to Congress on August 2, 1977, "I support legislation amending federal law to eliminate all federal criminal penalties for the possession of up to one ounce of marijuana." President Abraham Lincoln once wrote, "Prohibition... goes beyond the bounds of reason in that it attempts to control a man's appetite by legislation and makes a crime out of things that are not crimes... A prohibition law strikes a blow at the very principles upon which this government was founded."

In the early 1930s, ganja fell into disfavor with Americans mostly due to the efforts of the controversial newspaper magnate William Randolph Hearst. Hearst had condemned the herb since the pot-smoking army of Mexican Pancho Villa seized 800,000 acres of his prime Mexican timberland in 1898. Soon thereafter, he began to portray Mexicans in his newspapers as "lazy pot-smoking layabouts." Thirty years later he escalated his anti-ganja campaign by pandering to Americans' fear. His newspapers called pot the "killer weed from Mexico" and told stories of "ganja-crazed negroes" raping white women and playing "voodoo-satanic" Jazz music. His newspapers reported blacks driven insane by ganja, who "dared to step on white men's shadows, look white people directly in the eye for more

Rasta Heart

than three seconds, and even laugh out loud at white people."

The death blow to ganja's legal use occurred in 1937 when the Marijuana Tax Act was signed into law. The bill, riding on the coattails of Hearst's thirty-year anti-marijuana campaign, was shepherded through Congress by House Ways and Means Chairman Robert L. Doughton. Doughton was a key Congressional ally of powerful industrialist H.B. DuPont, the U.S. Government's primary manufacturer of munitions. DuPont also held patents on synthetic Rayon and other petrochemical manufacturing processes for making plastics and fibers. The industrial use of hemp for fibers was a direct competition to these products. Before its criminalization, DuPont assured the Treasury Department that petrochemical oils, made principally by DuPont, could replace hempseed oil, the most consumed lighting oil in America and the world. Making hemp illegal, even to grow for industrial use, wiped out Dupont's competition and gave him a clear field. Over the next 50 years, these synthetic products would give DuPont 80 percent of its industrial output.

As to the more recent chapters in ganja's long history, on May 14, 2001 the U.S. Supreme Court handed medical marijuana users a major defeat, ruling that a federal law classifying the drug as illegal has no exception for ill patients. The 8-0 decision was a major disappointment to many sufferers of AIDS, cancer, multiple sclerosis and other illnesses. Their decision was made in spite of the fact that on March 18, 1999, *USA Today* reported on the National Academy of Science study on medicinal marijuana, considered the most sweeping analysis ever and the strongest blessing yet of marajuana's potential medicinal benefits.

Fortunately, all this was not lost on voters in Arizona, Alaska, California, Colorado, Hawaii, Maine, Nevada, Oregon and Washington who have approved ballot initiatives allowing the use of medical marijuana.

On a more encouraging note Canada recently became the first country in the world to allow terminally ill patients to grow and smoke their own marijuana, overriding protests from doctors who said the decision could put them in an awkward situation.

"This compassionate measure will improve the quality of life of sick Canadians, particularly those who are terminally ill," Health Minister Allan Rock said in a statement. Groups working with the terminally and seriously ill warmly welcomed the change in rules.

Rasta Heart

Once again the United States' control over Jamaican internal affairs can be seen in this area. An August 20, 2001 article in the *Jamaica Gleaner* reported the Jamaican National ganja Commission "recommended that Government should amend relevant laws so that ganja can be used for private, personal use." Some of the recommendations were supported by the National Council on Drug Abuse and the Medical Association of Jamaica. However, the article went on to state that the US government has expressed disapproval and "opposes the decriminalization of marijuana use and that the island's final decision would be put under scrutiny." It went on to state that decriminalizing the plant would cause the island to lose most of their US foreign aid and would threaten assistance from the International Monetary Fund (IMF) and the Inter-American Development Bank (IDB).

The toll in human suffering for these repressive laws is immense. Just in the U.S. in 2000, the numbers are staggering. More than 2,100,000 people—almost 1 percent of the population and the highest percentage in the world—are in jail or prison, the majority for victimless drug crimes. The U.S. has only 5 percent of the world's population but over 25 percent of the world's incarcerated.

Though blacks make up only 15 percent of illicit drug users, they constitute 60 percent of those in state prisons and 42 percent of those in federal prisons for drug felons. In 2000, over 28,000 high school seniors in the States were denied eligibility for federal college aid funds due to their previous drug arrests, again mostly for marijuana. Because of this, many will never be able to receive a college education. Had they been convicted of rape or murder they would still have been eligible. In the U.S., where five times more funds are spent on building new prisons than new schools, the cost of the war on drugs is $19 billion annually and growing. Half of the criminal justice system's resources are spent fighting this war, a large part of this on marijuana violations.

Millions of people, mostly young people, are sitting in prison cells today for smoking a harmless plant. On average, these non-violent offenders will spend more time in jail than their violent counterparts. Many more have had their futures impacted because of a drug conviction on their records. In the last 60 years in the U.S. alone, people have spent a combined 14 million years in jail or prisons for using the plant. It is no wonder that 35 percent of U.S. citizens currently believe the plant should not only be decriminalized

Rasta Heart

but legalized—the highest level ever.

Clearly the trend toward legalization is quickening. Internationally things are even more promising. In June 1998, during the UN World Drug Summit, some 600 personalities, professors, writers, politicians, including ex-ministers and ex-presidents, and eight noble laureates, signed an open letter to Kofi Annan asking for an open debate on the future of international drug policies because they believed the global war on drugs is causing more harm than drug abuse itself. In August 31, 2001, Tim Boekhout van Solinge, a lecturer and researcher in Criminology at Utrecht University in the Netherlands told *The Jamaica Gleaner*, "The trend in the countries of the EU is clearly towards decriminalization, which is the general international trend," he observed, pointing to the annual report of the European Monitoring Centre for Drugs and Drugs Addiction. "The one big exception is the United States."

The Gleaner went on to report on September 9, 2001 that if legalized, Jamaica would find itself in the company of other countries that have moved in that direction. Holland has 900 cannabis cafes where adults can legally buy five grams of marijuana or hashish. Britain has instituted a six-month pilot project in which the police will caution users and seize their pot rather than book them for prosecution. In France and Germany local police, prosecutors and judges are allowed considerable discretion to be tolerant. In Belgium the government proposes to make arrests only if marijuana use is "problematic" to the puffer or to others, which includes smoking in front of minors. Spain no longer prosecutes users of any recreational drug, including heroin, as long as they do so privately. Even conservative Portugal in July 2001 embarked on a decriminalization approach giving first-time users of any drug suspended sentences.

Despite the relaxation on prosecution, European countries have kept marijuana possession statutes on the books to conform with a 1988 international convention that prohibits outright legalization and to avoid the political controversy of changing the law.

As in Europe, Jamaicans have flouted the ganja law with impunity.The Jamaica Gleaner reported, "Walk along the streets of downtown Kingston, especially in certain street-side vending areas, and one will find cured ganja neatly stacked on make-shift wooden stalls, with the vendors openly competing with each other, displaying their 'ware' just as they would any other legal commodity."

And in a final telling, and chilling, note, in a debate on National Public Radio between the governor of New Mexico, who had decriminalized marijuana and the new drug czar of the U.S., they both agreed that if the plant were ever legalized, it would only be sold legally through cigarette companies.

Nowhere is Babylon's greed more apparent than in its determined fight to keep ganja unavailable. Here is a renewable, fully-sustainable, non-pesticide-requiring plant. It is the most abundant source of paper, fiber and fuel on earth, with more benefits that any resource ever discovered, one that has no known side effects yet it is illegal. It is a plant—not a drug or a manmade substance—nonetheless, it is illegal. Obviously, "Babylon 'as more ta teach de people," as Scram would say. Or as Julia says, "Babylon is falling—one spliff at a time."

Rasta Heart

Poling down the Rio Grande on my second trip without Verley.

Israel reasoning at the Ital restaurant.

Dr. Dennis Forsyhe, author of Rastafari: *Healing of the Nations, with his son* Brian.

The Jamaica Palace Hotel in Port Antonio.

Rasta Heart

Scram at the beach during our first meeting, in front of his shop and at Reach Falls.

Rasta Heart

Renny at his stall at Reach Falls.

Scram and me at Reach Falls.

Rasta Heart

Khebo Pauling and his son, Jahmon, in North Carolina.

The pool area at the San San Tropez.

Rasta Heart

Scram, Julia and Clive chatting at a system party on the way to Reach Falls. Note the speakers in the background.

Ronald at the San San Tropez.

Swimming at Nanny Falls.

Rasta Heart

Scram in his shop.

JAH T and Scram at the restaurant at Foley Beach.

Rasta Heart

Scram hamming it up at the system party.

Bongo Roach telling us not to make our bodies "a walkin' cemetery."

Julia and Errol at his Ital restaurant.

Julia at the Rock House
Hotel in Negril.

The Devine Destiny
in Negril.

Rasta Heart

Julie, Alicia, Julia, Marc and me at the original Mayfield
Falls.

Ras Thomas
with Marc

Rasta Heart

Red at Rockhouse in Negril.

Alicia saying her second goodbye to Bongo Roach.

Rasta Heart

Scram,
Julia and
me on
the way
to Moore
Town.

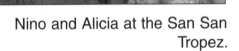

Nino and Alicia at the San San
Tropez.

Irman and Julia at Scram's
shop.

Rasta Heart

The Blue Mountains and the Rio Grande River on the way to Moore Town.

Julia and Scram stop for sweet water in Moore Town.

The ceremony for
Nanny at
her grave.

Julia at
Bath Fountain.

Rasta Heart

Alicia at Reach Falls.

All of us playing at Reach Falls.

Rasta Heart

Robert, Scram and JAH Priest at JAH Priest's stall.

JAH Priest at his best.

Julia, Scram and Robert walking down into Moore Town.

Alicia and Scram ham it up.

Rasta Heart

Jah LandSea

Rasta Heart

Scram and Alicia at the San San Tropez restaurant.

The Reasoning Tree.

Rasta Heart

Julia and Scram cooking some corn at The Reasoning Tree.

The author in 1970.

The view from The Reasoning Tree.

Chapter 11
Bongo Roach

*"Nothing will benefit human health and increase chances
for survival of life on Earth
as much as the evolution to a vegetarian diet."*
—Albert Einstein

The drive to Negril took almost eight hours. The highway from Port Antonio to Montego Bay had only a few potholes but the coast road from Montego Bay to Negril was horrible. They were repaving the road and rather than finishing one section at a time, they had torn apart the entire 90 mile stretch.

We arrived at the Devine Destiny at around nine at night. The hotel, like most of the older, smaller hotels, was in the West End of Negril. The facility is set back from the ocean a block or so in a beautiful garden setting. The handcrafted buildings are set around a large pool, complete with a pool bar and a romantic pool-side restaurant.

Until the 1970s, when it was discovered by hippies seeking paradise (and cheap ganja), Negril was a small fishing village. Soon, quaint hotels, restaurants and craft shops began to spring up on the cliffs on the West End. For twenty years, these establishments served the area and Negril grew to become Jamaica's largest tourist mecca.

In the last few years the large all-inclusive resorts have moved in on the East End along Negril's seven mile long beach. Thousands of tourists stay at these mega-resorts like Sandals, Beaches, and Hedonism (with its

Rasta Heart

"clothing optional" bar and beach). A stay at these resorts usually includes lots of alcohol, food and constant stimulation. Most guests never leave the hotel. The financial impact is devastating to smaller businesses in Negril. Many of the hotels, restaurants and shops are struggling. We saw few tourists when we were there.

Having only one full day in Negril, we decided just to relax at the pool and beach. We drove over to Changes, their private beach and restaurant, where we lounged and played in the ocean, refreshed by fruit drinks sold at a local stall.

As we headed back to the hotel, we passed a very tall man with full dreads under a very large Rasta tam carrying a large duffel bag that looked very heavy. He was colorfully dressed and walked erect with pride and purpose.

"Let's give him a ride," Julia said.

We pulled over ahead of him and offered him a ride. He waved and picked up his pace a little and got in the back seat. He was a very large, unusual looking man, with a wide face and eyes set so far apart it looked like he could look in two directions at once. He had Indian features but ebony black skin. There was a sweetness and humility about him that was instantly endearing. Looking at his face was both fascinating and pleasant. Though big boned, he looked trim and fit. He placed his very heavy bag on the seat next to him and we introduced ourselves.

"My name is Bongo Roach," he said. We later learned his proper name was Joseph Roach. Bongo Roach was a Rasta herb man. He traveled around Jamaica trading and selling healing herbs, tonics, roots, and plants with other Rastas, healers, and even doctors, from all over. He spent four or five nights a week on the road, catching rides or traveling on the island-wide bus system.

As he spoke he turned his head to the left and looked at us out of his right eye, which he slowly opened and closed. It reminded us of the scene from *Moby Dick* when the white whale breaks the surface and opens one enormous eye to look at Captain Ahab. We offered him a hit on our spliff.

"I doan't smoke herb anymore because I pulled a muscle carrying heavy loads of wood so I drink it now. I 'ave all kinds of herb and I do all kinds of research before I give a man an herb. I get a divine inspiration from de ALMIGHTY."

Rasta Heart

"So you are a healer?" Julia asked.

"Yeah. I 'ave spiritual contact from de ALMIGHTY and 'e tells me if someone should be healed or not. You cayn not 'ear it because it comes ta me direct from de ALMIGHTY. It's de power of life, ya know. It's de breath of life. I'm speaking about de ALMIGHTY dat give de breath of life dat manifest t'ru man, trees, animals and everyt'ing. I can speak ta de ALMIGHTY and if rain is to stop, it will stop. Anyone cayn live clean is a Rasta. Ya 'ave ta communicate. Ya cayn stop de rain from fallin'. If a man is comin' wit' someting fe ya, ya cayn use divine communication and bring 'im to you. I 'ear people say times are hard and dey caynnot get no work. I never beg no work fe 30 odd years now. JAH always provides. I just ask 'im fe clothes and t'ings and it come. Ya 'ave ta use natural herbs ta get it. Anyone cayn get it."

"Do you know a lot of true Rastas?" I asked.

"Ya, mon, a few dat know de ALMIGHTY and get de assistance from de ALMIGHTY. Ya see, anytime ya see someone suffer long, 'e doan't know de ALMIGHTY. A Rastamon cayn pass t'ru pain as a test.'E cayn pass t'ru sickness as a test. When I was sick, I saw Professor Hall and I got bettah. Ya cayn ask for a t'ing but you don't supposed to beg bread."

"What kind of sickness did you have when you saw the professor?" I asked.

"I did nah 'ave sickness. A women did damage ta me. She gave me poison and damaged me structure and she was a married women and I told 'er I cayn not deal wit' a married women. I doan't practice dos t'ings when I was a yout' and I doan't practice now neither. I am a free person."

"What do Rastas think of sex?" I asked.

"Well sex is a good t'ing but ya must not 'ave your own queen if you want to have ten or twenty women. But not sex wit' a married women and ya must not use dem and den lose dem, fe de ALMIGHTY is strongly against dat, ya know."

"Do Rastas take care of their kids?" I asked.

"Of course, mon. It becomes a part of ya and yah partner. Likewise ya take care of yah partner. I take care of nine youths and I doan't 'ave none fe myself but dey are children of family and some of strangers. I send dem ta 'igh school and send dem ta secondary school. Ya see, when ya meet upon a true Rastafari it's coming in like a food. Ya 'ave a lot of ones who just locks dere 'ead to achieve what dey see, de blessing of de ALMIGHTY restored upon Rasta. So dey feel dey cayn get it but dey doan't live clean. If ya do not live truthful you cayn not get de blessing from de ALMIGHTY."

At this point we had arrived at a house where Bongo Roach was delivering a couple of jars of honey. It was on a dirt side road a few miles from our hotel. We pulled up in the side yard where a couple of Rastas were chatting, surrounded by an array of cars with their hoods up or their wheels off. They came over and introduced themselves as Shepherd and Zion.

"I and I come in all forms because I would say JAH is all color in everyt'ing," said Shepherd.

"Yeah. Dere are no boundaries when it comes ta de ALMIGHTY," Bongo Roach chimed in.

"No boundary, just natural," Shepherd said. "It's just people dat make boundaries."

"We heard there were a lot of wolves in Negril," I said.

"Well in dis time, it's a serious time," Shepherd continued. "Ya're going ta see a lot of false priest and false prophets t'ruout de earth but, ya see, ya is a chosen mon, chosen by JAH, doing dis work. JAH send ya two wit' good 'earts. Ya will always find de real people."

"Every time I come to Jamaica my eyes go to the hills and I yearn to be there," Julia said.

"Yeah. Because JAH say lift up thy eyes unta de hills," Shepherd said. "I and I give strength and 'elp for ya upon de mountain. Ya see JAH if ya are a clean 'earted person. As I look unta de hills I and I get strength coming from JAH, who create Zion on eart'. We are all Zion because we are all Creation. De spirit of JAH live in I."

"So you don't have to go to Ethiopia as some Rastas believe?" I asked.

"Dey say dat because dat is de land of dere forefather," Shepherd said. "No, you doan't 'ave ta be in Africa, in America, or anywhere. JAH bless ya anywhere ya are. Ya understand? And dat de way it go. Ya see people talk a lot of t'ings, ya know. Ya see, de eart', de ALMIGHTY, create de eart' and anywhere ya on de eart', you cayn know JAH. If yah 'eart says go back ta Ethiopia, you cayn go. I and I Rastaman. I and I create His Majesty Haile Selassie I ta praise as our father, our founding father of Ethiopia. I and I say want ta be where our father is."

"If ya are going ta judge a Rasta by 'is locks, we are all born wit' locks whether we cut it off, ya are still Rasta," Zion said. "We are all Rasta. Ya see if you trim yah 'air, I call ya a trim 'ead man. When I say bald 'air, I mean Babylon. I mean de system."

"Yeah, mon. Dere works is what matters," Bongo Roach said. "As de ALMIGHTY say, 'JAH come in all forms.' Ya will even see de mon eating out of de garbage can and if ya know JAH, ya doan't disrespect 'im and ya doan't know who dat mon is because JAH come in all forms. JAH create all life and anyt'ing dat 'ave life. You doan't disrespect it. Ya would disrespect JAH because de eart' is de fullness thereof, is JAH Himself, de ALMIGHTY."

"If you doan't know JAH, ya doan't know 'alf of life," Zion added. "Dey say ta Bob Marley, 'Why do people suffer in de world?' Yeah. People 'ave ta suffer because if you doan't know JAH, ya must suffer. I could be suffering too because everybody who I know, dey fight against I but JAH nevah leave I alone, so I cayn't suffer."

"If ya 'ave JAH, ya are everyt'ing because I'm going ta tell ya somet'ing," Shepherd said. "I 'ave all dese stones. I 'ave evert'ing around me. Sooner or later I prove ta ya dat I 'ave not'ing. I 'ave ta go and leave everyt'ing. When I go, I leave everyt'ing behind and everyone else is de same way. So wit'out JAH, ya 'ave not'ing. Sometimes if ya doan't 'ave JAH, ya feel ya are suffering. Ya try somet'ing and ya fail. Sometimes ya even try ta kill yahself saying ya shouldn't fail but ya doan't know JAH. When ya fail, ya gain more knowledge so the next time ya do it, ya doan't fail again. It's easy, simple. We all 'ere ta protect one anot'er. I look at all de people and I say, 'Look inta de garden,' and I see all kinds of flowers. Look 'ow de eart' run. Dere are all different colors of mon upon de eart' but we are all mon. De color does nah matter."

"Babylon changes t'ings," Zion added.

"How do you view Babylon?" I asked.

"Ya see Babylon is from creation," Zion continued. "Ya see JAH created de eart' and created evert'ing good and evil. Everyt'ing cayn be good and cayn be evil. Babylon is de evil side of de system. In creation, ya 'ave de positive and de negative."

"Is Babylon going to change to the good side?" I asked.

"Babylon always stay negative," he said. "De People goin' ta live by de gun, goin' ta die by de gun. Babylon make war. Dey goin' ta die by war. So dat's de way it goin' ta fall. None of us know what JAH is goin' ta do so you just sit back and observe."

"And praise JAH when you see it," Julia added.

"JAH Rastafari," Shepherd said enthusiastically, loudly. "We have so much time dat we cayn penetrate and see t'ru Babylon. I work 'ere on dese cars and I'm doing my own work right and if I feel I need courage, I just go and light a spliff and meditate about JAH and come back and work again. JAH people keep ta demselves and meditate upon JAH. Once in a while we go ta Negril but most of de time I doan't go dere because de city is lousy. We doan't go ta de beach because ya 'ave too much gigolos on de beach."

At this point, Bongo Roach, who had gone inside the house to sell his wares, returned and asked if we could take him to his next stop and then to the bus area to get a bus to his home in Darlistown about an hour and a half from Negril. We said our goodbyes to Shepherd and Zion and headed out.

"Do you eat Ital?" I asked as we drove to the bus stop.

"Yah, mon," he enthusiastically replied. "Cookin' food is not a good t'ing and de water, de chlorine, is not a good t'ing. Ta communicate wit' de Almighty, ya 'ave ta be natural, ya know, mudder nature and herb. Ya 'ave to be Ital. If ya eat flesh, ya are nah goin' ta get communication. Flesh is a dangerous t'ing to your structure, mon. If ya eat flesh ya becomes a walkin' cemetery, a walkin' tomb, storing all dat dead flesh inside of ya. Dat supposed ta be buried in de ground, nah in de body. Ya take yah temple and ya make it a burying ground. Any type of flesh, chicken, fish. Go Ital, natural fruit, vegetable, natural grain like dat. If ya used dat, ya 'ave all de communication wit' de Almighty."

"No fish?" I asked. The image of being a "walkin' cemetery" was one that would stay with us.

"No fish neither. Fish carry blood and it's alive. Ya are not to kill life dat carry blood. It becomes a parasite. It becomes a blood sucker. Ya cayn nah introduce dat to de ALMIGHTY. Ya introduce dat to man and king and queen but ta de ALMIGHTY, you caynnot use dead. Natural t'ings ya 'ave ta use. 'E shall provide food—wheat, green and food of de earth. I doan't want no more animal or no more dead flesh. No more sacrifice. Do not accept dat again. Natural kingdom, natural t'ings to communicate wit' 'Im. Cancer, all dos t'ings cayn get better. Ya know I saw a Rastaman come inta doctor wit' a gallstone. I told de doctor if 'e stop eating fish it get bettah and it did but as long as you use flesh and salt all dos t'ings, it not get bettah."

"Because you eat dead things with no livity?" Julia asked.

"Yah. Starchy foods creates mucus and it destroy ya."

"How about cheese?" I asked.

"Dos are dangerous t'ings because dey come from de cow. De only cheese ya cayn eat is from de bean, soy cheese. Anyt'ing dat come from animal or anyt'ing dat carry blood is dangerous t'ing. It will fatten ya and contaminate ya and carry harmful cholesterol side effects. Ya see when dey spray vegetables, it is a dangerous t'ing. If ya cayn grow yah vegetables, ya cayn get natural t'ings dat doan't use de spray. Dos are de t'ings dat destroy yah structure. Dis is de soul of a man. De body is de soul of a man."

"When we started this book, we stopped eating meat but now maybe we will stop eating fish too," I said.

"Ya 'ave ta stop eating dese t'ings wit' poisons and toxins. Dey feed dat ta de cow and a lot of pollution go inta de sea where de fish eat. Ya see de swine fever, it come from animal, hog. Chicken pox, it come from fowl. When I get burned in 1991, a white lady carry some books fe me ta read because I love ta read books and ya know, I read dat fish carry cancer to de head. It weakens yah immune system." We had once lived in a small coastal village in North Carolina where people ate a lot of fish from the polluted Pamlico Sound. There were so many cases of brain cancer that we alerted the health department about the problem.

"What happens if you are not eating a perfect diet. Will that slow you down some?" I asked.

"Dat will slow ya down ta guide ya ta a perfect diet and ta research fe health and de ALMIGHTY will 'ave someone ta show ya dat what ya are eating is not upful. Ya will pass dat stage ta know. Everyone born is a Rasta but dey do not know how ta manifest de work. Dey are not choosing ta. I want ta tell ya pain leads a lot of people ta de ALMIGHTY. It's like a whipping (laughs). When children know dey are going ta get a whipping, dey surrender. Pain make dem surrender."

"Bongo Roach, we'd like to spend more time with you in June when we return," I said as we dropped him at the bus stop. "Can you take us to meet other Rastas? We would be glad to give you some recompense."

"What I would like fe ya to do fe me, if it is in your power, ta carry fe me a Stihl chainsaw, wit' two-foot blade and when ya are 'ere I cayn give ya some contacts fe yah book."

"You got a deal," I said, writing our return dates and hotel on a piece of paper. "We'll see you in June."

"Goodbye, Bongo Roach," Julia said. "I just had a strong feeling that we should pick you up back there and I'm glad we did. I really enjoy being with you."

Bongo Roach smiled and seemed touched by Julia's words. There was something very endearing about this man, something noble and kind.

Early the next day we drove back to Montego Bay and flew back to North Carolina. Alicia returned from a Florida vacation with her friend, Carly, and her family and was in great spirits. It was nice to be back on our mountaintop. I jumped into writing the book as Julia transcribed the conversations we had with everyone. In the evening we would walk mountain paths and discuss various aspects of the book.

As we reflected back on the trip, we realized JAH was revealing many things to us, not only about others but about ourselves as well. We were asking to express One Love more clearly and JAH was showing us our blocks. During our return home, Julia and I kept encountering our own unhealed issues, often leading to arguments. As our journey continued these blocks were revealed, sometimes painfully so, and then healed throughout our family.

In seven weeks, we would be returning to the island for a month, our longest trip ever. The weeks flew by and before we knew it, we were back on a plane headed for Montego Bay.

Eating Ital

After a year totally immersed in the Rastas, I have now come to believe that this section, on the reality of eating meat, eggs and dairy products, is the most important information in the entire book. It is important for our health, for our mind and spirit, for the animals and for the future of the planet. Also, I can testify to this, in the first nine months that Julia and

Rasta Heart

I ate a meatless mostly Ital diet we lost more than 60 pounds combined. My blood pressure has returned to normal and I no longer need medicine to control it. All my previous lower back pain and occasional hip pain are gone and Julia's sense of smell has returned. We feel and look much better.

To put our "normal" western diets in perspective we must view our present attitudes concerning eating meat, eggs and dairy products in the same way we must view our previous attitudes regarding alcohol and ganja. Just as the powerful alcohol and tobacco industries have spent billions of dollars convincing the public, and millions more lobbying politicians, that their products are the wise alternatives to marijuana, so has the meat, egg and dairy industries, the "saturated fat industry," spent billions educating us that their products are safe, healthy and a must in every diet. In many countries, the saturated fat industry has become the nation's de facto nutrition educator. In the U.S., the dairy, egg and meat industries supply millions of "educational pamphlets" to the nation's public schools convincing us at a very young age that eating their products is essential for good health. Almost no scientific evidence now supports this core assumption and most evidence refutes it.

In these few pages I will attempt to offer current information as to why a diet including meat, eggs and dairy products is unhealthy for humans, cruel to the animals involved and threatening to our life on the planet.

First, let's start with the human. Many people believe that humans are natural carnivores (meat eaters), not herbivores (vegetarians). Let's look at the facts. Carnivores have several things in common. All have claws, sharp front teeth for tearing with no flat molars for grinding. They have no skin pores and perspire through their tongues. Also, carnivores have short, relatively smooth intestinal tracks (three times their body length) so that rapidly decaying meat can pass through quickly. Humans have none of these. Our greatly convoluted and textured intestinal tracts are 10 to 12 times our body lengths with infinite cavities where meat can lodge and putrefy. Our stomach acid is 20 times weaker than meat eaters causing incomplete digestion of animal products. Unlike carnivores, we have salivary glands in our mouths that pre-digest grains and fruits and we have an alkaline saliva with ptyalin to predigest grains. Carnivores have acidic saliva with no ptyalin.

Rasta Heart

The American Dietetic Association (ADA) states "most of mankind for most of human history has lived on vegetarian or near-vegetarian diets." Today both the ADA and the U.S. Department of Agriculture (among many more) strongly encourage a vegetarian diet. Quite simply, the human body was not designed to be carnivorous and eating animal products makes us unhealthy.

In addition to the toxic property of meat, eggs and dairy products themselves, we also ingest tremendous amounts of hormones, tranquilizers, antibiotics, pesticides and dangerous chemicals that are injected directly into the animals or added to their feed. Recent studies show that almost 90 percent of all toxic chemical residues in the American diet come from meat, fish, dairy products and eggs. This is even true of shellfish, such as oysters, clams, muscles, scallops and other mollusks that filter polluted water. The American Medical Association (AMA) recently passed a resolution opposing the feeding of medically important antibiotics to livestock because it poses a serious human health threat by creating resistant bacteria.

The United States, home of the most sophisticated medical technology and best-trained doctors in the world, also has one of the lowest life expectancies of the industrialized nations. It is also one of the highest consumers of meat and animal products in the world. Only a handful of the world's medical schools give our future doctors much information in nutrition and the effect on diet and health. Most give almost none.

We have been so brainwashed as consumers that the first thing that comes to mind when we consider being a vegetarian is, *How will I get the needed protein without animal products?* Almost every food contains protein and meat is only a mediocre source of protein at best. The average American consumes eight times the amount of protein needed. Only 2.5 to 10 percent of the calories consumed by the average human need to be in the form of protein. Unless you eat almost all junk food, it is almost impossible not to get the protein you need. There is no nutritional need for humans to eat any animal products; all of our dietary needs, even as infants and children, are best supplied by an animal-free diet.

Let's take a scientific look at the statistics linking the consumption of animal products to our health. Meat eaters are 60 percent more likely to die of cancer, twice as likely to die from heart disease and 30 percent more likely to die of other diseases. Studies have shown that vegetarians

Rasta Heart

have stronger immune systems than meat eaters. We have become convinced that strokes, heart disease and heart attacks are almost an inevitable byproduct of growing old. They are not. For every one percent increase in the amount of cholesterol in your blood, there is a two percent increase in your risk of having a heart attack. Every one percent reduction reduces risk two percent. Elevated cholesterol, anything over 150, promotes atherosclerosis, the buildup of cholesterol, fat, and cells in the arteries that feed the heart muscles.

In 1984, the United States Federal Government released the results of the broadest and most expensive research project in medical history to date. It concluded that the research "... strongly indicates that the more you lower cholesterol and fat in your diet, the more you reduce the risk of heart disease."

According to *The Journal of the American Medical Association*, a vegetarian diet can prevent 97 percent of coronary occlusions. One of the largest studies of lifestyle and health found the heart disease mortality rates for lacto-ovo vegetarians (those eating egg and dairy products) to be only one-third that of meat eaters; for vegans (those eating no animal products), the figure was one-tenth. Studies show that over 90 percent of former meat eaters that switch to a vegetarian diet report that it increases their energy, vitality and overall feeling of well-being.

Another myth is that as people age, they need greater amounts of calcium to ward off osteoporosis, a condition that causes one out of four women to lose up to half their bone density by age 65. The dairy industry would have us believe that the obvious solution to this problem is to eat more dairy products which are high in calcium. What they do not say is that this added intake of dairy products actually worsens osteoporosis by leaving a negative calcium balance. High-protein foods, such as meat, eggs, and dairy products, leach calcium from the body as excess protein is processed by the liver and passed through the kidneys, making the kidneys work harder and causing the loss of minerals such as calcium.

The good news is that switching to a vegetarian diet can often reverse health problems created by years of meat-eating. The famous diet and health expert, Dr. Dean Ornish, author of the bestselling *Dr. Dean Ornish's Program for Reversing Heart Disease: The Only System Scientifically Proven to Reverse Heart Disease Without Drugs or Surgery*, demonstrated that this process can be reversed in his 1990 study of patients with advanced heart disease. The plaque that had been growing in their hearts for decades actually started to dissolve within one year of adhering to a diet very low in fat.

The link between meat-eating and cancer is also scientifically proven. There is not a single population in the world with a high meat intake which does not also have a high rate of colon cancer. The meat is literally putrefying and decaying in your colon. Meat, eggs and dairy products also have no fiber, which acts like a broom in your intestines sweeping things along. The high fiber content of a vegetarian diet also helps "wash away" excess cholesterol in your digestive tract. Even the digestion of meat itself produces strong carcinogenic substances in the colon as well as extensive bile acids.

It takes only three or four hours to digest vegetables, fruit and grains but 18 to 24 to digest meat. So if you even eat meat once a day your body's digestive system is always working. If you've been eating meat your whole life your body probably has been continuously digesting since you were weaned. Your body has never rested and it can only really heal when it's resting. When it doesn't rest properly, we get sick.

It is also now known that breast cancer is directly related to fat intake. The National Cancer Research Institute in Tokyo monitored 122,000 people for decades. The results of this study were that those who consume meat daily face an almost four times greater risk of breast cancer than those who ate little or no meat. Similarly, the more eggs, butter and cheese consumed, the greater the risk of breast cancer.

Even diabetes, which is reaching epidemic proportions in the U.S. where 16 million people or 6 percent of the population now suffer with this disease, is tied to meat, dairy and egg consumption. It is even worse in Finland which has both the highest rate of diabetes in the world and the highest rate of milk and cheese consumption. In 1992 the New England Journal Of Medicine reported, "Studies in animals have suggested that bovine serum albumin is the milk protein responsible for the onset of diabetes." Recently, *Preventive Medicine* reported that sugar levels declined on a vegan diet, "despite decreased medication use."

Another health problem that is reaching epidemic proportions in industrialized countries is allergies, especially asthma. Over 3 percent of all

Rasta Heart

Americans now have asthma, many of them children under 10. Many children are having to get their ears surgically drained for mucous buildup. Millions more suffer from periodic sinus problems. One cause for allergies being so prevalent in children is that their bodies have not yet adapted to assimilating the poisons in their environment and especially in their diets.

Almost all research on the causes of allergies now points to animal protein as playing a major role. Milk especially is known to be a common pathogen for asthma. For instance, many babies break out in painful eczema if they ingest cow's milk as their bodies use the skin as an organ of elimination. Like many allergies, their condition clears up if animal products, especially dairy products, are removed from their diets. Even chronic asthma sufferers have been cured by switching to a pure vegetarian diet.

Early onset puberty is now linked to the intake of meat, dairy and egg products. The average American now consumes 666 pounds of dairy products per year. These products are laced with bioactive hormones (59 in cow's milk alone) such as pop estrogen, progesterone and prolactin. These hormones work on a nanomolecular level, which means that it takes only a billionth of a gram to produce a powerful biological effect.

In addition to this evidence, there is now conclusive scientific evidence that eating meat, eggs and dairy products causes or contributes to a host of other diseases and ailments. These include cancer of the cervix, uterus, ovaries and prostate, hypoglycemia, multiple sclerosis, ulcers, constipation and other intestinal problems, hemorrhoids, obesity, arthritis, gout, kidney stones, gallstones, high blood pressure, and anemia.

In addition to the problems associated with too much fat, cholesterol, and protein, consumers of animal products take in far greater amounts of residual agricultural chemicals, industrial pollutants, antibiotics and hormones than do vegetarians. The absorption of antibiotics through meat-eating results in antibiotic-resistant strains of pneumonia, childhood meningitis, gonorrhea, salmonella, and other serious illnesses. Dairy products are also the leading cause of food allergies and have been implicated in neonatal tetany, tonsil enlargement, ulcerative colitis, Hodgkin's disease, and respiratory, skin, gastrointestinal and behavioral problems.

Approximately 9,000 Americans die annually from food-borne illness and an estimated 80 million others fall ill. Meat contains 14 times as much pesticide residue as plant foods; dairy products, more than five times as many. Fish is another source of dangerous residues. The EPA estimates that fish can accumulate up to nine million times the level of cancer-causing polychlorinated biphenals (PCBs) found in the water in which they live. Ninety-five percent of human exposure to dioxin, a "probable" cause of cancer and other health risks, comes through meat, fish, and dairy consumption.

Chapter 12
In The Lap Of Luxury

"The power which you possess is but one side of the coin; the other side is responsibility. There is no power or authority without responsibility, and he who accepts the one cannot escape or evade the other."
—Emperor Haile Selassie I

In early June, Julia, Alicia and I went back to Jamaica. The three of us arrived in Montego Bay in mid-afternoon and headed for The Half Moon Club. The resort was one of the most expensive on the island and way above our modest means, but a manager there, who loves Bob Marley, had answered our e-mail requesting complimentary rooms. After we checked in, they drove us to our suite overlooking the ocean. The grounds were striking, with over 50 pools and gardens everywhere. There were two crescent-shaped beaches which gave the resort its name. An additional 270 acres are occupied by a championship golf course and its surrounding pastures and woodland. There was a horseback stable, squash courts, a fitness center, several restaurants and shopping areas, six bars, a disco lounge, a medical facility and thirteen tennis courts. It is one of the top facilities in the Caribbean.

Given the opulence of the surroundings, we assumed there wouldn't be many Rastas at the resort and we would have to look elsewhere. We quickly found out we were wrong. As soon as we told anyone working at the hotel what we were doing, their face would light up and they would tell us they were either a Rasta who cut their hair to get the job, that they had a "Rasta heart," or their brother or friend was a Rasta. This happened

163

over and over again during our stay at Half Moon. The people we talked to were enthusiastic and sincere in their love of Rasta and we soon realized that where 30 years earlier Rastas were a pariahs, now they were heroes and spiritual teachers to many.

The first day we walked over to a small shopping center across the highway from the hotel where we met Otelia, a fifty-something Rastalady with two-foot dreads that she had been growing for thirty years. Otelia was selling necklaces and bracelets on the curb in front of the stores, aggressively hawking her wares. She was a Nyabingi Rasta and her husband, her "kingman," put on Nyabingi celebrations around the island, where hundreds of people would come for a couple of days.

"It's good to meet a Rastalady," Julia said.

"Ya doan't see de Rasta women so much," she told us. "Dey are usually home taking care of de babies but most of de Rastamen I know 'ave a Rastalady and dey treat dem very good and a lot of de young girls are growing locks and even when ya see dem wit'out de locks, dey hailin' 'Rastafari' becuz dey know it's de truth. Even in de schools dey trying ta teach it. But a lot of men 'ave de natty 'air but dey are wolves."

"Do you come to this area a lot?" I asked.

"Everyday I come 'ere ta sell," she said. "I want ta stay at 'ome but if I did dat, we wouldn't eat. I would sell my stuff ta de stores but dey doan't pay enough. I could not even buy a good meal wit' what dey pay. So I sit 'ere and I sell."

"How did you become a Rasta?" I asked.

"I used ta go ta church, ya know," she began. "But not'ing goes on dere fe real. Not'ing in de 'eart. Dey not real. I always searchin' an I nevah find de reality until I saw JAH thirty years ago. I used to grow my 'air straight and wear dos high heel shoes and pluck my eyebrows. I used to eat pig, fish, chicken. I weighed a lot more but now I jus' go natural, no meat."

We bought a few of Otelia's crafts, thanked her for her time and walked over to the shopping village on the far end of the Half Moon property where we had noticed a store called The Bob Marley Experience. They sold Bob Marley tee-shirts, CDs, DVDs, books, posters, hats and key chains and played a documentary about Bob Marley's life continuously in their small theater. We stopped by and bought a few things and talked with the young man, Ewan, working behind the counter.

Rasta Heart

"So what's it like working here?" I asked.

"It's great. It's de best job," he said. "You 'ave like youngster coming in here and dey seh, 'Oh! My God! I doan't want ta leave.' Some go inside and watch de movie and dey come out cryin'. We 'ave a lot of Japanese, Europeans, Americans, Canadians. Most come 'ere wit' a love of Bob Marley but some come in and ask, 'Who is Bob Marley' and den dey listen to him and dey love it and dey buy a few CDs. Especially de young kids. Dey love 'im as soon as dey hear 'im. People from Half Moon and The Ritz Carlton come 'ere too. Dey are older and rich and dey love Bob Marley."

At this point a middle-aged Japanese woman came in to buy several CDs that her son had asked her to get. She said Bob Marley and reggae are very popular with the young kids all over Japan but she didn't consider herself a fan.

As we were about to leave, the owners of the store came in, Jaime and Camille Delgado. Jaime is a native New Yorker and Camille is from the island. They looked to be in their forties, well-dressed and attractive.

"I've known his music since the 70s when we were raising our kids," Jaime said, after we explained why we were there. "They sort of grew up listening to Marley. When I came to Jamaica in '83, Marley was always in the background and we decided to do something here."

"It's his words," Camille chimed in. "That's what really got to me, if you really listen to his words."

"One thing that really hit me," Jaime said, "was the statement of a reporter after one of his concerts. He said, 'Bob Marley's fans come for his music and leave with his message.'"

"What made you decide to open this store?" I asked.

"Two things. The music and that it sounded like a good business venture," Jaime said.

"It's not making money yet but we're not closing the place," Camille added. "The average person may have closed it by now. My husband put so much love into the shop, the whole decor. He went to Trench Town and tried to capture something that Bob Marley himself would have been proud of. Even our Website carries this theme. I believe Bob Marley was special and he was put on this earth for a reason. And some of these dreads here give him a bad name."

We talked about Jamaica's growing reputation for violence. The problem was again in the local and international news that week because violence had flared up in the Kingston slums. Several dozen people had been killed and the police were forcefully and permanently relocating citizens in the worst areas and bulldozing down their homes to make a buffer zone.

"This violence is between the two political parties, the PNP and the JLP," Camille said "and these politicians do not really seem to want the violence to stop."

"Last month National Public Radio in the U.S. reported that the murder rate in the slums of Kingston had dropped by almost two thirds because a few of the gang leaders were meeting with the citizens and agreeing it had to stop," I said. "It's really a shame that so many people are judging Jamaica by the acts of a few people in the slums of Kingston."

"I know," Jaime said, "in Montego Bay crime is very low, almost non-existent in the tourist areas."

As we were wandering around the shopping village we met a handsome young Ras named Suga-T (Tony Shorter was his given name). We talked with him over a vegetarian lunch outdoors at one of the restaurants. He told us how several years before he had been a DJ and had become dissatisfied with the life he was living. He had a spiritual experience on the beach that redirected his life and made him decide to stop drinking alcohol, eating meat and sleeping with a lot of women. He stopped cutting his hair and beard and by now he had foot long dreads.

"A lot of people get dis feelin' like I got and go crazy, " he told us. "First dey must search fe JAH. So ya 'ave ta be prepared fe it. I t'ought I was goin' crazy when I just started to go natty."

"Why? What did you feel?" I asked.

"Feelin' like loneliness, like I didn't want ta talk ta nobody. Like I was different from all de rest of de world," he replied.

"Because they were not seeing what you were seeing," I said. "You began to feel like you were not like everyone else."

"Yes, dat is what I was feelin'," he said.

"That's very frightening because you begin to wonder, Where is my tribe? Where are my people ?" I continued. "There is a whole tribe of people around the world that don't really fit. We're fringe dwellers. Many of us have felt this loneliness since we were very young."

"Yes. Dat made me feel all alone until I met my wife. She is a Canadian.

Rasta Heart

She works as a flight attendant but she t'inks like me," Suga-T said.

The next day we stopped at the commissary on the property to get a few things to eat and Julia got into a conversation with Garfield, a twenty-something Jamaican with a beautiful smile. We happened to mention that we were thinking of going to Flagstaff, another Maroon village like Moore Town, about an hour's ride in the hills above MoBay. It is where the Leeward Maroon treaty was signed with the English in 1739.

"I'm from Flagstaff," he said.

"Really," I said, again amazed at the synchronicity. "Are there any elders there we could meet?"

"Ya, mon," he said. "My muddah and faddah live dere and ya cayn meet wit' dem and some of de leaders."

"We're going up on Sunday," I said. "Do you want a ride?"

"Ya, mon. Dat would be good fe me."

On Sunday, we picked up Garfield and drove up into the hills to his home in Flagstaff. As we entered the small village, we stopped to meet with one of the village leaders, Roy Scotte, a tall, thin, short-haired man, serious and intelligent.

We talked for awhile about Maroon history and he showed us a copy of the treaty signed by Cudjoe and the English. He told us the Maroons never really caught runaway slaves, even though the planters told everyone they did.

"Let me ask you guys," I said "is there a connection between Maroons and Rastas?"

"And particularly between Nanny and Rasta," Julia added.

"Well, our foreparents tell us," Roy began, "dat dey were told by dere foreparents dat when Nanny took de Great Trek from Nanny Town in Portland Parish to here to see her brother, Cudjoe, it took many months. She came with many of her warriors. De English and de planters seh in dere books dat she came to tell Cudjoe not ta sign de treaty and ta keep fightin' de English but dat is not what our grandparents told us."

"What did they say?" I asked.

"Dey seh dat de reason Nanny came was ta tell us only one t'ing and dat

167

t'ing was One Love," he continued. "She seh dat we must love de English even if we must fight dem becuz dey wanted ta kill us or enslave us. Sometimes you must fight yah enemy but nevah 'ate dem. It only weakens ya."

"So the Maroons and Nanny really are connected to the Rastas," I said. "The Rasta vision of One Love really began on this island with Nanny, more than 250 years ago."

"I've been feeling that there was a white woman with Nanny," Julia said, "and that she may have been Irish and that is why the Windward Maroons talk with an Irish accent. Did your foreparents ever mention a white woman with Nanny?"

"No, I nevah 'eard of dat," Roy answered.

"I've read almost every book on the Maroons there is," I said "and I've never heard of that either."

"When we were in Jamaica in April we were in Moore Town, where Nanny began the Great Trek," Julia said. "Now we are here where she stopped before returning. Since we arrived, I've been wondering what would Nanny do to solve this problem of the youth violence in the ghettos. I think she would light many fires across the island and at each fire there would be 12 Rasta men transmitting the power of JAH. The fires would be at 12 different locations on the island so that it would be 144, which is in the Bible in Revelations. Then all of JAH's people on the island that knew someone that owned a gun, would bring him to one of these fires to relinquish their gun and a Rasta mentor would take him and give him a spliff and guide him to feel the power of JAH. And those fires would be burning all over Jamaica. And then the guns would be taken and buried on Gun Hill. I can see this happening."

Gun Hill, directly behind us, was the location where the English placed their first cannons to fire on the Maroon village in Flagstaff. Now there were two Maroon flags on it, flying from tall natural poles.

"Ya, mon," Leon said. "It should be in a circle around the island. A circle of fires to be binding."

"If Jamaica could heal it's violence, then it could be an example to the world," I said. "And because tourism is the main industry here, the violence hurts everybody. Everyone here has a big stake in seeing it end. I've thought about setting up a radio station on the island and for one year play non-commercial Bob Marley, Luciano and Bushman music with Rasta DJs that really know One Love. We could call it WOMB. That way anyone could tune into that One Love consciousness with just a flip of a switch. I think that in that year you would see violence go down, the divorce rate go down, car accidents go down, the economy and health improve, even the weather would get better."

The next day was the last of our week in Montego Bay. My cousin Bobby and his son, Scott, were arriving late in the day and I promised that I would go with them to look at building lots before dinner. We were meeting them in mid-afternoon so we wandered over to The Bob Marley Experience where we ran into Jaime again. We soon fell into another discussion of Bob Marley.

"His lyrics meant something," Jaime started. "The fact that he was also a disciplinarian as far as his music was concerned is important. He had a vision of himself as a leader, as a musician, as somebody who took his work seriously, and, I wouldn't say a perfectionist, but he was trying to be as good as he could get. He had pride in himself. He had pride in his music," Jaime said. "In the movie, when you see him walk on the stage, there is such pride in his walk."

"He always came back to JAH, to One Love in his interviews," Julia said. "And as we went around the island there are so many different interpretations of what a Rasta is that it was starting to get confusing. But now we realize it's just this One Love. As soon as you get beyond that, it seems to start separating people."

We talked awhile longer about Jamaica's image problem and how that was impacting tourism. With the elections coming up in the next 16 months, everyone was on edge in the business community.

"How long has the economy been going downhill?" I asked.

"Well, basically since independence in 1962," he replied. "And the gulf between the well-to-do and the poor is getting greater. Even a couple who both teach school cannot afford a second-hand car. And a lot of the development you see around here like The Ritz Carlton and The Holiday Inn is funded by local investors, not foreign investment."

"My cousin and his son are coming in later today," I said. "He's planning to build a house above The Ritz Carlton but I don't know if these new reports of violence will chase him away."

"Look, why don't you come up to the house for a drink tonight?" Jaime offered. "Camille's out of town but I can tell your cousin what's it's like to build and live here."

We got directions to Jaime's house and headed back to The Half Moon Club for a meeting with Heinz Simonitsch, the part-owner and long-time manager of the resort. We were shown into Heinz's spacious office, decorated with his and the resort's many awards and honors. Heinz is in his seventies, but tan, fit and energetic like a man 20 years younger. He dresses casually, in tennis shorts and a knit shirt and rides a motor scooter around the property. He is confident but unpretentious and talks with an Austrian accent. He welcomed us with an air of European charm and hospitality.

We explained to him what we were doing and thanked him for welcoming us at the resort.

"You know, Heinz," I began, "when we first came here we thought we would have to leave the resort in order to meet people who are really thinking Rasta. We have found we really haven't had to do that. So many of your staff here are into One Love."

"Resting Rastas," Julia said. "And I love the silence and peace of this place."

"That's music to my ears," Heinz said. "Because my main attempt since 1963 is to recreate the nature that this land one time had before it became a sugar plantation and we plant the trees that were cut down in order to grow sugar. We make nature the number one priority. If you come from a concrete jungle in the city and you go to a concrete jungle in a resort, it doesn't mean anything. So I made it my goal to not build anything higher than three stories and buy more land rather than go up and use the land so that the human being can be a visitor to our little paradise, rather than having tourism destroy nature. I want to show that tourism, done correctly, can be a tremendous asset from the cultural, sociological, economical and natural aspect."

"And you can really feel that here," Julia said.

"As a sugar plantation," Heinz continued, "this land employed about 40 people for seven months a year, all at very low wages. We now employ 1,000 people, directly and indirectly. And yet we have improved nature, not destroyed it. One has to look after nature. We used to have about a thousand famous Jamaican coconut trees on the property—huge, magnificent trees—and they all died within four years. So we had to plant a different variety and these died too. So I gave up on coconuts and I'm now planting royal palms and now we are planting thousands of trees all over the property. And rather than spray DDT on our pond to control mosquitoes, I put fish in the pond and that controls them. Also we have built a school, a health center, a dialysis center and a chapel in the shopping village. We are trying to show our guests a holistic community where nature and tourism can live together."

"When you started this years ago, did you see this entire vision or were you just coming here to run a hotel?" I asked, always interested in how someone manifests their dream.

"Well, to be honest with you, when I came here, I came for only one reason, to prove a point to myself that I could do it. I only came here for one year to prove a point that this place, as beautiful as it was, as run-down as it was, which I didn't realize until I really got here, could be turned around. I wanted to do that just to satisfy my own ego, not anyone else. I wanted to do that and then go back to Bermuda and live happily ever after. And out of that one year, became this. Now I'm totally in love with Jamaica, Jamaicans and the whole philosophy. I am with my heart and soul and mind with Jamaica."

"Why are you so passionate about Jamaica?" Julia asked.

"Well, I have a pioneer spirit and Bermuda was too civilized and Austria was too regimented. Here I have an opportunity to develop, to be free. And here I told the government, whichever persuasion they are, that I'm going to succeed not because of them, but in spite of them. Because their bureaucracy is just as bad as it is in other places and unfortunately bureaucracies are stifling our progress."

We walked across the parking lot from Heinz's office to find Bobby and Scott were in the lobby, fresh off a morning flight from New York City. Bobby, called Robert outside the family, runs a publicly-held company in New York that manages buildings and hotels worldwide. Though deeply ensconced in the world of high finance, he is a generous and positive person and lifts the spirits of those around him. Sharing the same name, Bobby and I have been close most of our adult lives. Scott, around 30, is fit and handsome, with a kind and thoughtful disposition tinged by New York's dry sense of humor. Married to a doctor in the city, he was just finishing up several years at a struggling dot com company.

We hugged and greeted them and then Julia went off to spend the afternoon with Alicia while Bobby, Scott and I went to meet with his real estate agent and architect in the golf subdivision above The Ritz Carlton. Resembling a comic caravan seeking lost treasure, the five of us rode around in golf carts looking at half million dollar lots, with Bobby and I taking up the rear, smoking a spliff and reflecting on our lives.

Bobby picked out a lot with an unobstructed view of the ocean and we went back to the hotel to get the girls and head out to Jaime's for drinks. Before going to Jaime's, we stopped by Bobby's room so he could make his usual allotment of business calls. At one point he had his cell phone at one ear and the hotel phone in the other. It cracked me up.

Jaime's house was striking. It was open and spacious, set on a hill over-looking the ocean. The living room, with 28-foot ceilings, flooded out onto the veranda above the pool. Jaime had wine and cheese set out and we felt instantly welcomed. Jaime talked to Bobby and Scott about his love of Bob Marley and his music while Julia and I caught them up on our journey and what we had been learning from the Rastas.

After awhile, Jaime asked if we would like to see a new DVD that had just arrived at his shop. It featured a concert recorded a year earlier in Jamaica with several of the Marley children performing in Oracabessa, at Goldeneye, an estate once owned by Ian Fleming but now owned by Chris Blackwell.

We settled on the couch of Jaime's den that also adjoined the patio and Jaime put the DVD on a huge 6-foot square TV, transporting us to the concert.

"Hey, you see that group of people over there?" Bobby said excitedly, pointing at the screen to a group of people near the stage in a private box. "That's me, and my wife, Diane, with Chris Blackwell. We flew in for this last year as Chris' guests."

After dinner at the hotel, I turned to Julia as we walked back to our room through the beautiful gardens of The Half Moon Club. It was our last night in MoBay until our planned return in two weeks. The next day we would pick up our daughter Julie and our nephew Marc and all seven of us would head to Negril.

"You know it's been a great week. I'm discovering that I can't impose my view on One Love. It's equally present in humble settings and opulent settings. I keep expecting it to match my preconceptions and JAH surprises me everytime."

"And He seems to always reveal to everyone just what they're ready for," Julia said. "What better way could there have been to talk about Marley and the Rastas with Bobby and Scott than with a person like Jaime and in a setting like tonight. They were comfortable. There was nothing to resist."

Eating Ital

If consuming animal products is rough on humans, it's much worse on the animals. Each day in the U.S. alone over nine million chickens, turkeys, pigs, calves and cows are slaughtered. The description below of how these animals live and die is upsetting but necessary to explain in order for us to be aware of the impact our food choices have on other living creatures. As famed seer and psychic Edgar Cayce once said, "Destiny, or karma, depends on what the soul has done about what it has become aware."

For a vast majority of these gentle creatures, they are not "humanely slaughtered" (if such a process is possible) and they live their short lives in pain and terror with every natural instinct thwarted. The description on the PETA (People for the Ethical Treatment of Animals) Website (http://goveg. com) describes their living conditions:

"Simply put, the factory farming system of modern agriculture strives to produce the most meat, milk, and eggs as quickly and cheaply as possible, and in the smallest amount of space possible. Cows, calves, pigs, chickens, turkeys, ducks, geese, rabbits, and other animals are kept in small cages or stalls, often unable to turn around. They are deprived of exercise so that all of their bodies' energy goes toward producing flesh, eggs, or milk for human consumption. They are fed growth hormones to fatten them faster and

173

are genetically altered to grow larger or to produce more milk or eggs than nature originally intended (there are 59 different bioactive hormones in cow's milk alone).

Because crowding creates a prime atmosphere for disease, animals on factory farms are fed and sprayed with huge amounts of pesticides and antibiotics, which remain in their bodies and are passed on to the people who eat them, creating serious human health hazards.

Chickens are divided into two groups: layers and broilers. Five to six laying hens are kept in a 14-inch-square mesh cage, and cages are often stacked in many tiers. Conveyor belts bring in food and water and carry away eggs and excrement. Because the hens are severely crowded, they are kept in semi-darkness and their beaks are cut off with hot irons (without anesthetics) to keep them from pecking each other to death. The wire mesh of the cages rubs their feathers off, chafes their skin, and cripples their feet.

Approximately 20 percent of the hens raised under these conditions die of stress or disease. At the age of one to two years, their overworked bodies decline in egg production and they are slaughtered (chickens would normally live 15-20 years). Ninety percent of all commercially sold eggs come from chickens raised on factory farms.

More than six billion "broiler" chickens are raised in sheds each year. Lighting is manipulated to keep the birds eating as often as possible, and they are killed after only nine weeks. Despite the heavy use of pesticides and antibiotics, up to 60 percent of chickens sold at the supermarket are infected with live salmonella bacteria.

Cattle raised for beef are usually born in one state, fattened in another, and slaughtered in yet another. They are fed an unnatural diet of high-bulk grains and other "fillers" (including sawdust) until they weigh 1,000 pounds. They are castrated, de-horned, and branded without anesthetics. During transportation, cattle are crowded into metal trucks where they suffer from fear, injury, temperature extremes, and lack of food, water, and veterinary care.

Calves raised for veal—the male offspring of dairy cows—are the most cruelly confined and deprived animals on factory farms.

Rasta Heart

Taken from their mothers only a few days after birth, they are chained in stalls only 22 inches wide with slatted floors that cause severe leg and joint pain. Since their mothers' milk is usurped for human consumption, they are fed a milk substitute laced with hormones but deprived of iron: anemia keeps their flesh pale and tender but makes the calves very weak. When they are slaughtered at the age of about 16 weeks, they are often too sick or crippled to walk. One out of every 10 calves dies in confinement.

Ninety percent of all pigs are closely confined at some point in their lives, and 70 percent are kept constantly confined. Sows are kept pregnant or nursing constantly and are squeezed into narrow metal "iron maiden" stalls, unable to turn around. Although pigs are naturally peaceful and social animals, they resort to cannibalism and tail biting when packed into crowded pens and develop neurotic behaviors when kept isolated and confined. Pork producers lose $187 million a year due to dysentery, cholera, trichinosis, and other diseases fostered by factory farming. Approximately 30 percent of all pork products are contaminated with toxoplasmosis.

Factory farming is an extremely cruel method of raising animals, but its profitability makes it popular. One way to stop the abuses of factory farming is to support legislation that abolishes battery cages, veal crates, and intensive-confinement systems. But the best way to save animals from the misery of factory farming is to stop buying and eating meat, milk, and eggs. Vegetarianism and veganism mean eating for life: yours and theirs."

If there are any illusions as to how these animals lives ended, the following description—of killing cows in the "humane" kosher manner—will clear up this issue:

"Animals being ritually slaughtered in the United States are shackled around a rear leg, hoisted into the air, and then hang, fully conscious, upside down on the conveyor belt for between two and five minutes—and occasionally longer if something goes wrong on the 'killing line'—before the slaughterer makes his cut. The animal, upside down, with ruptured joints and often a broken leg, twists frantically in pain and terror, so that it must be gripped by the neck or have a clamp inserted in its nostrils to enable the slaughterer to kill the animal with a single stroke, as religious law allows."

Unlike picking fruits, vegetables, nuts and grains, slaughtering animals is repulsive to almost all humans. If we had to kill these animals ourselves, instead of buying their body parts in neat cellophane-wrapped packages, we would eat far less meat. This fact alone should indicate which food choices are best for us.

Not only are our diets having harmful effects on our bodies and on the animals but the effects on the planet are just as hazardous. If everyone were vegetarians there would be twice as much food as needed to feed the world's population. Ninety percent of all grain grown in the U.S. is fed to livestock, including 80 percent of the corn and 95 percent of the oats. Worldwide, 40 percent of world's cereal is fed to animals which alone could feed one and a half times the world's population. This at a time when it is estimated that over 40,000 children starve to death on this planet every day—a child every two seconds. Hunger is not caused by lack of resources but rather is a social disease caused by the unjust, inefficient and wasteful control of food.

By cycling our grain through livestock, we waste 90 percent of its protein, 96 percent of its calories, 100 percent of its fiber and carbohydrates. Over half the water consumed in the U.S. goes to irrigate land growing feed for livestock. It takes a 100 times more water to produce a pound of meat as it does to produce a pound of wheat. More is needed to wash away their excrement, often into rivers, streams and oceans. The production of one pound of beef requires 2,500 gallons of water. It takes less water to produce a year's worth of food for a pure vegetarian than to produce one month's food for a meat-eater.

In the U.S. alone, everyday livestock destined for our dinner tables produce 20 billion pounds of waste—twenty times as much excrement as the entire human population of the country. Much of the excrement from "food" animals flows unfiltered into our lakes and streams.

The meat industry alone accounts for three times as much harmful organic waste-water pollution than the rest of the nation's industries combined. In some areas of the world, the search for adequate clean water now threatens to undermine economic, social and political systems.

It also takes a tremendous amount of fossil fuels to produce meat. Corn and wheat provide 22 times more protein per calorie of fossil fuel than meat and soybeans provides 40 times. Between 1960 and 1985, nearly 40 percent of all Central American rainforests were destroyed to create pasture for beef cattle. The rainforests are the primary source of oxygen for the entire planet; the very survival of the Earth is linked to their survival. The forests also provide ingredients for many medicines used to treat and cure human illnesses, and these resources have yet to be explored for their full potential. Within a few years, this land becomes so eroded that a single steer needs 12 acres. After twenty years, a steer requires 20 acres. It is estimated that for every person that becomes a vegetarian, an acre of trees is spared from the ax every year.

More than four million acres of crop land in the U.S. are lost to erosion each year. Of this staggering topsoil loss, 85 percent is directly associated with livestock raising, i.e., over-grazing. One acre of pasture produces an average of 165 pounds of beef. The same acre can produce 20,000 pounds of potatoes. According to the U.S. Soil Conservation Service, a pure vegetarian diet makes less than 5 percent of the demands on our soil. In the U.S. alone, soil is eroding at more than 4 million acres of crop land a year. If Americans reduced their meat consumption by only 10 percent, it would free 12 million tons of grain annually for human consumption. That alone would be enough to adequately feed each of the 60 million people who starve to death each year.

History is full of wars fought because meat-eating societies needed more land to feed their stock. Meat-eating contributes to the anxiety in the world by making us fear there is not enough to go around. As long as people are starving we must all live in fear. This was noted over 2,000 years ago in Plato's *Republic* in which Socrates is speaking to Glaucon about the peace and happiness that comes from a vegetarian diet:

> **Socrates:** "And there will be animals of many other kinds, if people eat them?"
> **Glaucon:** "Certainly."
> **Socrates:** "And living in this way we shall have much greater need of physicians than before?"

Rasta Heart

Glaucon: "Much greater."

Socrates: "And the country which was enough to support the original inhabitants will be too small now, and not enough?"

Glaucon: "Quite true."

Socrates: "Then a slice of our neighbors' land will be wanted by us for pasture and tillage, and they will want a slice of ours, if, like ourselves, they exceed the limit of necessity, and give themselves up to the unlimited accumulation of wealth?"

Glaucon: "That, Socrates, will be inevitable."

Socrates: "And so we shall go to war, Glaucon, shall we not?"

Tom Robbins, in his bestselling book *Diet For A New America*, sums it up best:

"At the present time, when most of us sit down to eat, we aren't aware of how our food choices affect the world. We don't realize that in every Big Mac there is a piece of tropical rainforests, and with every billion burgers sold another hundred species become extinct. We don't realize that in the sizzle of our steaks there is the suffering of animals, the mining of our topsoil, the slashing of our forests, the harming of our economy, and the eroding of our health. We don't hear in the sizzle the cry of the hungry millions who might otherwise be fed. We don't see the toxic poisons accumulating in the food chains, poisoning our children and our earth for generations to come."

Most Rastas innately know that there will be war as long as humans kill animals and devour their bodies. They believe when we were told "Thou Shalt Not Kill" it referred to all of God's creatures, not just humans. They look forward to a time when the killing will stop and, as it is said in Isaiah, "The wolf will live with the lamb, the leopard will lie down with the goat, the calf and the lion and the yearling together; and a little child will lead them... And they shall beat their swords into plowshares... Nation shall not take up sword against nation. They shall never again know war."

Chapter 13

Ras Thomas

*"All revolutions attract mercenaries, thrill seekers,
and the unstable, as well as the truly committed."*
—**Marilyn Ferguson**, *The Aquarian Conspiracy*

The next morning we picked up Marc and Julie at the airport and drove to Negril. We arranged to meet Bobby and Scott later that night at Rick's Cafe. Julie, our thirty-year-old daughter, is one of the top real estate agents in the Research Triangle area of Raleigh, Durham and Chapel Hill, North Carolina. She is beautiful and vivacious, quick to laugh and loves being with people, which is why she's so successful in sales. Like her mother, she has an indomitable spirit. She was a hard kid to punish on the rare occasions where that was called for. If you banished her to her room, she'd go in and later you'd hear her happily humming to herself.

Marc is 29, with the bodybuilder's physique and a grin on his face which always makes you think he's about to crack a joke, which he often is. Since graduating from the University of Delaware several years ago he has been working in the sales department of a fitness center near his home in Maryland. Though sometimes troubled that he is not on his "career track," he just can't bring himself to work in a job that doesn't excite him. He reminds me very much of myself when I was his age.

Marc and Julie were looking forward to the trip, both needing a vacation. We had decided that Negril was the best area for them as it had an active

Rasta Heart

night life, something missing in Port Antonio and a little harder to find in Montego Bay. We encouraged them to relax and enjoy themselves and do whatever they wanted as Julia and I scouted out the local Rastas, including Bongo Roach.

With our rental car packed, we headed up the island toward Negril, once again along the coast highway. Near Negril we stopped at a fruit stand run by a dread. We were anxious for Marc and Julie to meet their first Rasta so I pulled over to buy some fruit. After a conversation espousing Rasta ideals, he tried to charge us twenty five dollars for a couple of cut pineapples and two mangoes.

After settling into our rooms and a swim at Devine Destiny, we drove over to Rick's for dinner with Bobby and Scott. Rick's, one of the most famous cafe's in the world, is a gathering spot for tourists, especially around sunset. With seating either under the sky or thatched roofs, the backdrop is breathtaking. The cafe is built on cliffs overlooking the crystal clear waters of the Caribbean Sea. Locals and tourists are always diving from different levels of the cliffs, which adds an element of excitement to the place.

After dinner we headed over to Bobby's hotel, The Rock House, a small hotel stretching across the cliffs of Pristine Cove, with thatched roofed cottages nestled in tropical lush gardens. Late that night, Scott, Julie, Marc and Alicia, all close friends as well as cousins, headed to The Jungle, the local tourist nightspot. The seven of us spent most of the next day hanging out by their pool and their restaurant enjoying the company of family until we had to take Bobby and Scott to the airport for their return flight.

The day after Bobby and Scott left, Julia and I were pulling out of the hotel when we saw Bongo Roach walking toward us. He was dressed in a homemade pants suit made of a shocking pink plaid, topped off by his multi-color huge knit tam. On anyone else it would have looked ridiculous but on Bongo Roach it looked magnificent. We were delighted to see him. We hopped out of the car and gave him a hug.

"Bongo Roach," Julia said enthusiastically, "it's great to see you! I've thought about you a lot since we left. What you said made me decide to really stop eating meat."

"I'm really glad to see you, too," I added. "I wasn't sure you'd remember when we'd be back."

"No problem, mon," Bongo Roach said. "I 'ave yah note and I come ta find ya. I knew de Almighty would bring me ta ya."

"We've got a present for you, Bongo Roach," I said. I popped open the trunk to give him a new chainsaw, in its own carrying case.

"Did you think we'd bring you the chainsaw?" I asked.

"Ya see I leave everyt'ing in de 'ands of de Almighty, ya know," he said in a way that you knew he meant it. "If ya bring it, no problem. If ya doan't bring it, no problem. I leave it ta ya consciousness. T'ank ya both fe dis. I glad ta know dat ya live up ta ya word. A lot of people doan't live up ta dere word."

Bongo Roach got in the back seat and we headed over to Errol's Royal Kitchen, a small Ital restaurant near our hotel. After we settled in he began to talk about his life.

"Fe t'irty years, I a Rasta. I pass t'ru trials and tribulation but I stand up fe de Almighty. I doan't 'ave not'ing ta lose."

"What kind of tribulation?" I asked.

"I go ta jail. I get poisoned. I get burnt up. All from people I do good ta," he answered with no bitterness in his voice. "De Chinamen and white people take care of me in my sickness. Professor Hall was a professor at de university, a white man and we like brot'ers before 'e die."

"How did you get burned?" I asked.

"Well now, I was readin'. I read a lot of books, ya know and I was readin' one night a book about cabinet work and I was tired and de kerosene lamp turn over and catch me clothes on fire." He showed us some very bad scars on his arms.

"Certain t'ings dat I passed t'ru, I get burned, dem burn down me 'ouse, dem poison me and all dos t'ings, de Almighty reveal to I and tell I what I needed ta know. When I got sick from de poison, no doctor tell me but de Almighty reveal it ta me. I go ta my Rasta doctor and 'e could nah 'elp me and I 'ave ta go ta de Almighty 'Imself and I said ta Him in my prayer I cayn't depend on de next mon so I want 'Im ta teach me de 'erbal medicine. Dat was years ago dat I asked de Almighty ta teach I 'erbal medicine. De time come ta teach I so I bettah myself and in a vision 'E showed me what 'erbs ta use and what ta eat."

"How long have you been a Rasta?" I asked.

"Since 1971 I been a Rasta," he answered. "Dat t'irty years. I 40 years old. I been a Rasta since I was a little yout', nine, ten years old. De first

Rasta Heart

Rasta I meet was a Rasta dat set up de lightning rods at my school. Dat de first Rastamon I see and talk ta. Dat mon resemble de prophets I saw in de Bible. Dat why I seek dat mon and 'is knowledge. My teacher and my parent did nah wan' me ta talk ta 'im. I go 'ome in de evening and afta I eat my dinner, I put on my ordinary clothes and I go ta wherever 'e is ta get 'is teachin' and de knowledge. 'E show me de fullness. 'E gave me food and t'ings but it was de knowledge I wanted. Dat mon was a learned mon and an intelligent mon. 'E told me about Rasta but 'e nevah told me to grow locks. 'E told me about Livity. But 'e showed me ta be Rasta. Dere must be a manifestation of One Love. Every action carry a reaction. Ya 'ave ta put in ta practice. Ya 'ave ta manifest. It 'as ta establish out dere. Ya cayn't just speak about love. Ya 'ave ta put it in ta action. Fe a lot of people it just words. Dey talk about love but dere action is nah reality."

"If you see a hundred dreads, how many do you think really express One Love?" I asked.

"One or two," he replied. "An dere are more wolves dan natural Rastas and I doan't wan' no wolf ta move amongst I becuz dey do damage behind ya back. De yout's give ya de most problems becuz dey t'ink dey know just as much as ya, dat dey 'ave same power. Dey did nah pass t'ru any tests. Now when I go ta Kingston, it is de livity of de person toward de community I look fe, nah de 'air. It might be a comb 'air mon. It is de discipline of de person. I must find people dat recommend dem. I live in Darliston t'irty years as a Rasta and police nevah come on my property. White people my friends. Chinamen my friends. Dem respect I and I respect dem. If de yout's come on my property, I'm not goin' ta bodder dem or influence dem to become a Rasta. I tell dem de fullness and if 'im want ta be a Rastamon, dey 'ave ta seek dat. I am nah goin' ta force 'im or influence dem inta bein' a Rasta. It 'as ta be on dere own will power."

Rastas do not proselytize their faith to others but rather allow others to seek them out. Almost everyone in Jamaica knows a Rasta in their extended family so anyone with an interest has easy access to their beliefs and lifestyle. In this way the faith is passed on person to person, much like early Christianity.

"Are things improving for Rastas?" I asked.

"Yes, mon," he replied. "Dey are bettah but if ya doan't know ya rights, dey still will cut yah locks when ya go ta jail. Now most of dem know it is against de constitution to cut our locks. But in dos days dey would shoot or beat ya and ask questions later. I lock up in 1971. I pass t'ru state of emergency. I pass t'ru curfew. I 'ave seen it wit my own eye and I see soldiers and police search locksman and den order anot'er locksman to cut 'is 'air. I doan't quarrel. I doan't make trouble. I doan't tell lies about people or t'ief people. I work 'ard ta achieve what I want and when I achieve it, I doan't keep ta myself alone. I share it amongst de people. Sometimes I buy food fe de old people or de yout's. De Almighty, my Fadder, take care of I. Me nah 'ungry and me nah naked. I nevah short of food. I nevah short of clothing. I nevah short of shelter. De Almighty always provide fe I."

"We've got to get our kids," I said after we ate. "When can we get together again?"

"I take ya ta meet Bongo Hu. 'E used ta be a doctor at de university in Kingston. Now 'e is an 'erbalist. Now 'e use only all 'erbal. 'E lives in Cambridge Retreat in de 'ills near MoBay."

We made arrangements to meet in two days and dropped Bongo Roach off at the bus stop in Negril. We headed back to the hotel and found Marc, Julie and Alicia in the pool.

"How's the trip going?" I asked my nephew Marc. I've always been close with him and his brother, Adam, and I was glad he could spend this week with us. Also I knew that without his company, I couldn't feel safe with the girls at the clubs alone. We had invited Adam, who worked for the San Diego Padres, but he couldn't get away.

"It's been great, Uncle Robert," he relied. "This is just what I needed. I'm really enjoying the beach and laying by the pool but the hustlers at the clubs can get to you sometimes."

"In what way?" I asked, already knowing the answer.

"Well ever time you go to the bathroom," he replied, "someone will follow you in and see if you want some pot or cocaine. And they're always coming over to see if Julie or Alicia want company. I mean, if I was just with one of them they'd figure she was my girl but with two of them, they figure at least one is available. And it's the off-season here and there aren't as many tourists so we attract more of their attention."

"Are they crude or just persistent?" I asked.

"No, not crude at all and not even that persistent," he answered. "Usually it's kind of sweet. They'll sit at our table and take Julie's or Alicia's hand

and say something romantic but they can usually tell by their response that they're not looking for a man so they cool out and just chat. But they're so many women here who are looking for a man. I see why they figure there's a good chance they are. If you learn to say 'no' firmly they get it but you can't be in any way hesitant and leave any door open. But, you know, in the States guys still come on at the bars but not as many and not as frequent and they're looking for romance and sex. These guys are looking for sex and money."

"What else have you thought about Jamaica?" I asked.

"Well, I wasn't ready for the poverty," he said. "I mean I've travelled in other parts of the world but I guess it's been more hidden or not as bad. I look at some of the places they live in and really feel bad for them. Sometimes I really feel guilty because we have so much and they have so little but you know in some ways they seem happier than people in the States."

"I know what you mean. Julia and I were thinking maybe we'd all go to Mayfield Falls tomorrow. It's about an hour and a half drive into the hills but you could meet some Jamaicans that aren't dealing with tourists and see more of the country."

"Yeah. Let's do that," he responded. "I'd like to meet people who are more like the Rastas you're dealing with."

Early the next day, we drove to Mayfield Falls. We had chosen Mayfield instead of another nearby attraction, Roaring River, because our guidebook said there were a lot of hustlers at Roaring River. We drove east along the coast to Sav-La-Mar and then veered inland into the mountains. Everyone was in good spirits, looking forward to getting away from the hustlers and seeing the area's natural beauty uninterrupted by hotels.

In Sav, I pulled over by the side of the highway to check the map. As we were sitting there, a young man on a motorcycle pulled up by my window and asked if he could help.

"No, not really," I answered, a little curtly, figuring he might put me on the spot for money just for giving directions. The last few days in Negril had hardened me somewhat.

"Ya, mon. I not a 'ustler," he said, picking up on my vibes. "My name

Rasta Heart

is Carlos. I work at Rick's Cafe. I t'ink I saw ya dere de o'ter night. I just trying ta help."

"Sorry," I said, feeling guilty for silently accusing him. "After Negril, we're on our guard. We're going to Mayfield Falls."

"No, mon, ya cayn nah go dere," he replied emphatically. "Yesterday, four little girls drown dere and de police closed it ta investigate. Ya should go ta Roaring River instead. I take ya dere because I pass right by dere on my way home."

"Give me a break," Julia said, laughing. "This is the worst scam I've heard yet."

"Nah, mon," he replied, overhearing Julia's statement. "De falls dere are closed. I would nah lie about sumpten like dat. I cayn take ya ta Roaring River."

"Look, Julia," I said, "I don't think he would make up that kind of lie. What do you guys think?" I asked Julie, Marc and Alicia in the back seat. They all seemed to think anything was possible after the Negril night-spots.

"Well, I know how to get to Roaring River from the map but we'll follow you," I said, deciding he must be telling the truth.

Driving behind him into Sav we all debated whether he was telling the truth. The guide book made Mayfield Falls sound more exciting and we wanted to go there if they were actually open. By the time we reached the turnoff to Mayfield, we all agreed Carlos was taking us for a ride. I turned off to Mayfield but the signs were confusing. I stopped a few hundred yards up the road and asked two little girls in school uniforms if this was the way to Mayfield Falls. They looked a little puzzled but said that I needed to go back the way I came and head toward Roaring River until I saw another turn off. Just then Carlos pulled up on his motorcycle having backtracked to find us. We all cracked up.

"Mon, why ya turn off 'ere?" he said. "Mayfield is closed. Just follow me to Roaring River."

Since we had to head back anyway, I obliged but now I believed him less than ever. There were no further signs for Mayfield so we followed him for another half hour. We were getting farther and farther out in the countryside, away from the main road when we finally arrived at Roaring River at the end of the road. It became clear this was not on his way home and we had been hustled.

"Pull over, mon! Ya park 'ere!" he shouted, as we turned around in the parking lot. I noticed a few other guys coming towards us from the reception area.

"Stop! Stop!" Carlos shouted, as I started to pull away. "Come back! Mayfield is closed!" As I looked in my rearview mirror, Carlos was standing there, his hands hanging loosely by his side, looking dejected. Then he cracked a smile, as if to say to himself, "Well, ya cayn't trick every sucker."

Trickery like this is common in Jamaica, so much so that it is almost ingrained in parts of the culture. One of Jamaica's primary folk heroes is Anancy, the devious spider featured in folk tales, originated with the Ashanti tribe of Ghana, but has since become localized. His tales are still told to many Jamaican children at bedtime. Like slaves of old and the downpressed today, Anancy survives in a harsh world by his quick wit, sharp intelligence, cunning and ingenuity. For many of the underprivileged in Jamaica if someone can get away with something they earn respect among their peers.

We headed back to Sav, pissed at being had again. It turns out the first turnoff I had made was the right one. We finally arrived at Mayfield Falls after another hour drive up into the Dolphin Head Mountains to the small village of Pennycooke. As almost all Jamaican back roads are, it was beautiful. Arriving at Mayfield Falls was confusing. There were several entrances with hustlers trying to wave us in. We chose the last one, which was marked "The Original Mayfield Falls."

We parked our car and headed down the hill where we entered a large open encampment that looked like a small African village, set in a grassy meadow, dotted by large shade trees. Scattered across several acres were thatched-roofed buildings including an open-air restaurant, several craft shops (one selling shirts trimmed with Bongo Roach's pink plaid fabric), changing rooms, playing fields, volleyball courts, a petting zoo complete with rabbits and goats, and a duck pond. It was immaculately kept, a real labor of love. Pheasants and guinea hens wandered freely. Hammocks were strung between a few bananas trees in a welcoming fashion.

Except for a few local guides and staff people, there was only one small group of tourists, who had just completed their tour. They were eating

Rasta Heart

lunch and chatting with their guide, a young Ras with long tight dreads. He was slim but muscular, wearing cut off jeans. A school group was having a picnic and soccer game in one of the playing fields. A very friendly staff person told us we could go on tour for 12 bucks or for 20 with lunch. We took the latter, ordered lunch and sat in the shade and awaited our meal. The place was serene and quiet.

After a few minutes, the guide that was with the other tourists peeled off and came over and introduced himself.

"I'm Ras Thomas. I'll be your guide," he said, holding himself proudly, almost nobly, with a serious look on his face.

We all introduced ourselves and he rejoined his other group as we awaited lunch. After the hustling of Negril and the scene with Carlos, we were all disappointed that we needed a guide. Ras Thomas' quick intro and poker face put us a little on guard. When we finished, Ras Thomas came over to get us.

Unlike Reach Falls, which is one big waterfall, Mayfield Falls is a series of small falls, from four to twelve feet high, strung along a mile or so of a cold, clear river, shaded by glades of bamboo. There are three major falls and 21 swimming holes. The place is breathtaking and magical, with the constant but pleasant noise of rushing water.

Ras Thomas, carrying our two small backpacks as well as a small cloth bag he brought, led us over a bamboo and log bridge to the river. As we walked upstream he would help each of us navigate the slippery areas, where a misstep could mean a painful fall. About every 20 yards, he would situate himself at the difficult spots and gently but firmly take each person's hand and guide them over, then move up again to the lead.

In our guarded frame of mind, we had all overlooked Ras Thomas' essence. We all figured he'd probably rush us up the falls and then hit us up for a big tip. Though he was rather quiet and didn't smile a lot, when he did, it was gentle and calm. He was very patient and caring with us, making sure that we were comfortable before we took each step in the precarious areas. But it was mostly his firm reassuring grip that endeared himself to us. It said, "Trust me. Just hold my hand and everything will be OK. I would never let any one of my guests get hurt."

We would stop every few minutes to play in the water and the farther we went, the happier we felt. Between the natural beauty of Mayfield Falls and Ras Thomas, the tension created by the hustlers lifted. Everyone was playing and laughing, especially Alicia, Marc and Julie, who were acting like silly kids. I was delighted. They had met their first real Rasta.

About halfway up, while we were swimming in a large pool, Ras Thomas took a chillum pipe, made out of a coconut and bamboo, out of the cloth bag he carried. He loaded it with ganja and motioned for us to join him as he stoked it up in billowing clouds of ganja smoke. Julie and Marc joined Ras Thomas and started to take a few hits off his pipe. The scene was so natural, three young people surrounded by natural beauty, passing a coconut and bamboo pipe, laughing in a cloud of smoke.

This created a dilemma for Julia and I. Though Alicia knew Julia, Julie and I had smoked a little ganja last time we were in Jamaica, she had never actually seen us smoke it before. Julia and I had always been ambivalent about this. I had to hide my ganja from my parents and now from my child.

Alicia was just fourteen and would soon enter high school, where ganja is prevalent. We knew she was going to encounter it soon. We both felt that we didn't want her using anything at this age and we were concerned that her seeing us smoke would undermine this. We had told her that even though she knew we smoked ganja in Jamaica, just as she had seen us drink alcohol before, she was still too young to do either. We had also explained to her the truth about marijuana and the inherent dangers in alcohol.

Finally, I looked at Julia and we both shrugged and headed towards Ras Thomas. We agreed there could be no better place for her to see her parents smoke for the first time than here, in this jungle, on this river, with this pipe, with this Rasta. As the five of us took a few hits off Ras Thomas' chillum, Alicia sat in the water looking a little sullen and left out. As we headed out, I turned to her.

"Don't worry, sweetheart," I said. "We're all just trying to get where you already are." She smiled. Another precarious step successfully maneuvered.

Farther up the river, we found a large swimming hole and everyone went in for a long dip while I talked with Ras Thomas.

"Thomas, how did you become a Rasta?"

"Twelve years ago, when I was 20, I 'ad a vision one day at my 'ouse."

"Were you smoking ganja at the time?"

Rasta Heart

Ras Thomas looked thoughtful for a second and said, "Well, no more than usual," and we laughed. "In my vision, I saw de Fadder. 'E looked like a Rastamon with full dreads and precepts and dressed in a long white robe. He was very loving and he said he had a message fe me, only one message. He said, 'Ya are ta tell de wurld about Rasta.' And dat was it. Den 'e disappeared. I nevah cut my 'air or eat meat from dat day. I talked ta ot'er Rastas and became a Rasta den."

I couldn't help but wonder if it was like Renny said at Reach Falls, "In ev'ry nation 'E makes mon and 'E prove 'Imself to dat nation in dere color."

"Did you have any idea how you were going to do this?" I asked. "Were you feeling any pressure to find out how you were to accomplish this assignment?"

"Nah, mon," he said. "I knew dat JAH 'ad given me dat vision and dat JAH would show me de way in 'Is own time. Fe seven years I wait and den I 'eard dat some people dat used ta live 'ere was goin' ta open dis place as a tourist attraction. Den I knew dat I was ta be a guide 'ere so I could meet de tourist and teach dem dis love. I knew dese falls well. I played in dem all my life and now JAH would bring people like ya and yah family 'ere ta see dem and be wit' me."

I told Ras Thomas about our book.

"The book includes the history of Jamaica and slavery here. Without this history, my culture cannot comprehend the level of forgiveness that the black Jamaican Rasta is practicing by not hating, but loving, the white man, after all the slavery, the poverty and exploitation," I said.

"Poverty, 'atred and guns," he said. "Dat what dey force us ta be. It's like dey lost de love fe humanity and 'ave love fe vanity."

"Why?" I asked.

"Becuz dey 'ave love fe material t'ings, fe cocaine, drugs, power."

"Do you think people are learning?" I asked.

"Ya, mon. Slowly but surely. Dey still 'ave more ta learn. JAH's plan reveals itself and it is always good over evil and de truth always reveals itself. De truth come 'ere wit' no clothes. Naked. Babylon cayn nah 'ide dis truth always. One day dey will 'ave ta come and tell us."

"But do they really know it? Do they really know One Love?" I asked.

"No. De 'eads of Babylon doan't know love becuz if dey know it, dey

189

Rasta Heart

would put away dere guns. No, dey doan't really know it. Dey in darkness," he said.

We continued up the falls and then headed cross country back to the village where we could hear African drumming. Twice a week they had the drumming there. Along the path we encountered three Rastas with machetes, friends of Ras Thomas. They chatted in patois, laughing a lot.

"Dey been up in de 'ills takin' care of de ganja fields," he said as we continued on. "Dey puttin' de likkle plants in now."

As we crossed an open field we came to a huge mango tree, spread wide, maybe 50 feet high.

"Do ya want some mangoes?" Ras Thomas asked us.

"I love mangoes," Julia replied.

With that, Ras Thomas gently placed his cloth bag on a bush limb and scampered up the tree with grace and quickness. He went higher and higher, shaking various limbs vigorously until the ripe mangoes fell to the ground with a thud.

"There's a truly natural man," I said as Ras Thomas climbed down from the tree. "He exists not only in a natural state in his body and his world but he exists in a natural state of love in his mind."

Laughing and talking, the six of us enjoyed our mango feast.

For the next half hour we wandered back to the village, through beautiful open hills and shaded jungle paths. Everyone was in great spirits, laughing and kidding with each other. It had been a perfect afternoon. Up until meeting Ras Thomas, Alicia and Julie, like many of our friends and relatives, did not really understand what we were doing and were worried about us spending time back in the mountains of Jamaica with people we barely knew. After meeting Ras Thomas, they were no longer afraid.

"Between Mayfield Falls and Ras Thomas, I feel renewed," I said as we approached the village.

"Ras Thomas let's you know very soon on the trip that everything's OK," Julia said. "It's like he was saying, 'You can settle down here. I know you've had a bad experience with other people but just look at my eyes and look at my action.' Many times I've had a vision of a very spiritual natural man guiding me through a path and in my vision I say, 'No, I want to go on my own path.' But with Thomas there was the same image but I didn't resist. The vision came full circle."

Rasta Heart

"How long have you been having this vision?" I asked.

"For many years," Julia said. "The best part of the trip was when he pulled me into the falls he called 'the washing machine.' He took my hand and the water was rushing so fast and I looked into his eyes and they assured me, 'It's OK.' His hands were holding me strong and I knew because of his strength this was safe. He pulled me into the waterfall and it was as if I was being plugged in to a power source and could surrender to the sensation. He pulled me farther into little small cave and then pushed me to another spot where I could sit and watch him meditate. We stayed there like that and the meditation intensified, energizing the cave. Then he pulled me under the waterfall and held me under it and then he pulled me out. The whole experience was an exercise in trust. For so long I've had this vision of a natural water park and that's what Mayfield Falls was and Ras Thomas was my guide, to show me the world I had glimpsed in my dreams. Thank you, Ras Thomas."

We relaxed around the village for awhile and then drove toward Negril, giving Ras Thomas a ride to Sav.

"Ras Thomas, what will you do tonight?" I asked, curious about his everyday life.

"Maybe I go see my girlfriend or play dominoes wit' my friends. First I go see my mudder an' stay wit' 'er awhile. I catch some fish fe 'er an' cook dem jus de way she like it. Sometimes I watch TV wit' 'er. I like de cartoons an' Dynasty. Dat program shows me why Babylon messes up de minds of de people. But afta awhile I t'ink de TV's watchin' me so I cut it off. Sometimes on de weekends I go ta De Jungle in Negril or a system party an' dance wit' my girlfriend."

We dropped him off near his mother's house, promising to visit him and Mayfield Falls again on later trips. It had been a perfect afternoon. Just as Bobby and Scott had gotten an experience of Rasta in a backdrop in which they felt relaxed, JAH had arranged this day so that our daughters and nephew could also.

Chapter 14

Red

"The day that hunger is eradicated from the earth there will be the greatest spiritual explosion the world has ever known. Humanity cannot imagine the joy that will burst into the world on the day of that great revolution."

—Fredrico Lorca

The following day we were eating at The Royal Kitchen when we met Red. Red was in his sixties. He had a long yellowish gray beard with long dreads wrapped around his head like a turban. He looked exactly like an Indian Sadhu or wandering ascetic. He walked with a limp. In his youth, he had broken his leg and the doctor wanted to amputate when it became infected. Before this could happen, he was hit by lightning and the infection was cured.

Red was articulate, intelligent and loud. His sentences were punctuated with profanities, even in mixed company and in public. Whenever he saw another dread, he had a habit of yelling "FIYAH!" at the top of his lungs, in a sharp, grating voice, that scared the hell out of you. If he saw two dreads he yelled "FIYAH! LIGHTNIN'!" He was committed to his faith but still carried some bitterness from years of mistreatment. However, there was a sweetness to him and he seemed to form personal friendships almost immediately. We were also amazed to find out that he had once been a US Marine.

Red had been friends with Bob Marley when he was a teenager. They had appeared together on The Opportunity Hour on the radio. He told us

192

about how against his advice, Bob never went to the Rasta doctors for his cancer. He felt this shortened his life. We talked about how Bob never wrote a song about the importance of an Ital diet. He believed that Bob was eating meat which added to his health problems. We told him we were picking up Bongo Roach in nearby Sav to visit Bongo Hu. Both Bongo Roach and Bongo Hu were old friends of Red's so we invited him to join us and he instantly accepted.

The three of us headed to Sav to meet Bongo Roach. As we waited on the main street, Red showed us his copy of a rare OAHSPE Bible. Though printed in 1884, it was supposedly first written more than 9,000 years ago. The intro page read, "Zarathustra, whose biased and partial history has come down to us from the lessons of Zoroaster, lived in Persia about 9,000 years ago. The first Bible ever given mankind was given to Zarathustra. All bibles since have been a restatement of the basic spiritual principles and laws embodied in this Zarathustrian Bible." It went on to say that man's warlike, aggressive nature, as well as all diseases and sickness, began when we started to eat meat.

As we were waiting, three of Red's Rasta friends rode up on bikes and we all started talking. Soon Bongo Roach arrived and joined us. He was dapper in clean black dress pants and a long-sleeved dress shirt covered with sparkles. As he walked up, Julia and I were talking with a young Rasta with bright eyes and a winning smile. He was telling us how much he loved his island and his life here.

"I love it, mon! I love it!" he said. "I go ta Kingston, de concrete jungle, and I cayn't wait ta get home ta Sav."

I thought, Here is an adult man on an old bicycle, probably his most valued possession, and he has a greater passion and joy for his life than most people I've met in years. We encountered similar reaction from many of the Rastas and other Jamaicans we met.

After awhile we headed out for Cambridge, an hour drive inland toward Montego Bay. As we drove, Bongo Roach and Red started talking about the effect getting money had on some people who claimed to be Rastas.

"Ya are rich if ya 'ave yah 'ealth," Red said. "Money will show if a mon is a Rasta or not."

"Of course!" Bongo Roach chimed in. "Dat is why de love of money is de root of all evil."

Rasta Heart

"What is it like for you to see people like us come here with similar beliefs as you?" Julia asked.

"Ya are growin'," Bongo Roach said emphatically, his large eyes closed in thought. "Ya came 'ere ta get knowledge. Dat's why ya 'ave been sent 'ere. So step-by-step, when de time come, if ya are a chosen one, chosen by de Almighty, ya will 'ave ta be a Rasta like I and I too wit'out de influence of I and I ta tell ya ta put on de locks. It is inborn and de inner mon will speak ta you but no Rastamon nevah tell I ta lock. It is de inner mon in I dat tell dat. No Rastamon cayn tell ya becuz if ya be influenced by one ta lock, afta awhile ya goin' ta change. Becuz dere is certain oppression and tribulation ya are goin' ta 'ave ta pass t'ru wit' a locked 'ead, ya know and when ya doan't 'ave de Almighty and if ya weren't chosen and de test come up on ya, ya cayn nah pass it. When ya 'ave been chosen, ya 'ave all dese powers."

"Now de Almighty protects me," Red said. "Three years ago I was in a bus with seventeen people dat had an accident and JAH took me out of de vehicle before de accident. I was in de bus and I saw a car was comin' across de road in front of us and before it ran inta our bus, I yelled, 'NO, JAH! NO, JAH! NO, JAH!' and my door opened and I flew out. Den it hit and everybody went ta de 'ospital except I. I was in de front seat and de engine went right t'ru de seat dat I was in."

"De Almighty will protect ya," Bongo Roach agreed. "Fe four years, I was sick and I doan't 'ave a month I was 'appy out of de four years. I went ta Babylon doctor and 'e could nah 'elp I, but he was a Rastamon and 'e sent me ta Bongo Hu and Bongo Hu 'elp me in some ways but dere were certain t'ings 'e could nah do and de Almighty 'Imself 'ad ta do dat."

We drove through the mountains impressed by the incredible beauty of the island. Around one in the afternoon, we arrived at Bongo Hu's. His house was in the countryside a few miles from Cambridge. We parked on the road and crossed over a small metal bridge spanning a clear, strong creek than ran in front of his property. The bridge made a tremendous racket when you walked or drove over it—a roots alarm system. The house was a well-built one-story concrete block home surrounded by heavy shrubbery. There were a few other buildings visible on the property includ-

194

ing a smaller octagonal house, in which someone was listening to a cricket game at high volume.

As we approached his house, I began to notice a few things that indicated this was no ordinary home. It was painted a reddish pink and high on the walls, in large, neat yellow letters in an arc were the words "Rastafari Selassie," "King of Kings," "Lord of Lords," and "Divine Theocracy." The front of the house, where a front door would be, was wide open, with no wall at all. Inside was a large room, 20 feet wide and 40 feet long. A colorful cloth drape cut off the back third of the room. The ceiling was maybe 15 feet high, with its two sides sloped, coming into a flat area at the top, maybe 10 feet across. The walls and ceilings were concrete and the floor covered with tile. Inside were several pieces of wrought iron lawn furniture, including a couch, several chairs covered by comfortable cushions and a table in the middle with neatly stacked copies of *The Jamaica Gleaner*. Several ornate wooden doors lead to side rooms.

Every inch of the ceiling and walls were covered with vivid pictures and words painted directly on the surface. On one sloping ceiling section across from the entrance was a huge painting of a Rasta with enormous Medussa-like dreads. Four feet high and six feet wide, it was painted in such a way that the dreads merged with his precepts so that his entire head was circled by locks, except for a crown. He looked very much like a young Haile Selassie. Above it was written, "The Immutable Living Master Piece." This portrait appeared again on the adjoining panel. On a sloped ceiling section on the opposite end above the entrance, was a huge portrait of a queen, black but with white features, in full royal dress. Above her was written "Grace Divine."

On several other of the sloped sections of the ceiling were spiritual texts handwritten in neat, one inch white letters on a black background. On the right hand wall there was a mural with a Daliesque picture of a city, full of tall buildings, freeways, cars, obviously depicting Babylon. The buildings and freeways were at rakish tilts—Babylon, on the verge of falling. On the opposing wall was a huge ocean liner, loaded with Rastas on the deck, as if heading back to Ethiopia. The whole effect was commanding, mystical, almost overwhelming.

Rasta, Bongo Hu's wife, met us and invited us in. She was tall, slim and graceful but reserved. Her dreads were wrapped in a large scarf. She

Rasta Heart

explained that Bongo Hu was out and she wasn't sure exactly what time he was coming back. After a few minutes of somewhat strained conversation, we all agreed we would wait around awhile for Bongo Hu and Rasta retreated into the kitchen.

The day was hot but the tall ceilings and concrete walls kept the room rather cool. After awhile, Julia, Bongo Roach, Red and I continued our conversation.

"Over de years, one of de things that I 'ave realized," Red began, "is dat de reason we doan't 'ave more daughters dat come inta de faith, is dat we are attracting a lot of young people. It should be de same behavior if it is boys or girls but it's not. The Rastafari energy dey are puttin' out to the I's dey are nah puttin' out ta de daughters. Dese wolves, dey are not real Rastas, try ta seduce dem so dey leave not knowing dey 'ave not met a real Rasta but a wolf and dey didn't come 'ere fe dat. Dey came fe spiritual knowledge and reason and dey didn't get dat and den dey doan't come back ta Rasta. When I meet a young daughter, my intention is ta encourage 'er ta be a Rasta, nah ta 'ave sex wit' 'er."

"So that is why there are fewer Rastaladies then men?" I said.

"Ya, mon," Red replied. "De wolves are chasin' dem away."

"So I guess it's the same story as it was with King Solomon and the Queen of Sheba," Julia said.

"What ya mean?" Red asked.

"Well, in the Bible, the Queen of Sheba sought out Solomon because she had heard of his great wisdom but when she went to meet him, he tricked her and seduced her, leaving her pregnant. It was really the same with Bob Marley. He had great spiritual power that drew women to him and then he misused that for sex."

"Ya. It is de same t'ing," Bongo Roach said thoughtfully.

At this point it clouded up, so we all moved outside where there was a cool wind blowing. We sat on a wall and continued our reasoning.

"Maybe since Rastafari is such a pure expression of the truth, of love," I said, "it attracts a lot of negative energy, like the wolves. What do you do when you find out someone is a wolf?"

"De Almighty will remove a wolf from amongst you," Bongo Roach said, his eyes closed, thoughtful. "De Almighty will do dat work fe ya. Dat wolf dat come amongst ya will 'ave ta move or 'e's goin' ta do somet'ing ta 'urt ya. No family, no mudder, no fadder, no sister, no brudder, no friend cayn come amongst I if dey are a wrongdoer. If dey cayn do dos t'ings and if dey nah movin' right, I tell dem dat dey got ta go and if I doan't tell de individual, I tell my Fadder ta move 'im and dey's goin' ta move. But ya 'ave ta be de one in charge ta initiate any change. Becuz if ya findin' 'im nah changin', den 'e 'as ta go."

"A leopard cayn't change 'is spots," Red added.

"I guess that's the big question," Julia said. "Is a wolf going to change?"

"A one is not too quick ta just lick someone becuz 'e do a wrong ta ya," Bongo Roach continued his reasoning. "Fe everyone makes mistakes but if it is continuous den dey must go. If a mon is a sick mon and 'e is corrupt, I must use Divine power and get rid of 'im or ot'erwise tell 'im physically ya cayn't stay amongst me now."

"When I go ta an area and see a locksmon," Bongo Roach continued, "de people around must cayn recommend 'im. In t'irty years, no police come on my land. I am de only Rastamon in de whole center of Darliston. I am de only one de police cayn look upon fe anyt'ing dat dey want to ask. I am de only Ital Rastamon."

"How many dreads are there in this area?" I asked.

"A couple of hundred dreads in dat area," he replied, standing up for emphasis. "I am de furst Rastamon dat send a yout' wit' locks ta dat secondary school an dey accept 'im. It was in 1980. Not my son, de next mon son, but 'e like my son."

"Where you surprised that he was accepted?" I asked.

"Of course, mon," he said, sitting back down. "When I went dere, I talked ta de principal an reason wit' 'im and 'e seh, 'I am taking dis yout' under yah influence, under yah aspiration.' An afta two years, 'is fadder take 'im out of de school and de children 'ave nah stop asking about 'im and now ot'er children go dere wit' locks."

"When I was a kid, t'ings were different," Red said, changing the subject, reflecting back sixty years. "Money didn't matter. It was really love in dos days. Dos were de days of love. Dere were no 'ard feelings. People loved each o'ter. Am I right Bongo Roach?"

"Of course!" he replied, emphatically.

"Was there more money around then?" I asked, wondering what it must have been like on the island in the 1940s.

"We didn't 'ave money but we 'ad love," Red continued. "Some of us nevah know what shoes are. Our parents could nevah buy shoes, could nevah buy me a shirt. But it didn't matter. Dere was so much love. When we were kids, we 'ad eight, nine places ta eat every evening. Sometimes we 'ad ta 'ide. Yah belly was so full of food, ya could nah go ta de ot'er yards becuz dey want ta feed ya again. If ya do sumpten wrong, any parent would flog ya. But dey nevah ill treat ya. Ya always deserved it. But now de parents get mad at de teacher if dey discipline dere kids. De TV is 'aving a bad effect on dem and now wit' satellite dishes, even de kids way back in de hills see it."

"An' Babylon keep showing all de guns," Bongo Roach added, "and den all de boys wan' de guns. De kids cost money too. Up my way it cost seven hundred dollars (U.S. $15.00) a week ta send ya kids on de bus, fe one kid and dere parent earn maybe one thousand a day (U.S.$23.00) plus dey 'ave ta pay fe book rental and uniforms."

"And when I was a kid," Red said, "I used a book an' de next year my brudder use de same book, but now it doesn't go like dat. Dey change de books every year and if ya kid doan't 'ave de uniform, dey cayn nah go ta school."

"I've noticed that all the uniforms are different," I said. "At least if they were all the same, you could buy used uniforms because kids always outgrow them before they wear out. Probably some uniform company and book company paid school board members to pass these rules."

"Yes, mon. Dat is de Babylon system. It is a system," Red said.

"The system is the same in our country. We get bigger crumbs from the table but our crumbs are loaded with saturated fat" I said and we all laughed. "But I'm not sure that's better. We buy cars, TVs, computers, and clothes but a lot of that stuff just isolates us. In Jamaica everyone is outside or in the shops or on their porches talking to each other, being together. And when you go somewhere, you're either walking or on your bike so you're still out in the community. Even if you're going in cars, it's usually a taxi or bus full of people you know. People are working hard in both cultures. Many Jamaicans look at the U.S and wish they had more cash, more things, and given the poverty here, I don't blame them. But when I look at Jamaica I wish we had the sense of community, the aliveness, the heart that you have."

"An de water and de food is all polluted," Bongo Roach added. "An dey eat de flesh dat make dem aggressive."

"Yes, mon," Red said, "and dat is where de Rastas come in and Babylon is very weak now. Dey are at de end of de road. Dey are looking for answers."

"But not all the leaders are getting it yet," I said. "Just yesterday Bush said he would not sign the Kyoto Global Warming Treaty because he feels that our American lifestyle is a blessing and we should not have to limit it in any way. What he is saying is that this consumer lifestyle, which produces 25 percent of the world's pollution—pollution that is negatively altering food growing patterns everywhere and causing food shortages for a lot of people—is our divine right and we do not need to change it, even if it threatens the entire planet."

"Yes, mon, it is de Babylon leaders, nah de people, dat mess it up," Red said.

"And de U.S. sell all dos weapons all over de wurld," Bongo Roach said. "and all dos weapons just ta make more war. Jus' ta get power. But dese leaders are locksman too. Dey jus' doan't know it. It in everyone. De leaders are like I but many 'ave an inner spirit in dem dat is an evil concept."

"Do you think everyone has that evil spirit in them?" I asked.

"It approach us too," Bong Roach said, nodding his head with his eyes closed in thought. "It approach everyone whether 'e is Rasta or nah Rasta but you doan't need ta maintain it. If a criminal come ta ya 'ome, ya doan't 'ave ta let 'im in, ya know. So afta ya analyze 'im and see 'e is a wrongdoer, ya get rid of 'im. Ot'erwise 'e will destroy ya or damage ya. It is de same way wit' evil t'oughts, greedy t'oughts."

"Why do some people maintain it?" I asked.

"Evil carry attraction," Bongo Roach replied. "and some people like dis attraction. But evil also come t'ru eatin'."

"De main t'ing is dere eatin'," Red interjected. "Dey 'ave pig consciousness. If ya ever watch pigs at de trough, every pigs wants it all. Dey keep trying ta push de o'ter pigs away so dey cayn eat it all. If ya eat pig, ya 'ave pig consciousness."

"You have a pig in your head," Julia said and we all laughed.

"A good person cayn still eat meat but dere will be more sickness and dey will die," Bongo Roach answered.

"De body cayn live much longer if ya stop eatin' meat," Red added, "and be much 'ealthier. To live ta 70 is nuttin'. Ya cayn live much longer den dat. In ancient times, before people ate meat, women would 'ave children at 70 and people's skin was golden."

"So do you guys feel like you will not physically die"? I asked.

"I do nah 'ave t'oughts of dying," Red said.

"I'm nah lookin' fe death," Bongo Roach replied, nodding his huge head. "De sun live fe' ever. De moon live fe' ever. I know my body will live fe ever. Ya mediation must be on life. What ya eat destroy ya, mon. Dat Babylon. So if ya 'ave dat belief dat ya 'ave ta die, ya do de t'ings dat is dead an ya goin' ta be dead."

"But it is nah everyone of us dat seh we are Rastas really know de medicine, like I and I," Red said, touching Bongo Roach lightly on the knee. "So dey doan't use it and if ya doan't keep ya body clean, ya be dead. Dere are certain t'ings ya must use, de roots. Clean ya colon, clean yahself. But de mon dat is nah livin' Ital, 'im cayn't see de life dat is in us. We know of life becuz we are feelin' life becuz we used ta be dead and we know what life is now. Changin' from dat carnivorous eatin' ta dis 'erbivorous life, we feel de difference. We know it and we tell ya about life. De o'ter people cayn tell ya about death. When ya eat meat, ya break one of de Ten Commandments—thou shalt nah kill. Dat means animals and 'umans, nah jus' 'umans."

"Power alone is nah goin' ta work," Bongo Roach added. "Ya need de Almighty ta guide ya."

"And now even de cows are carnivorous," Red said. "Dey are chopping up parts of de cows and feedin' dem back ta de dem. Dat's why dere is dis mad cow disease. Dat's not normal. A vegetarian cayn't eat flesh. An dey put female hormones in de chicken feed so dere will be more chickens den roosters and dese 'ormones get into us. All dese female 'ormones we are eatin' is nah good."

"And now there are a lot of genetically modified foods and no one really knows what problems these will cause down the road," I said.

At this point, we heard a car come over the metal bridge with a loud metal, "CLANG! CLANG! CLANG!"

After a few minutes, Bongo Hu came down the path, holding the cover

Rasta Heart

of our book that Rasta had given him. Bongo Hu was a thin, wiry man, medium height, in his mid-seventies. He had dreads stuffed in a leather tam and black precepts. He looked very tight, like he was mad to find us in his home. We said hello but he didn't look me in the eye and seemed distracted, irritated. He greeted Bongo Roach and Red more warmly, talking with Red for awhile, catching up after years of not seeing each other. He sat down next to Red and lit a spliff. I asked if I could record our conversation for our book.

"Don't tape I!" he snapped, angrily pointing his finger at me. "And even if you did, it wouldn't come out on your tape." He spoke with an educated Jamaican accent. He seemed arrogant and condescending. I felt like I was being dressed down by an impatient Sunday school teacher.

"So you want to write a book about Rasta?" he started. "You don't know Rasta. There are only a few Rastas on this entire island besides I and Red and Bongo Roach." I don't know if he really wanted to include them or was just saying it to be polite.

"How many other Rastas are there?" I asked.

"Maybe five or six at the most," he continued. "And there are just a few like that in other countries, too. One day, all these few real Rastas will take a cruise together on a boat that cost millions of dollars. We will travel the world. The other dreads, they are still eating fish or meat or Babylon's food. You can't be a Rasta and eat that. But one day when they are painfully dying in the hospital and I am still healthy and Ital, they will know."

"That doesn't sound very compassionate," I said. "It almost sounds like you'd be glad to see them suffer for their misunderstandings."

"It is not I," he said, defensively. "It is them. They have made their decisions and now they must pay the price for those decisions. Also, many dreads make the mistake of believing that Haile Selassie was divine. It was not Haile Selassie but Tafari, his brother, that was divine. Not Ras Tafari, but Tafari. Haile Selassie was the administrator, the governor. Tafari was the spiritual leader. He was a locksman and a vegetarian. Very few dreads know this. That is his picture on the ceiling in there."

"So you believe that unless you eat no flesh and believe in Tafari, you can't be a Rasta?" I asked.

"It is more than that to be a Rasta," he said, standing over me, looking down at me. "To be a Rasta, you must be a locksman. I made a covenant

201

ten billion years ago with the Almighty that in this life I would not die. That I would be with the Almighty forever and my locks and precepts are here to show that covenant. We are the ancients. We are not like other men. We look like the ancients, the prophets of old, because we are them. And if you want to say you are a Rasta, you must lock up."

"Some Rastas say it is the heart not the hair," I said, thinking of Scram. I also thought back to what Bongo Roach said on the way there that no Rastaman should tell you to lock up.

"They are wrong!" he said, almost shouting. "And you do not need to write this book on Rasta. Be Rasta! Become Rasta! Be the book! Become the book! Make your covenant with the Almighty and become a locksman. Then people will see you and wonder why you look like an ancient and they will come and ask you why you look like that and then you can tell them. Do not write the book. Be the book!"

"Maybe you're right. Maybe the book is all ego, all Babylon," I said, intrigued by the idea of being the book. "Maybe I need to just let go of the book idea, of teaching others, and just teach myself."

"Yes, mon, just do that," he said. "And to be a Rasta, every night before you go to sleep you must think of all the evil thoughts you had during the day and throw them out of your mind and just keep the good ones. And a true Rasta is prosperous financially, very prosperous. Money is no problem for a true Rasta. I drive a BMW. So now why do you think you can be a Rasta?"

"I believe to be Rasta is to know and express One Love," I said, liking this particular question. "I am not always doing that but there is not one person on this planet I cannot look in the eye. There's no one I hate. There is nothing I have ever done that I am ashamed of or would care if all of you knew about. And I am reaching to always show love to everyone."

There was a long silence after I said this. Bongo Hu didn't seem to know what to say. I couldn't tell if he liked my answer and was thinking maybe he judged me too harshly, or whether he realized he couldn't make the same statement. Everybody was looking at him, waiting for his reply.

"Well, now, you become a locksman," he finally said, his voice and attitude softening, "and stop eating flesh and then we see. Next time I see you, I will know."

"You mean if you see me again and I have locks?" I asked.

Rasta Heart

"Not just by that but by other things as well," he said mysteriously as we rose to leave. I thought I detected a slight smile as he shook my hand. I was taken aback. Had it all been an act? Maybe it was a test, a push to get me to not just write about Rasta but to be Rasta. Was he an angry, judgmental dread opposed to a white couple writing about Rasta or was he a concerned teacher, pushing me to reach higher? If that was his intention, it had worked but I wasn't sure I would ever come back.

As the four of us drove to Darliston, we started to talk about our interchange.

"Maybe he's right. Maybe I shouldn't write the book," I said.

"De Almighty will reveal it, ya know," Bongo Roach said loudly, firmly from the backseat. "Follow ya conscious. De conscious is de Almighty."

"You should make the decision fe de work dat ya are doin'," Red replied.

"I think Bongo Hu was saying 'claim your natural self' in the writing," Julia added.

"'E's nah figtin' ya. 'E's nah sayin' doan't write de book if ya want ta write de book." Bongo Roach said. "'E was sayin' tek care of yahself but write de book if ya want. A lot of people who write books den doan't live it."

"It's a lot easier to write it than live it," I said.

"Ya. It's bettah ta write it an' live it," Bongo Roach said. "Ya learn a lot from 'im today."

"And when ya know it, ya live it," Red added. "Bongo Hu was pushin' ya to live it. 'E was gettin ta ya, ta ya soul. 'E wasn't in love wit' ya. 'E loves ya when 'e sees ya makin' de changes. 'E is a very lovin' guy."

"You have to remember that sometimes you need that vigor, that commitment to be a Rasta here with all the opposition they get," Julia said.

"I understand and that's true," I said, "but I want this book to be about the Rastas who have been through all that and come out the other side still focused on One Love. I didn't get that sense from Bongo Hu. He didn't use the word love once."

We dropped Bongo Roach in Darliston, telling him we would come back when the book came out. It was a long goodbye and I knew that we had endeared ourselves to him just as he had to us.

The next day Red joined us for lunch at the cliffside restaurant at The

Rasta Heart

Rock House. Julie was laying by their pool and Marc and Alicia were out on a kayak. Julia, Red and I started talking.

"Suppose we could get a few t'ousand of us healers toget'er on one day," Red said. "We could do magic, mon, if we meditated and chanted."

"The real world would begin," Julia said.

"We could do t'ings even by our meditation," he said. "We could come ta dis oneness. We could become so powerful dat we could heal de planet."

"We now have this chance to be the total manifestation of One Love," Julia said.

"Bongo Hu said we are different people now," Red said. "Yah awareness and yah wife's awareness is like ours. We are de ancients, de elders. Others are free ta chose dis too but dey are nah choosing dat. JAH is using ya ta get dis message out. Once ago Rasta could nah even be around ta get any message out. We were rejected so even though we tried ta get de message out, no one would listen. And we got ta get de message out dat womon is equal to mon. Dis male supremacy, dis masculine stuff, must stop. Dat is nah de essence of Rastafari. But now dis essence is comin' out."

At this point we borrowed the restaurant's copy of *Yes Rasta*. It is a black and white picture book recently published showing pictures of Rastas, many living way back in the mountains far removed from the "real" world. Many looked quite young but very wise, joyous and peaceful. There were a couple of pictures of Red in the book and he had also acted as a guide for the author/photographer Patrick Cariou. I asked him to take us on a guided tour of the book.

The book's intro read, "High up in the mountains and the forests, resides the conscious of the world—bearded men close to God, living off what God provides, praying, meditating, often thinking about what it is like down there in Babylon, the Babylon system, where nothing is free."

"De work dat de author is doin' is only de material part," Red said. "It's nah about de money. It's so people cayn see us and 'ear us. Some of the Rasta in dis book are Ital Rastas. When we say 'Ital' we mean dey eat all organically. It is not everyone dat is Ital. Some eat a little fish or sumpten on de way up. But dis carnivorous way of life must one day end. We're still goin' to 'ave all dese wars an' killin' on de eart' as long as we are killin' de animals to eat. De meat makes us aggressive and violent. De fear de animals felt goes into us when we eat dem. True peace won't come until we stop dat. Dat's de way I see it."

"Do you know most of these Rastas?" I asked.

"Yeah, mon. I took dis guy around ta meet a lot of dem. Nah all de Rastas are from Negril," he said, pointing to a picture of a young Rasta with a tightly wrapped turban and celestial eyes. "Dis Ras is a Bobo. I respect de Bobos. De Bobos 'ave a respect dat carry fe each ot'er more den de ot'er Rasta groups. De stick toget'er. De are workin' people. Dey make brooms. Dey nevah beg. Many Rases come to Negril becuz it is easier ta live 'ere becuz we share a lot more wit' o'ter Rastas. But dere are a lot of wolves 'ere too and dey are chasing away some tourists and when ya hippies came 'ere in de 70s, it was only de Rastas dat would deal wit' ya. If ya drank from a glass, de bar would t'row it away. Dey took ya in eventually fe de money. We took ya in fe de love."

"Some of de I's I am not fully acquainted ta know if de are fully organic or Ital and t'ings like dat," he said pointing in the book at a bare-chested Rasta with full dreads and a serious look. "But dis young Ras I know. I taught 'im 'ow ta make roots. We 'ad a lot of spiritual time toget'er. 'E is in France now."

"Ahhh! Dis is my farm and dis one is tryin' ta go ta de States wit' 'is lady," he said, turning the page to another young dread standing in a ganja field full of ten foot high plants. "Dis is a nice I."

"Are the Rastas having any respiratory problems from smoking ganja?" I asked.

"Ahhh, dat why I use de steam pipe," Red answered. "By rights, smokin' isn't good fe yah lungs. Ya know dat. So wit' de steam pipe, ya nah takin' in so much smoke but steam. It is a different high. Keeps ya cleaner inside. I created de steam pipe. Ya cayn eat ganja but burnin' it is bettah, more power, potent."

On the next page was a picture of an older Rasta with the longest dread we had ever seen. It began in the back of his head and draped over his shoulder and hung down his front and on to the ground another foot in one solid dread about an inch thick and twelve inches wide. It was incredible.

"Dis Ras nah so very wise," Red said.

"FIYAH! LIGHTNIN'! Now dis family are very good friends of mine. Dey live in the interior," he said turning the page to a group picture of several adults and children. They all had joyous grins on their faces.

Rasta Heart

"I was just up dere last week," pointing to yet another young Ras. "From 'e was a little boy, I've been givin' 'im inspiration about dis way of life. Dis Rasta, someone came and shot 'im up ta get 'is money. 'E almost died. I took de photographer ta meet 'im. 'E gave 'im only twenty Jamaican dollars (fifty cents). Dat was all. 'E was a good photographer but 'e was cheap. 'E nevah even gave me a book but 'e brought one 'ere ta de 'otel. But we doan't resent 'im. But maybe one day 'e will come and give us some money. 'E's learnin' too."

"Strange face, ancient face," he said, smiling broadly as he got to his picture, one of three in the book.

"Red, how many true Ital Rastas do you think there are?" I asked, always interested in these answers.

Red slowly rubbed his head and thought for a long time. "Twelve, fourteen maybe, dat I 'ave met" he finally said. "Maybe more, more younger ones comin' up. It's growin'. I t'ink in de next ten years dere will be t'ousands of dem."

"Long ago I know you people," he said, a mischievous look in his eye. "I knew ya were comin' as 'Is messengers. Some Rastas are saying white people cayn't be Rastas. I doan't know where dey gettin' dat from. All of us were messengers and got elected and some of us elected ourselves. We didn't realize dat we did dat but we did dat. Like ya. Ya people chose yah life. It's nah easy. It's a struggle. Ya been t'ru a lot and ya prepared ta go t'ru more. Ya are a realist. No one save ya. Ya saved yahself and I know of herbal cures, root medicine, dat cayn cure people of colds, asthma, sinus, t'ings like dat with one drop. One of my nieces died right in my arms from asthma. I could 'ave saved 'er but nobody was listenin'. De doctor seh de asthma cayn't be cured but it's a lie. Ya got ta be Ital. Ya got ta be organic. If ya are not livin' organic ya must get sick because dat's de game."

As we continued through the book I was struck how, in many ways, the Rastas, thousands of them spread across the island, were like one large tribe, almost an extended family. They were constantly networking, meeting, reasoning together, going to Nyabingis and concerts. It truly was the "movement of JAH's people."

During lunch Red started talking about a personal situation that reminded us how many Rastas, like all of us, struggle with expressing One Love in their close personal relationships. Sometimes it's just easier to love the world than our mother-in-law or neighbor. Red had 14 children with many different women and had personally raised four of them when their mother died. One of these, his teenage son, Paradise, whom we met, was very affectionate toward Red.

Red told us how a few weeks earlier his 31-year-old daughter, whom he had not seen since she was a few months old, located him and came to Jamaica from the States to meet him. Understandably, she had some bitterness toward the father she had never met.

During her month-long stay, tensions escalated between them until he would not see her or talk to her at all the last two weeks. He admitted it was "the worst t'ing dat I 'ave ever done and I 'ad awareness dat de silent treatment is very awful but I did nah want 'er ta see de o'ter side of me. My name is nah Red fe not'ing. I know I did nah 'andle dis well."

At this point in our odyssey, we had learned that the Rastas in Jamaica had much to teach us but we were beginning to see that we had something to teach them as well. They had mastered their bodies with exercise and a clean diet. They had, to varying degrees, removed themselves from Babylon's influence. They had a deep understanding of its effect in keeping people enslaved mentally, financially, physically and spiritually. Their love of the the natural world and its importance in creating joy and balance and Livity in their lives, was inspiring. And they knew JAH.

However, many seemed not as far along in their close human relationships, something that many spiritual seekers in our culture had worked on intensely. As hippies in the 1960s and 70s, many of us grew our locks, smoked ganja, lived in the countryside and left "the Establishment." In our culture, we pioneered the "New Thought" and "New Spirituality" movements, women's rights, holistic healing and all forms of humanistic psychology and body/mind healing techniques. Though we shaved, cleaned up, cut our hair and rejoined our larger society, something that the Rastas never did, we have been working hard nonetheless to advance consciousness on the planet.

Because we have re-entered Babylon, we understand it from a different perspective than our Jamaican counterparts. We understand the thinking, the illusions, the values created within the people of the affluent, and therefore exploiting, societies. The Jamaican Rastas understand the perspective and thinking of the people of the exploited societies. Because of this, each group is better equipped to help free their respective people from these illusions. Also, understanding how the business community and mass media work, those of us who have worked within the system know how to get the message out on a mass scale. Having been raised in an environment of almost infinite possibilities, many of us have experience in manifesting our visions on the material plane.

That these two groups would come mainly from Jamaica and the U.S. seems almost destined. The ties between the U.S and Jamaica are deep and often unnoticed. Both countries fought the English for their freedom, one from economic and political bondage, the other from physical bondage. Jamaica is one of the poorest countries in the Western Hemisphere, the U.S. is the richest. Jamaica, with a population almost exactly 1% of the U.S., was the port of entry in the Western Hemisphere for almost all the slaves imported into America. The U.S. government, through its foreign policies, financial leverage and covert operations, has heavily influenced Jamaican politics and economics for decades.

Julia and I are beginning to believe that JAH assigned these two groups different tasks, two spheres of learning, in creating a complete expression of One Love. Both groups hold that vision. The Jamaican Rastas bring the love of the planet and the natural world, the diet, the exercise, the freedom from the commercial world, the love of JAH and Livity. We bring the understanding of modern systems, the training in healing relationships and a commitment to gender equality. It is the merger of the wisdom and understanding of these two groups that now offers our world a more complete perspective—the fusion of the work of these two clans of the Tribe.

Chapter 15
Returning Home

"Many discouraging hours will arise before the rainbow
of accomplished goals will appear on the horizon."
—Emperor Haile Selassie I

Early the next morning we loaded everyone and everything in the car and headed out, this time going through Sav-La-Mar and over the mountains, a detour that cut an hour off the coastal road to Montego Bay. Everyone was in good spirits even though Marc and Julie's vacations were ending. Julie was leaving the next day, so, after dropping Marc at the airport, we checked back in the Half Moon for the day and hung around the pool.

The next day we dropped Julie at the airport about mid-day. Before she boarded the plane, she turned to us and said, "I really love you guys and I think what you're doing is amazing."

We headed for Port Antonio, a five hour drive at my slow speed. We were looking forward to the upcoming week and being back in Port Antonio with Scram. Alicia was not as enthusiastic, thinking she might get bored and a little lonely.

As we drove the road from Montego Bay to Port Antonio, a road that was quickly becoming very familiar to us, Alicia, Julia and I fell into a rather metaphysical conversation.

"Whenever I looked at Ras Thomas," Alicia said, "I felt like I wanted to cry. It wasn't that I felt sad or anything. I just felt emotional."

Rasta Heart

"I think when you meet someone like that it can bring up a lot of emotions," Julia said.

"And when that Rasta at Errol's gave me a flower, I felt like a spark in my body," Alicia continued. We had stopped at Errol's restaurant and a young Ras brought her a flower.

"And then I came out from the pool to say goodbye to Bongo Roach a second time. Something just drew me to him. I wanted to see him again." We had brought Bongo Roach and Red over to the hotel to meet Alicia, Marc and Julia. Alicia had liked Bongo Roach very much.

"Well, Bongo Roach is a very powerful guy," I said. "It doesn't surprise me that you picked up on some of his energy."

Alicia is a very old soul. Energetic, happy and positive, she loves people. Slow to anger and never holding a grudge, she is mature way beyond her years. Like her mother, she picks up other's emotions, ones I often miss. In 14 years, we have never had to discipline her, not because we are permissive, it's just that she makes good decisions.

"Sweetheart, we're going to stop at Scram's on the way to the hotel," I said. "Do you want to hang out there with us for a few hours or just stop to say hello and then we'll drop you at the San San?"

"I'd like to meet Scram and then go to the hotel," she said. "When you guys are talking I don't want to hear it all but I like it when you come back and tell me about it."

"So you want the executive summary, huh?" I asked laughing.

Before she fell asleep in the backseat, she said, "I think when I get home I'm going to try to eat more Ital, maybe only chicken once a month."

We arrived in Port Antonio late in the afternoon and stopped briefly at Scram's before driving to the hotel. It was great to be with him again. It was like no time had passed and we had all been close friends forever. We only stayed a short time, promising to return in a few hours after we had settled in. Alicia and he hit it off immediately, something I was thrilled to see. I had hoped he would become a big presence in her life as he had become for Julia and I.

"I really like Scram," she said as we drove from his shop. "He's really handsome. Even though I saw his pictures and video, he's more handsome in person."

After a warm welcome by Nino and Lisa at the San San, we settled into our suite, went for a swim in the pool and then ate dinner in the restaurant. As we expected, Alicia also instantly hit it off with them. We left her hanging out by the pool in their company and headed over to Scram's.

We all settled around his table catching up on each other's lives. He talked about his vision to develop tourism in Moore Town and Nanny Falls by building cabins and a restaurant there. We told him about the way they had developed Mayfield Falls in a very roots fashion.

"Scram, what are you doing for money?" I asked, noting how few customers he had.

"Well, now, I doan't watch it," he began, laughing. "Sometimes I get 'ungry and I go and get banana before I get a proper meal. But I not worry about it. Sometimes I plant plantain, coconuts and I live off dat. Dere's always bananas, breadfruit (he points to a stalk of small green bananas hanging over his head) and I doan't give myself de problem about money becuz, 'ear me now, I am a real rich spirit. Dis rich spirit dat I have feed me even if I doan't 'ave no cash. Yasee? An' sometimes I take my plantain, my bananas, my corn, my cane and I put it in my two wheel basket and I walk t'ru town an sell it ta de people."

"Do you enjoy that?" I asked.

"I love it, mon. Sometime I give some sugar cane ta de kids and it make dem 'appy. Or maybe a mother, she doan't 'ave much money but I give her something ta feed 'er kids. I'm not ashamed becuz I'm poor. I'm not ashamed. When I go ta my village, I believe it's one of the poorest regions, I know dat I am rich in de spirit. We are not ashamed of our poor livity and sometimes I would work to clear up all dis mess."

"What mess are you talking about?" I asked.

"All right, good. When de Livity is poor, I call it a mess. But it is a revelation when I view it becuz of 'ow I view ot'er people and myself. We are so poor yet so rich becuz we cayn 'ave dis love, ya know. Dere is lots of love and we jus' try ta grow de kids ta be 'umble and nice and dey only sin when de television came and dey lookin' at de bad t'ings dat dey doan't even know about. When we are poor, it takes many years ta get bettah and sometime we die and slip out of our shell and change in de spirit wit' a good 'eart and de t'ing not yet complete. But I doan't wan' all dis pressure on my people and I 'ave 'ad a great idea, FE YEARS! And it comin' true and whatever I do, I go toward it."

Rasta Heart

"What is the great idea?" I asked.

"De great idea is dat I 'ave a feelin' dat t'ings are goin' ta get bettah some day," he said and laughed. "I doan't push it. But I workin' toward it. I know somet'ing good comin'." He stops a few minutes to chat with a young woman who has come in to buy some breadfruit.

He then told us a story about how he helped a white woman that he saw wondering around Port Antonio looking very sad. He learned she was thinking of killing herself before he intervened, giving her some food and kind words. Immediately her lucked changed and she came back to see Scram.

"She told me, 'Scram, you's a prophet and it's good fe someone ta go by yah vibes.' So ya see all along de way, I am a firm believer in somet'ing up ahead and ya go around a corner and dere somet'ing good around it every time."

At this point Irman came in. We all hugged. It was great to see him. He was glad to hear we had brought him a weedeater he had asked about. He settled in to listen to our reasoning.

"Scram, what is your next week like? Are you available?" I asked.

"Ya, mon. When ya in Portland Parish ya right 'ere wit' Scram. If ya want ta go private, ya go private but still I watch yah back," he said laughing. "Whenever ya are 'ere, it is like a vacation fe me."

I told him about our visit to Bongo Hu's. I had not totally assimilated what had happened there and I was interested in his feedback.

"If ya go ta anot'er Rastamon, ya will find a different view, yaseewhatImean? Dat is 'is belief," Scram said. "About eating de animals, a lot of people eat dem until dey realize dat dese animals are not ta be eaten. Maybe dat 'appen over a period of time. If ya 'ave a child and ya raise dat nevah ta eat meat, dat would be a different type of yout'. Dey would be different from a kid dat eat meat. But dat not ta seh dat dis child could not be a righteous child, de one dat eat meat. Becuz dat meat, it kill slowly and when people get ta know all dese t'ings dere is a change in dem. So meat an o'ter t'ings, de sugar, de flour, de pesticides, fertilizers, processed foods, do not give strength ta de body. But I would not seh dat a mon dat eat meat is not a Rasta. I wouldn't seh dat becuz my belief in Rastafari, my firm belief, is de love of de 'eart of such one dat would make 'im ta be a Rasta. Dat is my belief."

Rasta Heart

"But the vessel, the structure, can work better if you eat well," I said.

"What ta eat and what not ta eat is very much important," he continued. "If ya keep reaching ta live an upful life at some time ya would not want ta kill de animals ta eat dem. Ya will not want ta cause dem dat sufferation and to hurt yah structure as well."

"What you are saying," I said, "is that a Rasta life will lead you to an organic, meatless diet but an organic, meatless diet will not necessarily lead you to Rasta. Do you think that your body could live forever as he does?"

"Well, de spirit of a mon cayn nevah die but de physical body is 'ere ta fade away. It is like a butterfly. When I was a kid, a teacher taught us about de caterpillar. We went outside and we got a worm, a caterpillar, and we put it in a bottle and we fed it branches and leaves and soon it becomes a chrysalis and it is dere fe a few days a' when we look one day it gettin' taller and taller and startin' ta grow wings and it started to shake out into a butterfly and dat was just a worm. An' a human who is so intelligent is de masterpiece fe de eart'. Womon and mon are de masterpiece fe de eart'. A mon supposed ta change in de spirit."

"We're not supposed to be limited to a body forever. We must transform into the spirit," Julia said.

"So if we keep evolving spiritually, we drop the body?" I asked.

"Yeah, mon. And change inta a new body," Scram said. "Dat means if it's up ta de power to exist and someone else ta born, ya live, mon."

"Do you mean in another physical body, like reincarnation?" I asked.

"Yeah, mon. Dat is my belief."

As Bob Marley said, "I've been here before and will come again, but I'm not going this trip through."

"So what is a Rasta?" I continued. "Everyone has a different definition."

"Rastafari is a great power word," he began, "and ya couldn't tell me about Rastafari and Nyabingi becuz ya need a teacher ta reveal de real love dat de people supposed ta 'ave, ya know. Dos guys out dere will tell ya dat Rasta is dis and Rasta is not dat becuz dey demselves preach against demselves becuz if dey demselves know dat Rastafari is a One Love system den dey would gather in one accord and ya nevah 'ear any problem amongst dem. De person got ta be filled wit' dis love. T'ings change and if t'ings doan't change from de bad ta de good, dey change from de good ta de bad.

Dat's de only two changes we got," he said, breaking into a big belly laugh. "So if ya know dat t'ings were so bad den and ya want ta change de system, ya not goin' ta change it wit' more bad. Ya goin' ta change de system fe good, wit' love."

"De leaders dat came 'ere from England did not treat our foreparents good. We are de generation dat come forward wit' a certain amount of love dat we should be able ta change de vibes. So when we see English kids come now wit' white skin, we should take dem and share wit' dem as well and teach dem de love. One time, dis guy come from England and stay at Dragon Bay and 'e see me take some white girls t'ru de jungle to Winifred Beach and 'e tell dem, 'Why ya go wit' dat black bastard?' But I didn't pay 'im no mind and one day 'e saw 'ow everyday we 'ad a big pot of soup on de beach and we give soup fe free ta de people and we throw fish in de fire and roast and give ta de people and everybody jus' live like brudder and sister. 'E see dat and when 'e was leaving 'e seh 'Guys, dis place cayn really change a person.' We show 'im love and 'e change. So bit by bit ya find people knowing each ot'er and workin' toget'er. So, dis Rastafari business is love, is de true 'eart of love. It business built up on love and anyone of dese guys dat doan't know it den dey doan't know de love. Dat why ya find so many wolves in a sheep's clothing. An dey believe it is what ya eat and what ya drink is de true love. Dat is what dey t'ink. But dat is not de true love. Where I am now an' ta my feelings, I know dat a few 'eart Rastamen cayn change de whole place."

"Since only a few, like the leaders that make war," I said, "can cause suffering for millions then it must be that only a few can create healing for millions. If only a few can destroy the planet, a few can also save it. Just as the destroyers, Babylon leaders, can now use weapons of mass destruction, the builders, those inspired by One Love, can use means of mass communications, like the Internet and Bob Marley's music to heal it. And all enlightened movements began with a few people like Christ, Gandhi, Martin Luther King, Nelson Mandela and their disciples."

"So it is," Scram replied, shaking his head.

As Luciano sings "Even when JAH's children may seem outnumbered, it's good over evil everytime. And even when you see JAH's flock is scattered, is InI save mankind."

"So, to you," I continued, "Rasta is not even a particular expression of

Rasta Heart

this One Love, an expression that would include dreadlocks and not eating meat. To you a true Rasta is also a true Christian or a true Jew, anyone expressing One Love. Rasta is just One Love, the same One Love that is at the heart of almost all major religions. And just wearing a cross or dreads is no indication that someone is expressing this love."

"Dat is de way I see Rastafari," Scram responded.

"As soon as you start to separate, you lose this One Love," Julia said. "Only with One Love can there be no argument. And I truly believe in the mind of every single person on this planet is a remembrance of One Love but we get so confused and so distracted that we don't know who we are anymore. I think that all it requires is for us to sit here and trust that the power of JAH in the heart, in the mind of everyone, is so powerful that it will prevail because it is such a natural state. It is a state of grace, It is our Home that we've been looking for all this time."

"If God is love, pure unconditional love, One Love, and we are made in His image, than we must be this same love," I said. "We've forgotten our Divine nature and think that we are not part of God, part of everyone. We think we are separate, which makes us fearful. And we spend our lives looking for something outside ourselves to make us feel whole again. Our only function is to remember we are created by love and help everyone we interact with remember. If we treat them with love we help them, and ourselves, to remember that is who we are. If we react with fear we just cement the illusion of separation and perpetuate the pain. It's like Bob Marley said, 'You think you're in heaven but you're living in hell.' It's the same as Christianity and Judaism and every other religion in its purest form. Once you remove all the dogma, it's just One Love."

The next day Julia, Alicia and I hung around the Dragon Bay Resort beach. After a crowded week in Negril, it was nice to have a day to ourselves. Dragon Bay Resort is one of the few large resorts in the area. The resort consists of several buildings set into the hill overlooking the ocean. The property is secluded, quiet and serene. We swam, snorkeled, sun bathed, ate and read.

That night we left Alicia with her new friends at the San San Tropez and picked up Scram for dinner. We drove back to eat at the restaurant in the

Rasta Heart

Fern Hill Hotel, on the hill directly above the San San. On the way over we noticed about 10 teenagers setting up drums in a parking lot on the side of the road.

"Dat Sister P's daughter and 'er friends," Scram said as we pulled over to watch. "Ya said ya wanted ta meet Sister P so maybe we seh 'ello ta 'er now."

Sister P was standing nearby, regally dressed in full African attire: a brightly patterned long dress with matching turban. We introduced ourselves and, since she was busy, agreed to come visit her in a few days. We stayed and watched for a half hour or so. The drumming drew us in. What impressed me even more was how powerful these teens looked, proud and confident, especially Sister P's daughter. Each played their own rhythm on their own drum never overshadowing each other, blending in one unified voice. At times they would turn to each other and smile, an acknowledgment of their mutual pride and pleasure.

When it was over we went to the restaurant. The Fern Hill sits high on a breezy hilltop, looking over the pool to the hills and coves of Portland. We settled into to the dining room and ordered vegetable chop suey. It was a mild evening with a light breeze and the sun setting into the ocean.

"Ya know dis poverty dat Babylon cause us ta live in gotta end," Scram said as we waited for our food in our opulent setting. "I 'ave found a way ta live wit' it but fe most people it causes much sufferation."

"It seems that a few like yourself can rise above it," I said, "but for most people it is just crushing them. I can't imagine working in a cane field 10 hours a day just to earn enough to get food that day. It wears you out physically."

"Even in my case," he said, "my family 'ave ta go up ta de States wit'out me. All becuz of lack of money. Becuz while we were here I 'ad ta adjust myself to a level where I doan't get my eyes too red."

"What do you mean by that?" Julia asked.

"It means I doan't let myself want too much. And I doan't let my ears get too dizzy by listenin' ta t'ings dat are goin' on and I know I doan't really 'ave what it takes ta go dere. I just keep myself very much calm. I go ta de United States ta get money fe my family. I pick oranges, celery, corn. I cut sugar cane—all dos t'ings. But on my island I would go fe days askin' every middle-class person fe a little work and I cayn't get it. It was crushin' my spirit so I decided ta just take odd jobs and use all my money ta buy de clothes and books and food fe my wife and kids. So I would 'ave to adjust myself ta a certain level ta know dat months and years could go by and I doan't ask anyone fe a job."

"Why wouldn't you ask?" I said.

"Becuz askin' dem and not gettin' it was too 'ard fe me. So I just find myself livin' like a king supposed ta. I doan't go around lookin' fe work and I just eat de 'erbs from de field and de food in general dat grow and not lookin' fe much t'ings dat ya buy fe money. Even when I worked fe de council, de politicians, de didn't pay me. And I see dat Babylon is very 'ard even fe demselves, much less ta me. Dey doan't even treat each ot'er good. So dat is where I said I 'ave ta just stay as a spiritual person in my 'eart."

"What did you do about your wife and kids?" Julia asked.

"Oh, gosh. I bring my wife and my three kids down from de mountains, from Bellvue, ta Port Antonio but dat was a time dat I was very much alone 'ere and people t'ought I was a madman. I wear only a turban and shorts, no shoes, no shirt. If I go down de street, I stand alone but I was myself. At night I plant food. I plant pumpkin. I plant melon. I plant yams. In de daytime I get what work I could. My wife sell some of de produce. I told my wife and my kids dat dey must dress normal, not like me. I didn't want anyone ta 'ave anyt'ing ta seh about dem. All I want de people ta see is dem lookin' clean and nice and if someone lookin' dirty, it must be me. I know dat if my kids doan't look good in school, dey tease dem and den dey cry and it 'urts dere spirit. So I spent everything on dem and not'ing on me. Dat was very 'ard fe me. Durin' dos times, no one know my 'eart. I was 'iding my clean 'eart under my dirty clothes. After awhile I got work fe three days a week at de 'ospital. I 'ad ta trim myself up and look good ta 'ave dat job. Until my wife took de kids ta de States, I took any job and nevah quit. I give all de money ta my wife. And it was t'rough de Almighty dat calm my spirit so dat I cayn view all dese t'ings properly. And I could see in de future dat t'ings were gettin' bettah."

"Did things get better?" I asked.

"Yeah, mon. When I was in de States I sent dis mon money ta build us a 'ouse and when I get back 'e did not build what we agreed. De 'ouse was so small dat I could not open de door when I put my bed in dere. And I tell 'im dat 'e must give me some money back, some recompense, becuz

Rasta Heart

'e did not build what we agreed. But 'e would not give me anyt'ing. One night I 'ad a dream dat 'is house was fallin' down de 'ill inta de river and I woke up and told my wife what I dreamed. Den two weeks later a big rain come and 'is 'ouse fell inta de river and 'e 'ad no where ta live. So I told de people dat were still workin' on my 'ouse dat dey should go and build 'im a new 'ouse first. And den years later 'e could not afford dat 'ouse so I let 'im live in my house becuz my wife and kids were gone and I did not live dere anymore. But even den 'e did not pay me de rent money dat 'e get from de government. And 'e was a deacon in 'is church. An one day I was visitin' my brother and I was goin' by 'is 'ouse and 'e was sittin' on de porch tryin' ta make some juice. But 'e was old and blind and 'e was gettin' dirt in it so I went and 'elped 'im. And he seh, 'Who are ya?' but I didn't seh anyt'ing but 'e knew. And den years later 'e died in dat 'ouse, de 'ouse 'e didn't want ta recompense me fe. Me 'ave a great love fe dat mon."

Like Scram, many Rastas are confronted with two choices. They can spend a lifetime in backbreaking labor for ridiculously low wages only to live in Babylon in grinding poverty. Or, by growing their own food and living with minimal materialistic needs, they can live as much as possible in JAH's world where everything is free and joy and freedom is obtainable.

The next morning Julia, Alicia and I picked up Scram to go to Reach Falls. Like most 14-year-olds, Alicia wasn't particularly interested in our long spiritual discourses. She brought her portable disc player and headset so she could listen to her music as we talked on the long drive to and from.

At the falls, Alicia finally put her headset aside and started to frolic in the water with Julia, Scram and I. The magic of Reach Falls is just too powerful to resist. Within minutes, she was climbing up to the top of the falls with the lifeguards and a teacher from the local school and jumping off. We stayed for a couple of hours, swimming, snorkeling, reasoning and talking with Renny.

On the way back we stopped at JAH Priest's stall where we ran into some people from Italy, three twenty-something college students, two with dreads, that we had seen at Dragon Bay Resort the day before. We had noticed them because they had on Bob Marley tee-shirts. We showed them and JAH Priest the cover of the book and they instantly wanted to know where they could buy a copy. It reminded us once again of the groundswell of international love directed toward Bob Marley.

It was late in the day so we headed out, making arrangements to see JAH Priest the following day. He said he would be at Dragon Bay Resort the next night doing Nyabingi drumming and African dance for the tourist. Before leaving, I bought one of his wall carvings, a powerful countenance of a Rastaman with dreads in a Medussa-like fashion.

With Alicia plugged into the tunes on her headset, Julia, Scram and I talked about the world situation on the ride home.

"Right now it's a force, where in people who are at war," Scram said, "dey are forced by dere leaders. Dese leaders 'ave got ta stop it. Dese leaders dat are givin' de command ta kill one anot'er 'ave got ta stop, ya know. De need a touch of love in de 'eart of dem. So right now, Robbie 'ave ta go and work on dat fe dem. Ya 'ear me, Robbie. I t'ink dis book will reach ta de leaders, from dis small person sending such a message t'ru ta dem dat de poor people need ta be more secure and dey need ta 'ave de love fe de people ta save demselves. Dat's de only t'ing ta switch ta. Dere is no o'ter word ta go over Love. No law is 'igher dan One Love. Not'ing is more powerful on dis eart'. It is a converting word. It converts de 'earts of people. If ya tell someone about love an dey doan't respond in some way, ya know dat dat person must be a wolf and when de government leaders doan't know dis love, I believe dat when dey go in dere bedrooms, dey drop on their knees and cry fe what dey 'ave done."

"But Babylon is so huge, how do you see the shift to One Love occurring?" I asked.

"It's like de ear of corn dat is so fat," he said "but even when Babylon eat it, dey cayn't get fat. Dat is de system dey are running on now."

"What the hell does that mean?" I asked, laughing, knowing we were about to learn another parable.

"Well, dat mean dat even though Babylon get de fat corn, it not goin' ta work fe dem, it not goin' ta make dem fat. Regardless dat Babylon is so large and regardless dat de people wit' de strong faith is so less but dey goin' be overthrown by dese small people."

"Because they are so powerful?" Julia said.

"Yeah. Yeah. De power of de Almighty is so strong dat dey not goin' ta survive in doing all dese t'ings always. Dey killin' off people day by day but dat system, dat feelin' dat people 'ave in dem is not goin' to survive too long and dey know dat de time fe dos t'ings, dat killin' of people, is very much short. Becuz dey cayn not keep gettin' people ta go ta war. And soon all de big guys in de U.S. and in England will want de violence ta stop becuz dis violence will be in dere land. And when dese big guys, like Bush and Blair, want de violence ta stop, den it will stop becuz den dey will make all dere enemies into dere friends to stop it. Den de whole wuurld will be friends—nah more enemies."

As Bushman sings, "Tribal war won't solve the problem. Only love of the heart can solve it."

"I think you're right about Babylon getting weaker," I said. "You know in the 60s and 70s, at the same time Rastas were catching so much flack here, the hippies were too, mostly for opposing the Vietnam War. And anyone who opposed the war—housewives, doctors, clergymen, business people—if they opposed the war, they were considered traitors. There were 'Our country-love it or leave it!' bumper stickers everywhere. The leaders barely bothered explaining to us why we needed to fight. If people questioned or opposed the war, the hippie counterculture was their only refuge. Smoking ganja helped a lot of us see the craziness of these wars, of all wars. But since Vietnam everything has changed. Today it seems reasonable to question our government's decision to go to war. We debate it in Congress and in the press. We have a national conversation about it. We demand to know why. So at least in our country, and I think many other places in the world, Babylon leaders can't just get us to agree to kill and be killed because they've decided we have an enemy. Now they must convince us they are right. And now everyone knows that if a war escalates into a nuclear confrontation there will be no winner."

"Ya, mon," Scram said. "Ya see, Robbie, everyt'ing is wit'in de people an ya 'ave ta first love de people sincerely ta keep dem out of war."

"So that would be a leader like Nanny?" Julia said.

"Yeah. Yeah. Because Nanny was very much provoked before she get angry and all dese people dat try ta fight her, dey are very much warriors and dey fight wit' gun and dey fight wit' bayonet and Nanny fight wit' a spiritual force. Dere are all different types of leaders on dis planet now but ya 'ave great leaders dat look shabby," he said, laughing. "Ya 'ave great

Rasta Heart

leaders lookin' very shabby, like John de Baptist, ya know. Dey doan't 'ave no clean suits and shiny shoes. Dey just goin' t'ru de place and sehing 'JAH!' and t'inkin' 'bout love, ya know. Becuz JAH is so great. So dos men are so great, ya doan't even know if dat is a great king ya pass by, dey lookin' so shabby."

"And the Rastas here in the Blue Mountains are some of these leaders?" I asked.

"Yeah. And ya will find all dem guys will ride up a n' down wit' ya. I will tek ya to meet dem sometimes. Becuz ya 'ave de Rastamen on de ridges all de way to Negril. Dey are sending dis One Love ta de four corners of de eart'. Mostly dey are doing farming in de mountains. Even if dey go ta de town sometimes, dey go down inta de ghetto in Kingston becuz as a Rasta ya cayn not go where de rich people live so ya 'ave ta go ta de ghetto."

"Meeting them will be our second book," I said. "We'll come back from our Blue Ridge Mountains and meet them on the ridge of their Blue Mountains."

The thought of meeting Rastas that were removed from the world and holding the vision so strongly was very appealing. I began to wonder if Scram was the one sent down into the town to await us so we could get their message out into the world.

"RESPECT!" Scram shouted out the window as we passed a Rasta.

"Scram, what do Rastas really mean when they say 'Respect'?" Julia asked.

"Well, right now some people seh 'Respect' and dey doan't 'ave any. Becuz respect is a t'ing dat ya must 'ave fe yaself before ya 'ave dat ta distribute ta other people becuz is a t'ing dat is all de good t'ings fe ya. Respect is a t'ing dat people should 'ave in abundance so dat dey cayn give it ta ot'er people becuz ya cayn't run out. Respect is de foundation of holiness and is not a word ta just speak easily. Ya 'ave ta 'ave it confirm in de 'eart becuz dat where de love vibe start from."

The next day, Alicia, Julia and I planned an outing to Somerset Falls near Port Antonio. We decided to take Irman without his father, who is always a dominant presence. Scram could not go that day anyway as he had to appear as a witness at a trial involving O'Neill, a friend of his who owned a

221

tiny battery shop on the adjoining property. A prominent contractor in town refused to pay O'Neill for some batteries and when O'Neill demanded the money the contractor hired four guys to beat him up and burn down his shop. Fortunately, Scram happened by in the midst of the fight and broke it up before O'Neill or his shop were badly hurt. Now Scram was a witness in the trial against the four thugs and the contractor. Surprisingly, Scram said that was the only violence he had ever witnessed in his life.

We picked up Irman at Scram's and drove 30 minutes west along the coast before arriving at the falls. Like all the waterfalls we went to in Jamaica, Somerset Falls is magical. After paying a four dollar entrance fee, we wandered up the path with our guide through a beautiful gorge with the crystal-clear Daniels river rushing through. We were the only people around. After passing a small thatch restaurant and bar, we came to a large pool where a boat and boatman awaited us. Overhung by thick foliage, the falls were hidden at the end of a deep gorge. Leaving our guide behind, the five of us paddled through the ever-narrowing gorge about a hundred yards to the main falls. The rock walls formed a 40-foot high jade-colored grotto with the river plunging over a precipice into a pool.

When we returned to the boat dock, a Jamaican Indian family was waiting for a ride up. The family included a man, three children and three women who were dressed in long Indian cotton gowns and shawls. The women stayed behind as the others went up by boat. It was very hot so Alicia, Julia, Irman and I went for a swim. Soon two of the women decided to join us and began to slowly walk down the steps into the water, their beautiful dresses and long shawls gently floating around them—totally comfortable swimming fully clothed.

After a delightful afternoon playing at the falls, we dropped Irman off and headed back to the San San for a swim and dinner. Alicia and Irman really hit it off. With Irman's playful nature, even with the 20 year difference, they were like brother and sister.

We returned to Scram's around sunset to pick him and Irman up to go to the Dragon Bay Resort where JAH Priest was putting on a show. We all settled comfortably into chairs the hotel had set out on the beach and ordered some refreshments. JAH Priest had been working with some of the local youths, including three of Marcia Henry's daughters, teaching them African dance and Nyabingi drumming. They were incredible, their music

Rasta Heart

and dance infused with confidence and power. All the while, JAH Priest stood on one side of the stage, dressed in beautiful African fabrics and a turban, playing gourd rattles and rhythmically dancing like a teenager. As a man in his late sixties, he was a testament to Ital living.

After the show, we headed to The Oldit, a bar Scram went to occasionally in Port Antonio where they played a lot of old reggae music. The Oldit, a huge concrete bunker type of building on a back street in downtown Port Antonio, was almost empty when we got there. The music was so loud that after a half hour I was ready to go. Jamaicans love loud music, really loud music.

On the way back to the San San, Scram started talking to Alicia about our book. He was in a vibrant, expansive mood, even more so than usual. "Ya know dis Rasta life, Rastafari, is like none ot'er in de world," he said, with a joyous grin on his face. "Dis One Love t'ing is like no other livin' in de wuuurld and dis book dat yah mudder and fadder are doin' is goin' ta lead many people ta dis life. Dis is a very much important book dat we are all doin' and ya are doin' it wit' us," he said hugging her and laughing.

We had decided, at Alicia's request, not to return to Montego Bay for our last week but stay in Port Antonio the rest of the trip. She asked us if we should even consider moving to Jamaica. Every night she wanted to go to Scram's to hang out with everyone. Here's a 14-year-old kid about to enter high school who three weeks earlier was bugging us about taking her to a bigger shopping mall and now she's wanting to leave the hotel, with its air conditioning, its pool, its restaurant, its cable TV and all the friends and go spend hours hanging out in a small shed with poor black men with long dreads. I felt if nothing ever came from all our trips to Jamaica it had been worth it just to see the changes "dis One Love t'ing" was creating in her.

We dropped Alicia at the hotel and went over to Scram's. For awhile he talked more about developing Moore Town and Nanny Falls for tourists.

"Babylon used ta 'ide de philosophy of Nanny," he said, "becuz in de school in early my time, we didn't 'ear anyt'ing about all dese warriors and all dese people dat try ta fight fe de freedom of dis island and Nanny 'ad a power, spirit power and she know de ways ta disguise wit' de cocoon leaves ta wrap demselves so dey look like a plant. Even now at de celebration de still do dat."

"Yeah, the books we read," Julia replied, "said that they were so well disguised that the English couldn't see them even if they were standing right next to them. And Nanny kept them unified at a very high level."

"Yes, she would just turn 'er back and go like dat ta gather de shots in 'er," Scram elaborated, "and she would toss it ta de direction of de English. Becuz 'er spiritual movement is more powerful den ta shoot guns. She worked wit' de Almighty. But Babylon doan't want ta establish all dese t'ings. Dey want ta drive it out of de memory of de people."

The conversation drifted to what it was like to be a Rasta in his youth.

"De love started to diminish from the 1940s ta dis time, becuz of de TV. Back den people on dis island could nevah speak too loud 'bout Rasta becuz ya 'ave Babylon ready ta trim dem, ta tek a dull weapon ta cut dere 'air and ta do ta dem everyt'ing dat is so bad. But now we cayn speak freely about Nanny and all dat Rasta business becuz now dey need de love dat all dos heroes used ta speak about." Or as Bob Marley said, "Rasta, I and I got brutalized fe jus' sehin' right' t'ings."

"You guys were courageous," I said. "You didn't sell out and buckle to Babylon's pressure, just like the Maroons didn't."

"Yeah, mon. Babylon need ta seh dey are very much sorry," he said, "and den dey will no longer be Babylon but Rasta."

"But here it's about exploitation. How much money do people make here in a day?" Julia asked.

"Maybe five hundred dollars a day. Dat's maybe twelve dollar U.S. But ya find guys still workin' fifteen 'undred dollars a day if ya cayn use a 'ammer or a trowel and 'ave a trade."

"But everything costs the same here as it does in the States," Julia said. "Sometimes even more."

"In my yout', de people in my village, Bellvue, my people nevah used ta work outside de village wit' no o'ter person. Dey did everyt'ing fe dem-selves and dey do dere own farmin' and we live off de old roots, de roots dat de grandfather plant fe a very long time. So we nevah rush it ta look fe work. But now if we leave our land we 'ave ta negotiate wit' Babylon and askin' fe jobs and t'ings like dat."

At this point Clive came by with Pom Pom and Michael. Pom Pom was proudly wearing some of the clothes we had brought her.

"So, Clive, how goes it?" I asked.

"Well, since I saw ya last," he said, "I still cayn't find a job even t'ough

Rasta Heart

I look every day. So fe what ya brought we are very much thankful."

"That's sounds pretty tough," I said. "How are you handling it? Are you enjoying life?"

"Ya, mon, I love it! I love it!," he said with unbridled enthusiasm. "T'ings are good. Dis mornin' I tek Pom Pom and we catch some fish. It was fun."

By the time we were ready to leave, I was starting to experience a severe gout attack in my left toe, my first attack since I stopped eating meat five months earlier. Gout, caused by too much uric acid, often from eating meat and shellfish, comes on very quickly, causing inflammation and severe pain in a joint of your foot, usually in the big toe. There is no way to alleviate it. An attack can last six to eight days once it starts and it makes walking painful and difficult. Doctors say it is one of the most painful physical conditions known.

I was upset at the idea of being partially incapacitated and in pain for the remainder of the trip. Scram put some cooling roots ointment on my foot and gently massaged it for 20 minutes as we talked. He said he did have healing powers and maybe these would help.

By the time we left, it felt a little better but I was bracing for a painful few days. Before getting in bed, I smoked a spliff alone by the pool to see if it would ease the pain, which it did somewhat. I crawled into bed and put my throbbing foot on the pillow. Intense pain washed over me in continuous waves but then a strange thing happened. I noticed that it no longer felt painful—only intense. I stopped labeling the sensation as something negative, something unwanted, and just experienced it. Soon it became almost enjoyable as each wave wiped all other thoughts from my mind. For a half hour or so, I laid there amazed and captivated by the experience. Then my mind started to forget the pain and travel down other avenues. The pain was still there but had become irrelevant. After an hour or so, I fell comfortably asleep. When I awoke in the morning the gout and pain were gone.

Chapter 16
JAH Priest

"To become vegetarian is to step into the stream which leads to nirvana."
—Buddha

The next day we were to pick up our friend and my former business partner, Robert Davie, at the Port Antonio airport. Robert is intelligent and usually rather quiet but quick to laugh and kid around. He is strongly committed to his spiritual path and always reaching. In 1997, Robert suggested that we start an Internet site where used computer brokers could list their inventories. It grew to be somewhat successful but was not really able to support both of us so I sold my share to him and moved on. Robert, in his mid-thirties, had remained close with our family, with Julia and I sometimes playing the roll of spiritual mentors.

Robert had responded to our adventures in Jamaica, reading my early chapters, looking at Scram's videos and visiting us in Blowing Rock to learn more. He was thrilled when we invited him to join us in Port Antonio to meet Scram. We were looking forward to his visit.

We went to the airport but no Robert. We later learned he had missed the only flight to Port Antonio and was stuck in Montego Bay overnight. Julia, Alicia and I headed to San San Beach for the day. Alicia and I plunged into the clear turquoise water and swam the half-mile to Monkey Island. When we got back from our swim, Julia, who had stayed on the beach, was very excited.

"While you guys were swimming," she began, "I started talking with

Rasta Heart

a young Jamaican tour bus guide. I thought maybe she knew Perine (the Rasta guide we met on the first trip). When I told her we were going back to Moore Town, she said that there was a lot of anger toward the Maroons for turning in the escaped slaves. I asked her if she had ever heard of a white Irish woman helping Nanny. She said, 'Oh, my God. This reminds me of an ancient story that was told to me a long time ago by a Rastaman. It was in his book that was so old that he can barely turn the pages. The book said there was a white woman with Nanny.' I got so excited when she told me that I forgot to ask her if she knew the name of the book."

Early the next morning Julia, Scram and I headed to Moore Town leaving word at the hotel for Robert that we would be back later. Scram was dressed in a rainbow colored tie-dyed African robe. He looked like a proud Ashanti chieftain. We arrived in Moore Town in mid-morning and went to attend Mother Roberts' healing service. There were already 20 or 30 people awaiting her arrival at her Redemption Tabernacle. We parked and bought some jelly coconuts from Sam, a sweet natured farmer selling his goods in front of the church. We asked Sam about Nanny teaching the Leeward Maroons One Love and he said he had heard the same thing from his grandparents.

As we were standing in front of the church awaiting Mother Roberts' arrival, two new mid-sized tour buses drove by, a very rare and surprising sight in Moore Town. Each bus was filled with 15 or 20 people, mostly locals who had moved away. They were on tour for the Portland Parish Homecoming Week presently going on, and Moore Town was on the tour. They were heading into the village for a ceremony around Nanny's grave. Since Mother Roberts hadn't yet arrived, we went into the village to observe the ceremony.

By the time we arrived, everyone had gathered around Nanny's Grave, directly across the street from the school. Most of the visitors were well-dressed, in their thirties and forties. The bus drivers kept their loud diesel engines idling in the background, a rather discordant note. Colonel Sterling was standing at the head of the group, one of only two or three Moore Town citizens at the ceremony. Rosemarie, one of the tour leaders, gave a short speech about Nanny, reminding everyone that she was not only a brilliant military strategist but also a healer. She closed with, "Let us embrace the ancestor spirit of Nanny as our rightful heritage. Let us use this tribute to resuscitate our spirit, to rejuvenate our energies, to reunite us as Portlanders. With the spirit of Nanny within us, how can we not identify with Portland, our beautiful parish? How can we watch day by day, year by year, the decline and decay in our culture, commerce, tourism and unity of our people? Portlanders, where is the pride of Nanny? We still have the blood of Nanny in our veins."

At this point, Miss Portland, a lovely young Jamaican woman, placed a large plastic wreath on Nanny's grave, while a local man blew the Abeng in a weak, uninspired manner. After that Colonel Sterling said a few words to the assembly. Then the tour guide, reminding everyone they needed to leave to go get lunch and a raft ride down the Rio Grande, hustled everyone back in the idling buses and they were off.

When the ceremony was over, we were going to the car when Scram walked up with two friends, Ovals and Nigeria (Japeth Deans). They both looked to be in their thirties or forties. Ovals, who lived alone on the outskirts of the village was tall, thin and very dark with long dreads and precepts. He was very intense and talked rapidly, stuttering at times almost as if to fill in any silence so no one would interrupt until he found his word and finished his thought. He was an accomplished Nyabingi drummer, singer and poet. Nigeria, whom Scram called Geria, was tall and solidly built, with close cropped hair and a clean shaven face. He seemed intelligent and rather sophisticated and was presently working and living in Ocho Rios.

"Scram says ya are writing dis book and we should talk ta ya," Ovals began. "T'ings are not as you see. De new colonel, Sterling, does not have de 'eart of Nanny. 'E does not hold de vision of de Maroons. He is a Babylon leader and Colonel Harris before 'im was worse. Colonel Harris stopped de drummin' after over two hundred years. Every night we 'ad Nyabingi drummin' in de village until 'e called de police and 'ad it stopped." (The police can only enter Maroon territory with the explicit consent of the Colonel.)

"Fe t'irty years, Harris was de teacher in de school, dis school right 'ere," Nigeria added, pointing to the school directly behind us. "And in all dat time, 'e nevah taught de kids about Nanny or de Maroon 'istory and now dat 'e is old and 'e may die soon, 'e try ta tell all de visitors like ya dat 'e kept de spirit of Nanny and de Maroons alive."

Rasta Heart

"I was on de village council wit' Colonel Sterling," Ovals added, "and I quit because what 'e is doin'. 'E 'as signed papers ta sell de Tichfield Trust land in Port Antonio dat 'as been Maroon land since 1739 and 'e did not ask all de council. Dey want ta tell de Tichfield School ta move so dey cayn build a 'otel."

"Well, I've got to admit this whole ceremony didn't show much heart," I said. "They left the buses running and after 15 minutes they left. And I would have thought they'd let the kids out of school to see why all these people were coming to their village. I mean the school is only 50 feet away. I think the plastic wreath says it all. And no one else in the community even showed up."

"Dey didn't show up becuz Colonel Sterling didn't tell anybody dey were comin', Ovals said. "'E doesn't want dem 'ere when people like ya are 'ere becuz so many people doan't like 'im and 'e doesn't want us ta talk ta 'im. And neither of dem do anyt'ing ta uplift dis place. Dey doan't do even as much as Scram who started to build de cottage up by Nanny Falls."

"Yeah, mon," Scram added. "De colonel should 'ave come out today in a big African gown ta show de spirit of Maroon. As 'ead of government 'e should look up, not down as 'e does. 'E must act like a colonel, a leader. 'E must look forward, not backwards. 'E 'as faith but no works. A true leader must 'ave works and dis government, dis Maroon government, caynnot be lost. It is de first government on dis island. De Maroons 'ad a good government before de English set up dere's. Dey cayn't afford ta let Babylon take away de power becuz de Maroon's fight fe dat. Babylon is still winnin' de peace." We later learned that Scram had been the village leader of nearby Bellvue until the administration of Bellvue and Moore Town was merged together.

"We were hoping to meet with Colonel Harris today," I said. "I'd like to ask him about this."

"I talked ta his wife while ya and Julia watched de ceremony," Scram said. "She said 'e caynnot meet wit' us today so we must come back day after tomorrow. Dese guys, Nigeria and Ovals, dey should be de next leaders 'ere. Nigeria should be de colonel. He spends time wit' de yout's and dey love 'im. 'E teaches dem de drummin' and songs and about dere culture."

Rasta Heart

Julia and I hiked up to Nanny Falls for a swim and then headed back to find Mother Roberts but she was resting after her service. A sudden downpour broke out so we took refuge under the awning of the health center in the middle of the village. Soon another of Scram's friends joined us. It turned out to be Ray Sterling, the colonel's brother. Ray, in his early fifties, had light brown skin, with short hair and a short gray beard. He was a quiet, thoughtful man, very kind.

"I 'ave dis vision. Dere will be a path up dat mountain and dere will be a flag at de top of the hill and people will go up dat path ta be healed," Scram said seriously, calmly, slowly raising his arm, his finger pointing to the top of a nearby hill, his robe sleeve hanging loosely from his outstretched arm. He truly looked and sounded like an ancient prophet.

"Scram, I'm not sure if I told you about a vision I had since I was a little girl," Julia said. "I've always wanted to create a natural park, where people could come and play in nature. After being back here today, I feel like it's supposed to be here, in Moore Town. I can just feel Nanny calling to me. I want to build a path along the river to Nanny Falls."

"So it is," Scram said. "We will build dat toget'er."

"Also I have this vision of there being 12 fires built all over the island," she continued, her eyes aglow like Scram's, "where ghetto youths can come and meet Rastas and smoke a spliff with them and learn about One Love. We invite anyone who knows a youth with a gun to sponsor them to come to these fires. And we have Nyabingi drumming at the fires and singing. The youths will leave their guns and we will carry them to Gun Hill near Flagstaff and bury them. And when you said you saw a path up that mountain, I saw the first fire there, on the top of the hill, and then Rastas can add on to this path until it extended all the way along the ridges to Gun Hill. And then other people could walk this path, like a spiritual journey, and meet these Rastas and learn from them."

"Dat is true," he said. "Right now I cayn see a great development comin' through yah vision. So ya see 'ow de t'ing should be arranged and 'ow it should be and dere is a hot spring near my village in Bellvue dat people cayn also hike ta. I wan' ta build a path ta dat hot spring."

"I've been thinking that we should have a ceremony here to introduce the book in Moore Town, with African drumming and dancing," I said. "We could invite the international and black press. This is the perfect place.

Rasta Heart

Nanny was the first teacher of One Love on this island and the Rastas in our book have continued that teaching. And this is the first place in the Western Hemisphere that the African slaves won their freedom. This is holy ground, but from what we've seen today the vision here is very dim, just an ember. This would rekindle the vision of Nanny and the Maroons, here and in the world. This would be a perfect place to launch the book."

"Yeah, mon," Scram said, his eyes still emanating his vision. "For many years I knew dat I would help ta uplift Moore Town. Dat is why I began ta build dos little cottages fe people ta stay when dey come ta Nanny Falls. Now I see dat ya, Robbie, and ya, Julie, will share dat vision wit' me."

At this point Colonel Sterling walked by under an umbrella and joined us in the shelter of the overhang. We all greeted each other and I updated him on both the progress of the book since our visit in April, as well as on the visions we were all having.

"Would you, as colonel, support these things in Moore Town?" I asked.

"Well, now," he began, weighing each word, "anything that will help my people and my village I would support, but of course that is just me speaking. You would still need to discuss this with the village council."

He continued down into the village and we all lapsed into silence, listening to the rain beat against the metal roof of the building. Ray looked a little bewildered. I realized that as Colonel Stirling's brother he might be offended by my comments of the vision being dim in Moore Town.

"Look, Ray, I hope you didn't take offense at this," I said, rather hesitantly, "but what I saw today up here troubles me. I've been thinking that the heart and soul of Nanny is weak here with the Maroons but strong and alive in Rastafari."

"Funny you should say that," he said. "I've been thinking the same thing. Before you leave Jamaica I want you to meet my father. He is the oldest Maroon and there is much he can tell you."

We drove back to Port Antonio and dropped Scram off in the late afternoon. Returning to the San San, we found Alicia and Robert eating by the pool. He had arrived around three and gone to San San Beach with Alicia. After they finished eating, we drove next door to the Fern Hill for dessert and to watch the sunset.

Rasta Heart

"I can't believe I'm here," he said, glowing with excitement. "This is so beautiful. It's like a dream come true. I really want to find out if this One Love that Scram is talking about is the same as the love that Jesus talked about. I mean a lot of people in my church when I was a kid talked about this but I'm not sure people really understood it. That's why I'm here, to see if people here are practicing His command to love your neighbor. When Scram said in the video that your neighbor is everybody on the earth, not just the man next door, I wanted to see how it was manifested so that I can practice it in my life."

"Did the fact that this might come in a form that is black and poor surprise you?" I asked.

"That makes me think that this is the truth," he replied. "I think if it had come in any other way it would have made me skeptical. This would have been the way Jesus would have come down, in the lowliest spot. The low will be made high and the high will be made low. So it would make sense that it would come from the poorest of the poor. But I've got to tell you, in MoBay I really got hustled with people offering me ganja, cocaine and women. I didn't know that was going on and I wasn't quite ready for the poverty I've seen, especially coming through Port Antonio."

"I know the facade is rather ragged," I said "and it looks like the rough areas of Durham but it's not the same at all. But one thing we've noticed, is that emotions get pretty intense here. What we're going through here has a way of revealing everyone to themselves and each other. Whatever you think the next few days will be like, they won't."

"I can't wait," he said enthusiastically. "What are we going to do?"

"Well, tomorrow the three of us and Scram are going first to Bath Fountain and then to Reach Falls," I said. "Then the next day we're all going to Moore Town to meet Colonel Harris, who was the leader of the village for 30 years. Are you tired or do you want to head over to Scram's and meet him?"

"Sounds great to me," he said beaming.

After dessert, we all drove over to Scram's. Scram was there with Bell and Irman and Haile Selassie, a young Rasta with dreamy eyes and a gentle nature. Haile Selassie was playing Nyabingi drums in the corner. Scram was fast asleep sitting in a chair, oblivious to the commotion around him. *The Bold and the Beautiful* was playing on the old TV behind him. Later we learned that people all over the island watch this program as a comedy, not as the melodrama it is supposed to be.

After awhile, Scram awoke and we introduced Robert. Alicia fell into a domino game with Irman and a talk with Bell about gymnastics, something they both enjoyed. Robert, Julia, Scram and I chatted around the table outside.

"Scram, what is One Love to you?" Robert asked.

"Well, now, One Love means great t'ings ta me. It means dis love toward everyone on de planet, everybody dat 'ave life. Everybody need ta 'ave dat love. Ya jus' want de person ta know dat de 'eart is so true. Becuz love is 'appiness, ya know, and love is everyt'ing dat people go down on dere knees and pray fe. Sometimes I pray ta 'ave more ta give. I really want more people ta be wit' dis One Love spirit becuz anywhere ya doan't 'ave dat love motivatin' dere are problems. When ya come 'ere ta Jamaica, to see Scram, I tek care of ya. Dat too is One Love."

"How do you feel this One Love?" Robert continued.

"What is important fe de people ta know is ta be dis true 'eart person. If ya didn't know de way of One Love, de day ya get in contact wit' dis feelin' is de day ya become a newborn. It's not 'ard ta find. It's real natural. Everyone dat is alive felt it but not everyone cherish it. Becuz de Creator, 'E do it so spiritually dat everyone gets it. So if one day ya 'eard dat people are mistreated in some place ya 'ave nevah been and ya feel sorry fe dem, from a distance, dat's de way ya cayn show ya love miles away and people cayn feel it and ya cayn assist dem and ya get inta dere 'eart and everyt'ing reveal in such a way becuz dis true love is so great."

"So what you're saying is that if we see a war on the news," I said, "and we feel sympathy for its victims, they feel these feelings and it helps them heal?"

"Ya, ya. Dat's what I'm saying. Yes. Spiritually dat cayn happen. Becuz when Nelson Mandela was in jail, dere was a cry from Jamaica, from artists, singers, in TV, in newspaper and dat went out spiritually to help free him."

"You said people in power need to know One Love to help the poor people," Robert asked, "but how do poor people express One Love?"

"Even dey must 'ave dis sympathetic feelin' fe dere neighbor too. But if de big guys know dis love, dey would not want to send de soldiers ta fight and de soldiers would not want ta fight. But dere is not much people feel like dat. Robert, how far ya believe dis One Love business goin' ta reach before t'ings take it ta a point dat it won't be so corrupted?"

"I think if more people find out there are people like you here," Robert answered, "and people like us there and that we're not so alone, things will get much better. When ya go by and yell 'Rastafari!' at your brother, then you both feel not so alone."

"The One Love dat Rastafari speak about is de same love dat everyone 'ave," Scram said.

We talked for awhile until our tiredness, and Jamaica's mosquitoes, let us know it was time to go. We made plans to pick up Scram early the next morning.

"When I was talking with Haile Selassie," Julia said as we drove home, "everytime he would say 'JAH I' for 'joy.' That's my Rasta name—JAH I. So Haile Selassie gave me my new name." We all laughed. We later learned that Julia means joy in Hebrew.

Early the next morning, Robert, Julia, Alicia and I picked up Scram. We travelled east along the coast past the Reach Falls turnoff and drove another hour to Bath Fountain, near the town of Bath. Legend has it that Bath Fountain was discovered in 1609 by an escaped slave whose wounds were healed by its hot waters. By 1699, the English gentry were coming up to seek relief from everything from colds to venereal diseases. Soon a hospital and a hotel were built and the area flourished as a cultural center for the English elite until local political infighting ruined the ambiance of the town. It is now regaining some of its lost luster and the 17-room Bath Fountain Hotel has reopened, complete with private hot baths and a small restaurant. Directly behind the hotel, the springs bubble out of the riverbank at a very hot 128 degrees and pour into the small creek. Anyone can go there for free.

We drove into the village of Bath and stopped for a cold jelly coconut. While we were there, Scram met a couple of local teenagers he knew and they ran ahead of us to the baths to be our guides. Refreshed by the jellies, we drove the mile or so to the baths, looking forward to a restful soak.

While parking in the lot, we noticed a half dozen young men sitting with our two guides, several with long dreads. As soon as we pulled up, our guides and four others descended on us like vultures. Within seconds we had lost all control and we were being jostled about, our towels and backpacks ripped out of our hands and, with a guide or two on each of us, we were noisily hauled up the path to the springs. None of us liked it but we were helpless to stop it. Going up the trail I looked back. Two guys were washing my rental car and another picking a bouquet of flowers.

Where the hot springs boiled out of the riverbank, there was a narrow concrete and rock ledge. Our guides almost forcefully grabbed us and pushed us down on the hard ledge, while they dunked our towels into the hot water. There was no permission asked and no explanation given as to what would happen next. Then, while we laid there helplessly, they spread the towels over us. It was hot! Painfully hot! They kept dipping the towels in the hot water and draping them over us. I was about to tell my guide to stop, when he started a hot water massage, very rough and not in the least relaxing.

After 15 minutes or so of this rough treatment, it was over and my guide said he wanted forty U.S. dollars for each person. I told him there was no way I was paying two hundred dollars for five massages and finally, after a lot of bargaining, gave them twelve dollars each, just glad to have the whole experience over with. I was disappointed that Robert's first adventure with us was a worse hustle than what he had gone through in MoBay. On the other hand, I couldn't help but feel compassion for the predicament of these young men. Someone once said poverty is madness and we had just witnessed some of both.

"Wouldn't it be wonderful," Julia said as we drove out, "if Jamaicans could come together and ask how they would like their island to be if they were a tourist here. Then if enough people could agree to just work towards that goal, to make this place a fun, loving, open-hearted place to visit, it would start to happen and tourists would flock here just because of the good vibes going around. This would be a place to go to renew your One Love, just like Verley said that day on the river."

"Jamaica could be the bad trip tent of the world." I said.

"What's de bad trip tent?" Scram asked.

"At the pop festivals back in the 60s and 70s," I said, "there was a big yellow tent you would go to if you were having a bad psychedelic trip. The staff in the tent had tripped before and knew what you were going through. So if you thought you were going crazy, you'd just go there and they'd talk you down. They'd give you a lot of love and just remind you that you'd come down and everything would be OK."

We arrived at Reach Falls after an hour drive. After Bath Fountain, it was an oasis of serenity. Renny, the only vendor, was there with his big smile and kind words. We chatted with him for awhile, bought a few bamboo cups and then hiked down into the falls. As always, Reach Falls worked it's magic and within minutes we were all frolicking in the water, the tension of the drive and the incident at Bath Fountain, draining away. Robert enjoyed snorkeling below the falls, exploring small caves in the company of tropical fish.

After leaving the falls, we stopped at JAH Priest's craft stall. He was sitting on a lawn chair reading *The Way of The Shaman*. JAH Priest is part guru, part playful child. He has long yellowish white precepts and his dreads were wrapped in a colorful turban. Wire-rimmed spectacles are set on a smiling, kind face. As Scram and Robert continued their dialogue and Alicia lay in the back seat listening to her music on her headset, Julia and I pulled up a split log bench and engaged him.

I told him about our day at Moore Town and asked him if he had ever thought about a connection between Maroons and Rastas.

"Not definitely," he began, speaking slowly, distinctly with an impish grin on his face, his eyes twinkling like that of a young child. "Because the Maroons and Rastas are going to the same place but in different ways. We are heading for the same thing, for that connection with the eternal that is energy. The only thing that can do better for mankind is mankind. My 2001 motto is 'Once I was blind but now I see that the light of this world is just us.'" And he breaks up laughing. "I'm looking to find God. I'm looking to find Satan. I'm looking to find a duppy (ghost). I'm looking to find an angel and all I find is man and woman. And where do they come from? They tell me that God made the woman from man's rib but what I have seen is man coming from woman and woman coming from herself. So I have concluded that when those two molds come together and make a child, there is God."

"What do you sense will happen in the next 10 years?" I asked.

"Yes, mon. Yes, mon. Hear me now. I would call it cosmic consciousness. What I think is that you will have a consciousness growing and you will have an unconsciousness growing because there must be a balance because it is by so doing we do not become stagnant. There are things official and artificial. The artificial will have to go."

"What do you mean?" I asked.

"The artificial is like a shadow. For instance, the kind of food we are eating. We can't survive on such. So the people will have to change to the natural thing to live. The food is what makes you. So if you are to survive in a certain way, you must be conscious of your environment, conscious of your food, conscious of the air you breath, the water you drink."

"JAH Priest," I said, "I've been thinking that the reason the Rastas here are so clear is because the highest consciousness might be created by the fire of slavery and poverty, not by abundance."

"Yeah, mon. My enemy is my friend," he said, "because every time he attacks me, he sends me a little higher. Sometimes I get a little lazy and that person can push me to learn a little more. I am bringing myself to the water, not being anything. I'm the tree. I'm the dirt. I'm the car. I'm everything. I'm nothing. I want to be like the spring coming from the mountain flowing into the sea. Sometimes it goes under. Sometimes it goes around. Sometimes it goes over. Sometimes fast, sometimes so slow. That's what I aim to be. And there is nothing that can wash water. Water wash everything. So nothing can touch me, but like water, I wash everything. Attached to nothing. Defined by nothing."

At this point, Robert and Scram joined us.

"Everybody ask me why I don't buy a lottery ticket," JAH Priest said. "I tell them I'm afraid to win." This cracked Scram up and he jumped around laughing clapping his hands. "If I get money easy, everyone will come and bother me because they want the money easy too, and soon I would have nothing again. It is like the story about a master and his disciples that were on a long journey so they put everything they needed for the trip into a big cart hooked to a horse. One day they come into a village where everyone was starving. The disciples said, 'Master, we must share our food with the people in this village.' The master said, 'The food we have would not even feed the village for one meal and, if we do that, then we will not have enough to finish our journey and we will starve here too.' Well, one of the disciples went into the village where he saw a mother giving suck to a baby and he stole some food from the cart to give it to her. And when the rest of the villagers saw that food is around they ran to the cart and ate all the food and the horse too." Again he cracks up laughing.

"Ya, mon, dey eat up ta de horse, too," Scram said laughing wildly.

We talked awhile longer, enjoying his wisdom and humor. Soon the mosquitoes came out and our hunger came on so we thanked him and started to leave.

"Ya should go visit my son, JAH LandSea. Sometimes I am de student and 'e is de teacher," JAH Priest said as we got in the car.

"Yeah, mon," Scram said. "I'll take dem to see 'im."

"Scram, how do you deal with hustlers like those at Bath?" I said, as we drove toward the ocean. "Every day several people here ask me for money. Not really hustlers but just people when I'm in town, or someone in Moore Town, or some of your customers. Sometimes it makes me so uncomfortable that just going into town to get film is a hassle. More people ask me for help here in one day than in my country in one year. I give some to almost everyone but if I lived here, we'd be broke. They'd eat my horse. How do you deal with it?"

"Well, 'ear me now. Dere are beggars and dere are 'ustlers and dere is a big difference. A beggar needs what ya give 'im. 'E caynnot provide fe 'imself everyt'ing dat 'e needs no matter 'ow 'ard 'e tries and when ya give ta 'im, 'e is very much 'appy and will love ya forever. Ya feel it in ya 'eart. But a 'ustler, maybe 'e cayn provide but 'e jus' doan't want ta or maybe 'e t'inks becuz ya 'ave somet'ing, ya owe some ta 'im and when ya give ta 'im, ya doan't feel de love like a beggar loves ya. But I told dat Rastamon Steve (a longtime guide at Bath Fountain who is known for his kindness) dat dos young guys need ta get demselves in line. Becuz wherever ya go, no matter 'ow nice people are ta ya, de wolves come looking like Rastafari. Dey knot up dere 'air but dey doan't learn not'ing about Rastafari."

"So with a wolf you feel it in your gut, not your heart, because he's emotionally tugging on you like you owe him something," I said. "It's like you feel in some way responsible for him, which is what he wants you to feel, like at Bath Fountain."

"So it is. So when I go down de street, every day I give somet'ing. But I doan't 'ave ta give ta everyone. Some days I cayn't give more den one person becuz I doan't 'ave enough. I 'ave ta save a portion fe myself. If I have five dollars, I know dat I cayn give away two and I doan't give one person dat ask me two dollars but I give maybe four persons fifty cents each but only ta de beggars, not de 'ustlers and when my two dollars are gone, I seh when de beggar ask me, 'I sorry I caynnot 'elp ya but I doan't 'ave not'ing ta give' and 'e know dat it's true and 'e cayn understand," he said and laughed. "Sometime someone seh, 'Scram, give me some money ta buy some cigarettes' and I seh, 'No' becuz I'm not goin' ta burn my money like dat.' It's so 'ard ta get money on dis island so ya come like a god and goddess dat people ask ya like dey ask de Almighty. Yeah, mon. Ya appreciate ta de people by givin'. But not every mouth cayn be fed. So if dere is not enough in a situation, ya doan't start. Dat what JAH Priest tried ta tell ya. Becuz o'ter people get jealous if ya get what dey doan't get. Money make friends and money break friends."

Or as Bob Marley would say, "Money make ya suffer and money doan't make ya suffer. It in de mind, ya know."

Everywhere we went Scram was always sharing what little he had with others, letting young Rastsas sleep at his shop, buying someone a beer or giving them a little cash from what we had given him. If we passed an old person selling a few things on the roadside, he would often ask us to stop and buy some bananas or vegetables. Once we saw an old man very slowly walking with a cane on our way to Moore Town.

"Ya got any of ya good pineapples, Mistah Pierce? If ya do, we'll tek one," he said. With that the old man dropped his cane and literally skipped 50 yards to his shack and skipped back with a big pineapple. He wanted 20 Jamaican dollars but we gave him a hundred. Because he was almost blind, Scram had to tell him it was a a hundred dollar bill not a 20, which brought a big grin and tears to his eyes.

"Did ya see de way dat old mon run?" Scram said laughing loudly. "'E skipped like a little boy. We make 'im very 'appy today. Everytime we go by now we buy a pineapple." And we did.

After this discussion, dealing with beggars didn't bother me. I actually enjoyed going into downtown Port Antonio. Each day I would give away what I thought we could afford in small amounts but never to the hustlers. I could always sense who was a hustler by whether I felt their request in my gut or my heart. Saying "no" became easy and saying "yes" became easy, both there and back home, where the financial problems are not always acute but the emotional ones often are. It became clearer on how to set my personal boundaries and feel comfortable with them.

Farther down the road we pulled over by a little shop to get Alicia some batteries. Across the street, a few teenagers were playing volleyball on a small beach.

"Ya see dat beach? Years ago I clean up dat beach so de kids 'ere would 'ave a place ta play," Scram told us as we leaned on the car. "And after 'Urricane Gilbert, I clean up Dragon Bay Beach so we could open stalls dere. Before de 'urricane, I ran de restaurant at de Dragon Bay Resort. I rented it from de 'otel and ran it fe myself. I 'ad six people dat work fe me and I was makin' money but when de manager's wife saw dat she wanted it so 'e came ta me and seh, 'Scram, I not married ta ya so ya got ta go'," Scram says, laughing. "And den I cleaned up Winifred Beach, all de junk, all de batteries and all dat stuff. It took months and den I opened a stall dere. Before den, almost nobody went ta dat beach. Now it is a public beach wit' many stalls. I do dis ta uplift dis area."

We drove awhile along the ocean and stopped at a thatched roof restaurant on the beach in Long Bay for dinner. It was beautiful. The sun was setting and the moon rising. A warm breeze was blowing from the ocean. As we awaited our meal, Robert and Scram talked at the bar, Julia and I sat at the table and Alicia frolicked on the beach, playing with the waves on the shore—a picture of beauty and innocence. Soon we all gathered at the table to eat. Scram started talking to Alicia.

"Dere were elder ones when I was small dat teach me and if it were not fe de instruction dat dos men give, I would ot'erwise grow up ta be lesser dan what I am and if ya came ta Jamaica," Scram said, pointing to Alicia, "like a 'eart person, like I would consider ya now and if we 'ad lot's more good people fe ya ta move around wit' while ya are 'ere, ya will 'ave bettah, bettah, bettah, bettah ideas all de way, fe all yah life. Kids grow like dat. Ya 'as a good intellect becuz we exercise our love in yah midst."

She nodded but looked a little quizzical.

"I was sehin' in plain words, I was sehin' dat if ya come ta Jamaica now, and ya find Scram, old mon who ya love so dear and if ya find more people like Scram in Montego Bay when ya go dere or Negril when ya go dere, ya want ta come back ta Jamaica becuz all de friends dat ya goin' ta meet, we're goin' ta love ya in a nice way and wish ya de best and ya like ta know dat if ya come wit' yah friends, we de same person ta treat dem de way we treat ya."

"I would like my friends to come here and meet you," Alicia said.

"Ya know what build dat love vibe so? Ya know when ya jump out of de water and ya come straight up ta Scram to see what is 'appening and ya come inta my kitchen and ya seh, 'Scram, ya alright?' I like dat. I like dat vibes, ya know and when ya leave, dat make me love ya more and I hopin' ta see ya quick time and we cherish all dos vibes and worship dem and we pray good prayer fe ya dat in yah school ya 'ave friends and ya doan't 'ave much enemies becuz ya are goin' ta be loved by everyone, Yes, so it is."

"How was your day?" I asked Robert as we drove back to the hotel after dropping Scram off.

"Well, Bath fountain was kind of scary but I really enjoyed Reach Falls. I mean if the Garden of Eden were to be recreated it would include Reach Falls. But I didn't care that much where we were, I just wanted to talk to Scram about this One Love. Man, it's been a long day and I'm bushed but I still want more. I don't think I'm at the heart of this One Love yet. Scram describes it as a sympathetic feeling in the heart but when I asked him if he felt it for everyone, he said he didn't. That kind of threw me because that doesn't jive with what he said about loving everyone in the four corners of the earth. I'm still trying to figure out if this is the same love that Jesus spoke about. On the road he would reach out to share with some people but not everyone. This kind of disappointed me. I asked him how does he distinguish who to share this love with. He said something like he recognized the vibe in them."

"Maybe he's just choosing not to connect with people with negative vibes," I said. "One Love doesn't mean not having personal boundaries. If you're not careful here people will eat everyt'ing and the horse, too." We both laughed.

"Well it was amazing how everywhere we go his heart just reaches out to these people," Robert said. "I mean everytime he yells 'RASTAFARI!' he gets pumped. He knows what it means and they know what it means. Their sharing this love with each other. There's responsibility in it. I mean if people read this book, I don't want it to sound like this One Love is some sappy thing. He was sharing with people who are responsible, not the wolves. I think it's multifaceted. What kind of love do you show to your enemies? Is it the same love your show your friends and family? But Scram reaches out to almost everybody all during the day. We don't do that in the States. There's so much suffering here but people seem to give what they can. Back home it's all me, me, me, my, my, my."

"I think when you live in an impoverished culture like Jamaica," I said, "there are a lot more opportunities to nurture and serve. The suffering is right on the surface. That's why Scram has such joy. He spends a lot of his day serving others in a way that really makes a difference to them. You develop much more compassion and understanding for human frailties because poverty can really push people to do desperate things they wouldn't otherwise do. Affluence hides a lot of sins and suffering. Poverty reveals them."

"Yeah. When Scram reaches out to these people," he said, "they're all in the same predicament and the least little bit he gets, he shares with other people. And those people come back and share with him. It's like one big family. And having experienced having a lot of money and then having the rug jerked out from under me and having none, I can relate to this. And I know what that does to you," he continued. "It builds your strength of character, like it does with Scram."

"And you," I added.

"And me. Or it turns you into the guys at Bath Fountain, who are just looking to get money from everyone. You're on the outside looking in at a banquet where you're not welcome. It really does a number on people here. It turns them into hustlers. It does the same number on the people in the States."

"Well, let's see what tomorrow brings," I said, as we pulled into the San San.

Chapter 17
Missing Pieces

"We ask ourselves, who am I to be brilliant, gorgeous, talented and fabulous? Actually, who are you not to be? You are a child of God. You're playing small doesn't help the world. There's nothing enlightening about shrinking down so someone won't feel insecure around you. We were born to make man into the glory of God that is within us. It's not just in some of us, it's in everyone."

—Nelson Mandela

The next morning, Robert, Julia, Scram and I drove back to Moore Town to meet with Colonel Harris. As we drove up we started talking about our journey.

"Sometimes ya 'ave ta take time ta mash de ant," Scram said.

"What the hell does that mean, Scram?" I asked, laughing.

"Well now, if ya wan' ta see de ant's guts, ya got ta mash 'im very slowly ta see de bottom of de belly of de ant. So ya 'ave ta take time ta mash 'im and dere is no rush because dis is a never-ending book dat we are writin' and ya cayn read dese books over and over, like listenin' ta Bob's songs. Dis is not only fe today or tomorrow. It's forever. Rastafari! And when dey put de two books together, de information is so straight from de first book ta de second book and de t'ird book, dat when dey look at de last word, dey gonna see a big comma," and he let out a big belly laugh.

Rasta Heart

As we drove into the village, I felt conflicted. I strongly felt we were following some circuitous path, clues to some mystery that would reveal itself eventually. I also wondered if this was just a wild goose chase, having nothing to do with Rastafari and the book.

Colonel Harris' house was in the middle of the village, a modest concrete block home. We were ushered into his living room, a well-lit but cramped room decorated with personal effects and pictures. A young woman let us in and then she retreated into the kitchen. Colonel Harris, seated in a large armchair, rose to greet us, giving Scram a warm handshake. Scram then wandered into the kitchen to chat with the woman.

Colonel Harris is tall and thin, with patches of short white hair surrounding a bald top. He was dressed in light-colored dress pants and a clean short-sleeved dress shirt. Though he moved slowly, he seemed to still have a lot of vitality. In this small village, he knew we had talked with Geria and Ovals and he knew what they would have told us. As Julia, Robert and I sat down, he informed us that he agreed to meet with us because of his fondness for Scram but that since we were late and he rested every afternoon, we could not stay long. We thanked him for seeing us and agreed to keep the meeting brief.

We chatted awhile, talking in generalities about his term as colonel. He talked about how he and all the colonels were people chosen because they had the welfare of the community at heart. He wandered all around, telling a long detailed story about how he was first chosen as the colonel. Finally, knowing our time was running out, I interrupted him.

"Colonel Harris, let me be honest with you. Several people we have talked with said that you stopped the tribal drumming before you were the colonel and that you did not teach the children about their own culture when you were the teacher for 30 years. They feel that this crushed the Maroon spirit. I do not feel comfortable putting that in our book without giving you a chance to address this."

"One of those statements is a lie and the other a half-truth," he said emphatically, his face beginning to twitch with nervousness. My heart went out to him. "I did teach the children about the Maroons. I have travelled around the world telling people about our tribe to Paris, to Washington, to The Smithsonian. Why would I not teach our own children? But I would not call myself an authority on Maroon history. The greatest Maroon that

244

ever lived was Grandy Nanny."

"What about stopping the drumming?" I asked.

"That is a half truth. Where the drumming is concerned, there was something that worked against the children's education. When I came back here to teach, no Maroon child had passed the third year examination for 20 years. The Maroons are all psychic people but of course you have degrees of this. And amid these great people who could cure diseases with the drums and the dancing, we also had some cheats who were assassinating the character of a few noble, honorable people and they were using the drumming to convince people that their children were not smart. These children had to pass the examination but couldn't because of these few cheats. So I had to put a stop to a section of the drumming. For more than 20 years, no child had passed the examination until I started teaching. Many of the adults forgot that their children could pass examinations."

"And the drumming was part of that somehow?" I asked.

"The drumming was a major part, the drumming and the dancing and the singing. The drumming was a part of our spiritual healing and so it was used by a few tricksters and as so often happens when things like this take place, you find that tricksters have the ability to convey their thoughts to make people believe them."

"Do you now regret that decision?" I asked.

"No, no, no. I have no regrets," he said loudly. "You must understand that the elders would not have chosen me to teach the drumming and the history. It is not what I know. It is their duty to keep the spirit of Nanny and the Maroons alive. They would not have chosen me. I was the colonel and the teacher and I did that well. When I came it was a small C grade school with fewer than 100 students. In a few years there was over 500. And while I was the teacher it became an A grade school in a shorter period of time than any other school in Jamaica."

He rose to let us know it was time to leave. Scram emerged on cue from the kitchen. Colonel Harris asked us to sign his guest book and showed us a picture of him with the King of Ghana, who had visited Moore Town recently. Giving us a goodbye in the native Koromantee language, he showed us to the door, probably as glad to see us leave as we were to be leaving.

We met Ray Sterling and Ovals by Nanny's grave and all wandered over to a small shop for some cold drinks. Robert, looking moody and detached, stayed at the store chatting with the locals while Ray, Julia, Robert, Scram and I sat under a large shade tree next to the church cemetery near Aunt Lizzy's grave. We told Ray about our meeting.

"I was a student of 'is fe 16 years an 'e never taught us any of dat about Nanny or de Maroons," Ray Sterling said.

"Ya, mon, when I was in school," Scram added, "durin' dos days dey taught kids about King George and dat de cow jumped over the moon and de dish ran away wit' de spoon," which cracked everybody up.

"De reason dat 'e stop de drummin'," Scram said, "is becuz it was goin' on next door ta 'is 'ouse and if yah 'eart is not right, de Nyabingi drummin' will drive ya away. Ya cayn't tek it. Nyabingi drummin' is de 'eartbeat. What we really like is dis One Love springin' up in de 'eart of everyone and de people in dis place 'ave dat 'umble spirit so ya know love is somewhere around and a few cayn see de o'ter side and dey cayn tell de people about dis becuz not everyone want ta see de light on de o'ter side."

"Colonel Harris said something in there that is very important for all of us," Julia said. She had been very quiet and thoughtful since we left his house. "I just can't get it out of my mind. He said that the elders would not have chosen him to keep the spirit of the Maroons alive. It was not his job. He was the colonel and teacher. He is not an elder. This is very crucial to understand."

"I'm not sure I'm following you," I said.

"He said the people who keep the tribal spirit alive, who teach the children about Nanny, who teach drumming and dancing, is not the duty of his tribe. He is from the administrator and politician tribe. He is not an elder. He did his job well. He administered the village and improved the education of the children. Inspiring the children and keeping the tribal spirit alive wasn't his job. That's your job. You're the elders, not him. You've been complaining for years that these colonels do not understand and uphold the Maroon spirit. It was never their job. That's what he told us. It's your job and you must now come forward and accept it."

"I see where you're going," I said. "There needs to be a council of elders to maintain the vision as well as a town council to run the infrastructure. And members of these councils would come from two different tribes, one from the administrator tribe and the other from a priest and priestess tribe."

"Who would be on the elder council?" Ray asked.

"Anyone who wanted to be," I answered. "Anyone that felt they were able to hold purely this vision and could communicate it to the people. By elders I don't mean physical age, I mean spiritual age. The council of elders would have to work in unison together, with very little ego. So if you weren't coming from that place, from One Love, it wouldn't draw you. You'd want to be a colonel or major. Elders wouldn't be elected. You would just come forward and share your vision and the people would be free to follow you or not. If you were coming from love and clarity, they would know it and follow your advice. If you weren't, they'd probably just ignore you or laugh at you."

"But now that I think about it, it's much, much bigger than that," Julia said, her eyes glowing with excitement. "This is the missing piece we've been looking for. It's the pivotal point of our journey and Colonel Harris just gave it to us. He didn't mean to but he did. It's the reason we've been guided to follow this out, to keep coming up here."

"Julie, why do ya seh it is de pivotal point?" Scram said.

"We've all been doing what Ovals and Geria's been doing," she continued. "We've all been complaining that Babylon is not teaching love to the people, the One Love that Nanny taught. It's not their job. We're the elders of this planet, not them. This whole tribe of people around the world that know One Love, the people we're writing this book for, are the elders. Most of us have been complaining that the leaders are leading the people astray and they are. But it's not their job to teach love. It's our's."

"So we need to stop complaining about the leaders, whether it's Colonel Harris, President Bush or Prime Minister Patterson and come forward and demonstrate to people what One Love is," I said, picking up on her thinking. "The political leaders can't do that. Usually they don't know One Love. Scram, you've said that a hundred times. The big guys don't know One Love so teaching it to the people can't be their job. Even the few leaders that knew it, like Jesus or Gandhi or Dr. King, weren't political leaders. Most political leaders lead people into fear, greed, or war."

"That's why we've been feeling that Bob Marley's music is like Nyabingi drumming calling together a global tribe of people to teach One Love," Julia said. "He's been sending us this message, instructions on how to teach this to the world. So have these singers like Bushman and Luciano. Now all we need to do is demonstrate how to make their words a reality."

Or as Luciano sings, "I look around in the world today, I see the children are going astray. I try to teach them how to kneel and pray and let your love be the only way."

We drove back to Port Antonio listening to Bob Marley, everyone lost in their own thoughts. We dropped Robert at the San San and connected with Alicia, who was having a great time with Nino, Lisa and a few Italian guests. Julia and I went over to Scram's where he cooked an Ital meal and we talked a few hours absorbing the impact of the day. Robert had said he was tired but I could tell it was something more. When I got back to the hotel, I went to his room.

"Are you OK?" I asked. "I wish you would have joined us under the tree in Moore Town. It was incredible."

"I don't know. I'm not sure I understand where you're going with all this in Moore Town," he said. He seemed distressed. "I mean what does this have to do with One Love?"

"A lot," I said, explaining what insights had taken place in our trips there but I could tell he wasn't really listening.

"It all felt like you were social engineering," he said. "Like you were imposing your own belief system on them. I thought you pushed Colonel Harris too hard. You were coming on too strong. And I was disappointed in Scram for not intervening."

"I see us as catalysts, messengers, connecting things," I said. "We asked him about statements made by other Maroons. And then we brought what he said back to them. And maybe it would be better if we were black but JAH sent white."

"And all this postulating about how to create these big events around the book signing and building paths up there bothers me," he said. "There seems like a lot of ego here. It's disappointing. I just feel like nature, and JAH, should take their course."

"Nature often takes its course through visions," I replied. "We're not forcing this. We're just letting this happen and watching where it's going."

Rasta Heart

"I guess I'm still wrestling with the fact that Scram still has some hold outs from his love. I mean Christ didn't have any hold outs. Or maybe He did. He didn't chose to heal everyone and He said if people don't honor you, you should brush the dust from your shoes and leave and don't throw pearls before swine. I'm just really confused. I think I'm just going to head back to MoBay tomorrow. I'll spend the night there and catch my plane the next day. I'm just not in a place to go back to Moore Town with you guys. I'm very uncomfortable with all this. I guess it's like when you told me the night I arrived that the trip would be different than whatever I expected and would bring up a lot of issues."

"Well, Scram's not perfect and maybe when we are looking to someone for wisdom we expect them to be," I said. "Scram still has his unhealed relationships, his hold outs, but that doesn't mean he doesn't have a lot of wisdom to teach. Bob Marley showed we don't have to be perfect to claim our place as teachers, as elders. Even though he was still human and wrestled with his own issues, that doesn't mean that his songs, his message, didn't heal a lot of people. I'm sorry you're leaving and I don't think you're really at the heart of what's bothering you. I don't think you've peeled this onion to its core."

"What do you think is bothering me?"

"Well, you're looking at two older men on whom you relied for guidance and wisdom and you're discovering we don't have all the answers."

"I need to get away and think," he said dejectedly. "This is too intense for me right now."

The next morning Julia and I left early to get Scram to return to Moore Town to see Mr. Sterling, Ray and Colonel Sterling's father. When we told Scram that Robert was leaving later that day, he asked to go to the hotel to say goodbye before we went. We arrived to find Robert by the pool having breakfast alone.

"If ya are in a serious position wit' ya job, we doan' wan' ta spoil dat," Scram began, thinking Robert was leaving early because of a job commitment. "Yah job is goin' ta secure ya to be back another time. I know de boss man's always feel corrupted about t'ings like dat."

"He is the bossman. He owns the company," I said.

"Oh, my goodness," Scram said, laughing loudly. "Ain't dat somet'ing, mon. It's yah turn ta relax on de planet, ya know. Ya time ta find yourself

249

an Ital river ta cool off in."

"So you guys are going back to Moore Town?" he asked.

"Dere are some people in de mountains we want ta see if we cayn get some information from. We want ta see if we cayn take one stone for Robbie and kill more dan five birds. But we try ta get dis goin' business out of ya mind, fe ya ta relax today. So we could tek ya ta a different place den Moore Town."

"No I don't want you to do that."

"Well, maybe when we get back, we cayn take ya ta a different region ta feel de same vibes. Dat what me wan' ta give ya. I wan' ya ta take dat vibe 'ome so ya wan' ta come back soon. We wan' ya ta cheer up de mind. We're workin' on de mind, ya know? And when we find a good friend like ya, we wan' dat ta be fe life."

"Well, you guys go on up. Maybe I'll still be here when you come back. I'd like ta spend more time with you, Scram."

"Dat sound good and when ya seh like dat, if ya even got ta go, I know what de 'eart is sehing. Me like dat speech."

Chapter 18

The Mystery Unravels

*"The ends you serve that are selfish will take you no further than
yourself: but the ends you serve that are for all, in common,
will take you into eternity."*

—**Marcus Garvey**

On the way to Moore Town, Scram told us a story about what
had happened between him and Poncho, a white friend of his. It
seems Poncho had wanted to build a house in Port Antonio and
he hired Scram to manage the project, handling everything from locating
the land to overseeing the construction. Scram had only taken a fraction
of his agreed upon wages, asking Poncho to save the rest for him until the
job was over. Because of personal and financial problems, Poncho stopped
the job near the end and returned to Europe without paying Scram several
thousand dollars that he owed him. Poncho later returned and finished the
house but was avoiding Scram and payment of his debt.

"I cayn forgive dat mon but I cayn nevah forget what 'e did ta me. Even
after dis, when 'e could 'ave 'elped me when people were tryin' ta frame
me, 'e wouldn't and now when I see 'im, I cross de street."

"Scram, obviously you haven't forgotten but really you haven't forgiven
either," I said. "In the Old Testament they said that justice was an eye for
an eye and a tooth for a tooth. If someone punches you, just punch them
back. Don't kill them. Don't escalate things. But that just creates a lot of
blind, toothless people. Then in the New Testament Jesus comes along
and he says if a man strikes you, turn the other cheek. If a man steals your

coat, don't stop him. However, there's even a higher level than this that says there's nothing to forgive. They never attacked you. They never did anything to you."

"Yeah. Dey did it ta demselves," he said, laughing.

"No, no." I said. "That's just saying you still want to see them suffer for their attack on you. I'm talking about seeing there was never an attack, that we only perceived it incorrectly as an attack. We become aware that we create the Ponchos in our lives who ask for our love in very strange ways so that we can give it to them. They're just looking for love in all the wrong places. Poncho thought love was your money, so he stole it. And if we say, 'You're a sinner but since I'm a better person than you, I'll forgive you,' that only increases their shame and makes them feel worse about themselves. They just keep doing what you want them to stop doing. But still you would have boundaries. You might sue Poncho in court but you'd do it with love."

"But what should ya seh ta dat person?" Scram asked.

"All right, good, as you would say," I said and we all laughed. "True forgiveness says, 'My friend, you've never harmed me. You simply forgot who you were, you forgot your own divine nature as a perfect child of JAH. And in this state you did something that appeared to be an attack.' This is forgiving to heal. It reminds people of their bigness not their smallness. That's what Jesus meant when he said on the cross, 'Forgive them Father for they know not what they do.' His whole life story was just to show this true meaning of forgiveness, not forgiveness to destroy but forgiveness to heal. Real forgiveness is *for giving* not *for getting*."

"And your mother said those exact words when Dolores stole all her jewelry," Julia said.

"That's right," I said. "Scram, you want me to tell you a great story about my mother?"

"Ya, mon."

"Five years before my mom died she went blind and lived alone but she had her own apartment and plenty of friends to help her and she was enjoying life. One of her friends was Dolores, an older woman who had been hit by a car a few years earlier. Since then her behavior was very strange and she started to steal things from friend's houses, from stores, even silverware from restaurants. Well, when my mother had a small stroke I went

Rasta Heart

to Florida to help her and while I was there she gave me all her heirloom jewelry, several thousand dollars worth, and told me which ring I should give to Julia and this pearl bracelet should go to Alicia and this gold broach to Julie. So she gave them to me and I put them in a drawer in her apartment. One day while I was still there, Dolores came over to visit and later that night I noticed the jewelry was gone. I told my mom, 'Mom, I think Dolores stole your jewelry as well as some of my money.' So my mom got on the phone and called Dolores and said, 'Dolores, sweetheart, I know you didn't mean to but when you were over here today you stole some of my jewelry and some money so I'll send Robert over to help you look for it.' I went over and Dolores was grief-stricken and we searched everywhere but we couldn't find it and she couldn't remember where she hid it. So, I went back and told my mom and she contemplated the loss of a lifetime's worth of heirlooms for about a minute and then said to me, 'Aw, it's just a bunch of old jewelry. Call Dolores and see if she wants to go out for dinner'. And ya know what, Scram, everyone is Dolores and everyone's been hit by a car and that car's name is Babylon," and we all laughed.

"Well, I couldn't answer dat jus' yet but I 'ear what ya seh. I still 'ave ta burn 'is 'eart a little before I talk ta 'im. 'E sehs 'Howdy' ta me and I jus' raise my 'and 'e doan't 'ear my voice. Dat is a burning, ya know."

"Yeah. But the ones that ask the loudest are the one's that need it the most," I said.

"I doan't believe 'e need it."

"He needs it," I said. "It doesn't mean you don't have boundaries. You don't have to spend time with him again or even like him as a friend. It just means that in your heart you love him and remember that he never really attacked you."

"He's your best reminder of all times," Julia said. "He's the biggest gift that JAH can give to you. Otherwise you're both in bondage together, you by your resentment and judgment and Poncho by his shame."

"Well, right now 'e is very much ashamed fe what 'e did ta me and I would like one day ta ask 'im ta sit down and consider what 'e 'as done."

"That's still forgiving to destroy," I said. "You must help him to love himself or he won't love others. We have to understand that the three of us are asking to express greater love and when we do that we are asking to be shown all our barriers to this love. Then all our unhealed wounds, our

253

ancient hatreds, our judgments and resentments, will be revealed to us and this is going to make us uncomfortable at times."

"Dat so good, Robbie. T'is true."

We drove through the village, dropping Scram at the store, and continued to Mr. Sterling's house, where he and Ray were waiting for us. Mr. Sterling was a feisty man in his mid-nineties and could easily have passed for 70. He was short and slim with white hair and a white moustache, a quick smile and a twinkle in his eyes. He spoke very slowly, emphasizing almost every word. His thinking was clear and crisp.

We settled onto his porch and he explained that before we could begin, he had to get the cooperation of the ancestors through a rum and water ceremony. This was to insure that he would be free from any harm by the ancestors. Speaking Koromantee prayers, he would alternately put white rum and water in his mouth and spray it across his threshold. Once the ancestors were properly appeased, we started talking. He said he would tell us things that no one outside the tribe had ever been told, except for one other American writer who had interviewed him several years earlier.

For a long time he told us personal and tribal stories, many of which we had heard. I was beginning to feel that this trip had been in vain when Julia interrupted his dialogue.

"Mr. Sterling, did your foreparents ever tell you about a white woman with Nanny?" Julia asked.

"That woman was a betrayer," he said, his face changing to anger, his body rearing back. "Her name was Missy Blay Washee."

"Why was she a betrayer?" Julia asked.

"She was a friend of Nanny but really a spy for the English and she betrayed us," he said, staring angrily at Julia as if she was Washee.

"Do you think she was an English woman?" Julia said, her excitement building. "What if you learned that she was an Irish woman, a woman who was an indentured servant for the English, almost a slave herself; a woman who saw her own country enslaved by the English. She heard the call of freedom and came to live free up here with the Maroons. She must have taught the tribe English.That's why I hear that Irish accent in your voices. I feel very strongly she really helped Nanny and was cast as a traitor in the myth told to the Maroons by the English."

"The English told us that she was their spy and during the treaty nego-tiations, Washee took messages to the white people from Nanny," he said, "And the white people said to themselves, 'If you are with Nanny and betraying her, what will you do to us?' and the English killed her."

"That is the story the English told the Maroons. Think about it. What would be the best strategy to weaken Maroons, to have them divide against each other? It made Nanny look like a fool and turned her own tribe against her. They turned you against each other and against the women who had helped you for all those years. I think she so loved the Maroons, she could never betray them," Julia continued. "How could she live for years up here, totally removed from the society that was trying to enslave people, and still betray you. Why would she? A white woman could only have lived up here in this remote area, with all Africans, if she loved freedom and their cause. The English had to say she was their spy or else her presence here would be a huge embarrassment to them. It said at least some white people thought the English were wrong. Why would they kill her if she had been a successful spy? They would have honored her."

"Mr. Sterling, the Maroons in Flagstaff said Nanny brought the mes-sage of One Love to them on her Great Trek," I said. "Did any of your parents or grandparents ever tell you about Nanny teaching One Love to her people?"

"That is what they told to us," he answered. "That movement served for years in the fighting."

"Even for those you had to kill?" I asked.

"Yes, One Love, One Love, that is what she taught," he replied. "But I did not read that in any book. It is what our foreparents told us. And when we signed the treaty with the English, we signed in blood, not ink. And that's where the One Love was linked. My blood is your blood. Your blood is my blood. We all have one red blood. Beneath the black covering or the white covering, one red blood."

"Did the Maroons start to capture other runaway slaves after the treaty?" I asked.

"After the treaty, the English said the Maroons were to fight alongside them if and when any force of the world should be against us because they were now blood brothers. So they went out according to the treaty signed and helped the government capture Paul Bogle." Paul Bogle was the leader of the Morant Bay Rebellion of 1865. He is now one of Jamaica's seven national heroes.

"The first treaty did not say they would capture runaway slaves. After the first treaty was signed and agreed and the praises were given to us for bravery, Washee went and signed the agreement with the English people to recapture runaways. Missy Blay Washee was cooperating with the English and betrayed us. And that agreement to capture runaway slaves was another agreement made by Missy Blay Washee and they even agreed to capture Maroon freedom fighters here in Portland."

"I think she went in there to talk with the English and make peace," Julia said, "and the English retold this whole story to make her look like a traitor. Then there would be no union. By making this white woman the betrayer, the English weakened you with your own anger."

"And this pitted the Jamaican people against the freedom fighting Maroons by making them capture runaway slaves," I added.

"I met a young Jamaican tour guide on the beach the other day," Julia continued, "and she talked about the Maroons with as much anger as you talk about Washee. She considers Maroons bad people because they captured runaway slaves. These angry stories continue to weaken everyone, even today. Nanny knew this hate and anger weakened her people. That's why she taught One Love. When Nanny caught those bullets and sent them back at the English, she was showing us how we must deflect people's anger and hate back to them and not absorb it ourselves."

"That is why we want to introduce our book here in Moore Town," I said. "And this valley, the place where blacks in this hemisphere first won their freedom fighting with One Love, is holy ground. Anywhere that ancient hatred becomes present love is holy ground."

"And that is why I am signing up with you, now," Mr. Sterling said, the smile returning to his eyes as the anger receded, an ancient hatred becoming a present love. "This is a wonderful story, a very wonderful story. The only story that compares with this story is the one of the Israelites."

As we drove back through the village we found Scram at the store talking with friends. Scram wanted us to meet with Bookson (Major Charles Aarons), a local man who had been on the village council for 49 years and had been the second-in-command for 12 years under Colonel Harris. He had been playing the drums and blowing the Abeng since he was three and had dedicated most of his life to upholding the Maroon culture.

Bookson was a well-built man who looked to be in his fifties but was in his seventies. He was quick thinking and serious but his occasional smile revealed a warm heart. He wore a plaid turban and was clean shaven except for a moustache. As we sat on his porch, he told us his view of what was happening to his tribe. He felt much was lost when the drumming stopped because the spirit of the ancestors spoke through the drums, telling the people not only of the past and present but, more importantly, of the future. When the drums could no longer be played in the center of the village the children stopped learning the drumming, dancing and singing of their tribe. Before the drumming stopped, celebrations in the village center could last for days.

We told him about our visions in Moore Town. He began to tell us of a vision he had for a museum and herbal clinic there. He showed us a letter he had written. It read:

"Crucial to our success in defeating the British, was our knowledge of herbal medicines from the plants that grew in our communities. This knowledge was handed down to us by our ancestors and our leader and our founder, Queen Mother Grandy Nanny. We still retain knowledge of these medicines today. As assistant chief of the Moore Town Maroons, I see the urgent necessity for the creation of a museum for the cultural preservation of my people's history—a museum, as well as the writing of books on Maroon history and culture from the perspective of the Maroons. Over the years many outsiders have come to the communities to conduct research on Maroon culture and history. A museum would allow us to call in all materials written on us and artifacts discovered by anthropologists that are presently in libraries and archives scattered around the world. The museum would greatly improve the economic conditions of the Maroons of Moore Town. It will create employment opportunities for my people in a manner complimentary to their culture and will be a vehicle in expressing their creativity. In addition, the museum will be of great value to the island of Jamaica as a whole to increase tourism and add Maroon culture to its present day life. It will also elevate the status of Jamaican women by fore-grounding the historical achievements of the illustrious founder and foremother, Queen Mother Grandy Nanny. In fact, the museum would be dedicated to the memory of this outstanding African woman. Organizations and individuals interested in assisting me to establish this museum or herbal clinic or in the manufactur-ing and marketing of herbal medicines, can contact me at: Major Charles Aarons, Moore Town Post Office, Portland, Jamaica, West Indies."

He had also written a letter asking for assistance with another issue. It seems that when Jamaica negotiated its independence from England in the early 1960s, the Maroons, who by treaty are part owners and rulers of the island, were totally disregarded. The British turned over the island to the Jamaican politicians without consultation with the Maroons thus violat-ing the original treaty. He was now looking for assistance in righting this wrong.

"When we introduce the book from here," I said, "we should have a special ceremony to ask for healing between the Maroons and the English. Actually between the Maroons and the Jamaican people as well as between the Jamaican people and the English. All these ancient hatreds need to be put to bed."

"You know, this would complete the circle of One Love," Julia said excitedly. "And that would be the healing of the nations," Julia said. "Make One Love a reality. You could play the Nyabingi drums that day."

Before leaving, Bookson showed us a copy of the treaty with the English. It had been signed by Quao, Nanny's brother, but not by Nanny. He also said that the original Maroons were not freed by the Spanish before the English invasion of the island, as the books claim, but rather received a spiritual message that people were coming to make war and that caused them to flee into the mountains.

The three of us walked down to the store to find the ever-gregarious Scram. Scram was roasting some yams for us in a small fire by the store. We got cold drinks and joined a handful of people hanging around. I talked with a man who said he had recently lived for two years in the village with no money.

"Fe two years, I doan't spend a dollar and I was nevah 'ungry," he told me. "I go ta de spring fe my water. I pick coconuts, breadfruit, star apples, bananas, all dos t'ings. I grow my own vegetables, even rice and I generate my own fuel fe de night, coconut oil. It burns wit' water. Maroons cayn make light wit' water and no wind cayn put it out. Durin' de 'urricane, dat is what Maroons used. I lived in Kingston and worked as a security guard and I left. I love it 'ere. I eat de best food, no fertilizer, no chemicals, no chlorinated water, no polluted air. Ital. I 'ave been livin' Ital fe 14 years."

By now it was late in the day and I wanted to get off the roads before dark. As we drove back to Port Antonio, we talked a lot about what Mr. Sterling had said. Julia had known in some deep part of her that this white woman was with Nanny, just like I had known there was a strong link between Nanny and Rastafari. But why had we known this? Coincidence? Reincarnation? Or were the ancestors talking to us?

Back at Scram's we continued our talk.

"It's hard for me to imagine what is must be like for you, Scram, living here your entire life," I said. "I mean all of us are living away from where we were raised and even if I went back there now, I wouldn't know anyone and a lot of things would look different. My entire family is spread all over the country. That's the way it is for many people now. And this is probably the first time in human history that so many people have no sense of home, of roots, like you still have here. It's so different for you. In your 57 years things here look pretty much the same and even though a lot of people have left, you've known hundreds of these people your whole life. But with so few jobs around, it's still almost like living in slavery".

"Well now, slavery really never ended. Dis PNP and JLP, we are under dere vibes de same way. Dey take de chains off our feet and off our 'ands but dey put it all around de pasture and dey 'ave dis big gate dey call de embassy and people never get out of dat pasture and t'ru dat gate. An de only way we get proper justice is ta leave de pasture. An dey jus' throw some slop in dis pasture and dat is all we get ta eat. Ya, mon, dat is de way it is now."

Or as Bob Marley would say, "JAH is de rightful ruler and 'E doan't run no wire fence."

"These business and government entities are so huge and so powerful, what can we do to stop this exploitation?" I continued. "They realized they can't get away with physical slavery any more so they're using economic and political slavery. It still get's them the money, only now they have to pay a little out. But it's just like Nanny said that if you hate your enemy it weakens you. You become enslaved by your hate, your bitterness, your resentment. They take the shackles off your feet and then you, not them, put them in your mind and heart. But as I talk about it, I think the way to look at it is through One Love."

"'Ow ya seh?"

"Well, we must love these leaders even as we work to change the system because it is only love that will change their hearts and then they will change the system. That doesn't mean we shouldn't reveal the greed or immorality of Babylon or fight to change it, but we must do it with compassion, recognizing that these leaders too are trapped by their greed, trapped in Babylon's values. So if there is more love going around, it will infuse into everyone, not only into the people fighting to change the system but also into the people fighting to maintain it. If we hate each other, it just hardens things. Bob Marley vacillated between bitterness toward the oppressor and One Love. He needed to point out the downpression, the exploitation, and to mobilize people to work against it. But sometimes he wouldn't remind us to do it with love. Sometimes he would, like in "Rastaman Chant" when he sings, 'You cannot win the revolution except with Rasta. If ya win it any other way, you going to fight again but with Rasta, dere's no more war.' He was telling us we can only triumph good over evil with Rasta, with One Love, not bitterness and resentment. Now Luciano and Bushman keep reminding us of this love in their songs."

"Yes, Robbie. So it is."

"Healing this global exploitation is even harder in some ways than ending the Vietnam War or corrupt racial laws," I said. "In those cases the goals are clear—get the politicians to stop the fighting or change the laws. But with this type of international exploitation the system is massive, involving billions of people, countries and treaties all over the world, multi-national businesses that we have come to rely on. There are few clear objectives to accomplish to correct it. You can fight a thousand small battles but it just reemerges somewhere else. The only way to change it is from within, by changing people's hearts, even those of the business and

Rasta Heart

political leaders."

Like almost all post-colonial countries, when Jamaica won its independence from England in 1962, it was left broke, with little help from the "Mother Country." It soon turned to the IMF (International Monetary Fund) and the World Bank for loans. In the 70s Jamaica owed $800,000. Today the island owes over $7 billion. Fifty-two cents of every Jamaican tax dollar goes to service this debt. The interest rates charged to Jamaicans by local banks and government agencies range from 19 to 40 percent, rates dictated by the IMF, an organization controlled by the U.S. and Western Europe.

Since the passage of NAFTA (North American Free Trade Agreement) things have only gotten worse. Being forced to abandon its trade duties and tariffs by the IMF, Jamaica must now compete with the world, something that is impossible for it to do. Produce from the U.S., subsidized by American government programs, have swamped the island. For many years the U.K. has given Jamaican bananas special purchase pricing to help the former colony that they exploited for over 300 years. Chiquita and Dole are now trying to get this arrangement thrown out so they can capture the worldwide banana market, where they already have a 95 percent market share.

In 1980, under a U.S.-backed program, the Caribbean Development Bank and the World Bank established "free zones" in the port of Kingston. Ships arrive daily from the U.S. with piece goods to be assembled by low-paid Jamaican labor. Most workers earn around $6-10 per day, keeping them in grinding poverty. Since these zones are not considered part of Jamaica, these companies pay no taxes or duties and they are not required to adhere to any labor or environmental laws. Unions are prohibited and many workers are not even allowed bathroom breaks. Like most multinational companies in today's global economy, if they find cheaper labor elsewhere, they move.

This situation is pervasive throughout the developing nations, due in part to the economic and political policies of the industrialized countries. Global communication has excited expectations and overturned centuries of traditions. But the global economy has not fulfilled these expectations or replaced traditions with anything of meaning. The IMF and the World Bank insist these countries slash their budgets to pay their debts, thereby gutting their social and humanitarian programs. The global economy has cut them off from its benefits, while enslaving them to low paying, tedious jobs. Over 2 billion people, a third of the world's population, earn less than $2 a day.

We drove back to the hotel and as we were pulling into the drive we saw Ronald, the waiter at the San San we had met on our April trip. He was walking down from the Fern Hill Hotel looking dejected. We stopped and asked him to join us by the pool for a cold drink. Alicia was eating with friends in the restaurant and Robert was gone. He had spent the morning with Alicia at the beach and then caught the two o'clock plane to MoBay. I was disappointed he had left.

We started to talk with Ronald and learned he had left the San San when it closed for a month earlier in the summer for repairs and was now looking for work elsewhere with no luck. I gave him some money to help him and he looked at me with tears in his eyes.

"Ya doan't know 'ow much dis means ta me today. If I did not get twelve dollars by tomorrow fe rent, I would 'ave ta leave my apartment. Before ya picked me up, I was watching dis worm try ta get across de hot driveway. 'E was almost dead and I knew 'e couldn't make it so I picked him up and put 'im in de cool grass an 'e started to wiggle and come alive. I just prayed to JAH dat someone would come and 'elp me off my hot pavement like dat and jus' den ya drove up."

As we were walking with Ronald toward the street, the hotel phone rang and Nino said it was for me. It was Robert calling from MoBay.

"I wanted to tell you what happened today," he said, sounding calmer, more assured. "When I left the San San, I was upset and disappointed and thought I had wasted my time and then I got into an incredible conversation with Brent Hill, the policeman out at the Port Antonio airport. The fact that this would happen during the very last minute of my time in Port Antonio was reassurance that I was hearing what I was meant to hear."

"What happened?" I said, intrigued.

"Well, I still didn't understand the concept of One Love. I was left wondering, *What does it have to do with the specifics of Jamaica and the people and their predicament? Why is it coming from Jamaica?*

Rasta Heart

And I didn't really understand what Babylon was. It never all jelled together until I started talking with Brent. Then I began to understand that these people are still oppressed. The good-hearted people here are oppressed and it's a challenge every day to send this love out into the world. Brent does it by going and teaching students to study and to obey their parents. It was meant for me to meet somebody who was really involved in the community and doing good."

"It seems that many of the teachers of peace in the last 50 years have been people of color," I said. "People like Gandhi, King, Mandella, Tutu, Sadat and Kofi Anan."

"When I came down here I was still trying to correlate what's going on here with what went on with Jesus," Robert said. "Why today? Why Jamaica? And why does the theory of One Love move me the way that it does? What is it? And now I see that it's so similar to what happened in Palestine in Jesus' time. People are oppressed. It's the people on the bottom of the rung that are the wise people. It's the same message. It's love your neighbor. Love everyone, even the oppressor. And Brent can see everything the matter with the Babylon system, but he's stuck. Scram's stuck. There's nothing they can do. Which is why it's time for a change. People's hearts are changing but still they're oppressed. The system is so abusive."

"So your epiphany was that you had put their level of service in context with their predicament?" I asked.

"The epiphany was that it's so much like what it was back then in Palestine. The early Christians' faith was transmitted verbally and in simple homes of the poor. Like the Rastas, they were persecuted by their government and society. These early Christians probably had dreads if they followed the Jewish law not to cut their hair or beards. And just like the Rastas think that Babylon will fall soon, the early Christians thought the second coming was imminent, which is really the same thing. Both groups had this historical perspective. The early Christians saw they were involved in the prophesied first and second comings of the Messiah. The Rastas see they are one of the tribes of Israel and that Haile Selassie is the foretold King of Kings, Lion of Judah. Even some of the individual characters are the same. Just like the Rastas Scram said are living way back in the hills, John stayed separate in the desert and mountains. And just like Paul came down into the city to teach, that's what Scram's doing. My whole experience here just raises my awareness of Christianity. It became human to me after I talked with Brent. He sees Babylon as all the leaders and politicians lining their pockets so that nothing gets down to the bottom. I finally asked him, 'Well, wouldn't you do that, too?' and he said, 'No!'"

"So what's your frame of mind now?"

"Well, I don't really want to get back into the material things. I was strengthened by having met this guy who is my age and doing really good things—what his heart is telling him to do."

"So you thought your teacher here would be Scram or me and it turned out to be a policeman."

"Right. He was just like me. And on the plane to MoBay I got to thinking about what you said about you're not really social engineering. And I realized you were right and that I had been judgmental without having all the information. Scram said something which I thought was very significant. He said something about so many misunderstandings occuring because of a lack of information. So many problems are just from people not having the right information about something or somebody. You may think you hate somebody but in reality you may just have the wrong information or not enough information. And I think this information is going to have a major impact. If it's had such an impact on me, it can influence other people."

"How has it changed you?"

"It's helped me realize that all over the world, in different situations, there are people like me who are working to do good. Sharing that feeling, what Scram was doing everyday which I didn't understand at first, will allow this to grow. One Love means cultivating a kind, sympathetic heart—a loving heart—toward your fellow man. It's reassuring to know that they're are people all around the world, in all kinds of circumstances, whose hearts are leading them to do these wonderful things."

"Has it reoriented your goals?"

"Totally. Everyone in Jamaica says, 'Don't worry. Be happy.' I feel like things are in someone else's hands. The great rewards in life are pursuing this heartfelt connection with other people who are fighting Babylon. I fight in the States. Wall Street just wrecked our economy and they came to me before it all fell. Four Wall Street firms came to me when I only had four employees and said, 'We've identified your Internet company as a company that can go public.' This is the kind of garbage these people were profiting from. They were just stealing money. There was no way my company was positioned to go public. And that's the Wall Street game. They make money just taking you public even though they know it's a bad idea and people will eventually lose. They continued to increase their personal fortune off of other people's vulnerability. I had to say 'no' to that. That's like Brent saying 'no' to padding his pocket with bribes."

"Whether you have to say no to someone giving you millions or someone giving you fifty bucks, it's the same."

"Yeah. It takes equal courage. It's the same trial."

"Anything else occur to you?"

"That One Love can lead to a more abundant life. I'm just beginning to understand this. But already I sense I'm at peace more—about relationships, about work, about my family. It's a peace that comes from understanding. My whole life feels like it's just starting to open to living."

"I know," I said. "It's like Babylon spins you counterclockwise and One Love spins you clockwise and when they meet, you're either going to reverse your polarity or there are going to be sparks."

"I guess I had a few sparks before my polarity got reversed," he said and we both laughed.

Chapter 19
JAH LandSea

"We must become members of a new race, overcome petty prejudice, owing our ultimate allegiance not to nations, but to our fellow men within the human community."

—Emperor Haile Selassie I

We spent the next day playing with Alicia, who wanted to go snorkeling with Lisa and Bruce, a couple we had met at Dragon Bay. They ran Too Canoe Cruises, a large catamaran sailboat that took tourists around the area and snorkeling on a reef near Monkey Island.

Leaving Julia on the beach at Dragon Bay, we boarded the boat, along with a few other tourists. I soon fell into a conversation with one of them, Georgia Berland, an attractive and articulate woman around my age. Georgia was a professor of humanistic psychology at Sonoma State University in the wine country above San Francisco. I had briefly studied there in the 70s when I was living nearby as a hippie in my school bus. We even had some mutual friends. Georgia was in Port Antonio for several weeks as part of a Canadian International Development Agency grant to train locals in the tourism industry. She was organizing people and community groups to oversee the training and make sure it met their needs and goals. She was also working with the Portland Chamber of Commerce to

266

Rasta Heart

help them support and develop the local economy.

As we talked, she told me that the Americas' Sail Tall Ship Event was to be in both MoBay and Port Antonio the following summer in June of 2002. This event, held every few years in different locations, featured the large masted sailing vessels built in the 18th and 19th centuries. She went on to say that this would be a very big event for Port Antonio, with a new marina being built and international press attention.

"Another piece of the vision was revealed today," I told Julia when we returned to shore. I told her about the upcoming event. "The Tall Ship event is going to draw the international press here. We could introduce the book that weekend. We could have another healing ceremony then. I am going to tell the Tall Ship committee while they are down here in Port Antonio honoring the civilization that created those ships, the civilization that forced the Maroons to be runaway slaves in the mountains, that we will be in the mountains honoring these slaves that these ships brought over. We would like to invite them to join us in One Love and have a 'Healing of the Nations' ceremony where the Tall Ship crews and the descendants of the slaves will come together and ask for forgiveness and healing so that some of the animosity can be healed. This would complete the One Love that Nanny said Maroons must show toward the English. After a ceremony with African drumming and dancing in Moore Town, we could all march down to Tichfield Fort and light a healing bonfire with the tall ships anchored behind us in the port."

Julia loved the idea and the three of us went directly over to Scram's to tell him about it. He listened wide-eyed and kept punctuating my dialogue with "So it is!" (This event, *The Fires of Forgiveness*, was heald in Port Antonio on June 14, 2003)

"Robbie, Julie," Scram said with a twinkle in his eye as we were leaving later, "dis morning I saw Poncho in town. I 'aven't seen 'im fe almost a year. But I talk wit' 'im and hug 'im and 'e told me, 'Scram, if dere is anyt'ing dat ya ever want ta do, ya come see me and I will 'elp ya.' So I t'ink now everyt'ing fine wit' me and Poncho. I feed 'im but I still use a long spoon."

The next day, Julia and I picked up Georgia from her hotel. She was staying in a cottage perched over the ocean at the Frenchman's Cove Resort, directly across the street from our hotel. We went to visit her friend,

Rasta Heart

Bent Kristensen, or Kris as he is called, in downtown Port Antonio. Kris, a Danish man in his sixties with a white beard and white hair surrounding a bald top, has lived there for three decades and runs General Business Service LTD., a small company that assists local businesses with consultation and support. He is well-known in the area for his commitment to helping others.

We liked Kris immediately and told him about our plans. He could see that it had the potential to not only bring much needed positive attention to Jamaica, but to Port Antonio and the Maroons of Moore Town as well. He agreed to discuss the idea with the Chamber of Commerce. We really wanted these two open-hearted people to meet Scram, so with Kris' stipulation that he could only stay a few minutes, we drove the few blocks to Scram's.

As soon as we walked in Scram greeted Kris like an old friend, which he was. Kris knew Scram by his other name, Thomas. We all settled around Scram's table and Scram served some wonderful Ital food.

"So you know Kris?" I asked Scram.

"Ya, mon. Dis is a good mon. 'E is like a revolutionary fighter fe de Almighty. 'E is a Rastamon."

We discussed our ideas to encourage everyone to heal their relationships.

"Can you imagine if that could become a large movement?" Kris said with a gleam in his eye. "It could change the world. I believe that when creation took place and God formed the planet earth, He started in Jamaica and in Jamaica He started in Portland."

"Yes. So you know it can happen, too," I said. "I think Jamaica is where this is supposed to begin and then emanate out from here. There is something very dynamic about this island. It birthed people like Nanny and Garvey and Mutabaruka and Colin Powell and Marley. Some of the proudest and bravest African tribes went through hell here and are still going through it. But out of this fire something very phenomenal and pure has been created. The sufferation had to be there. JAH knew what he was doing. It takes millions of years of pressure to turn a lump of coal into a diamond and that diamond is Rastafari! And its vibration imbues this island and its people. There is something special going on here, some destiny fulfilling itself and I think a lot of people sense this. If enough people here will step forward to heal their relationships, something very powerful will happen that will be a pattern for the world."

"He's been giving his life to this the last 20 years," Georgia added.

"I had the pleasure of meeting Bob Marley a couple of times," Kris said. "When Pan American airways opened the Intercontinental Hotel I was there with Sister P. Bob Marley and the Wailers were playing. Early the next morning, I was down at the front desk and there was this person sitting all alone, doing nothing, in a huge chair at six o'clock in the morning. So I went over to him and said, 'Mr. Marley, is there anything I can do for you?' And he said, 'No sir, I just want to sit here for a minute and enjoy this beautiful morning breeze that is blowing and to realize that I had the privilege to be in a place like this.' Those were very important words from one of a kind."

One can only imagine what could have been going through Bob Marley's mind that morning. Here's a man who lived his entire life in poverty and only a few years earlier was homeless and eating from the dump. Now he's the toast of the town, with wealth and fame.

At this point Scram rejoined us after serving his food.

"Do you know they're building a saffu yard in Charles Town (another Maroon village near Port Antonio)?" Georgia said. "It's an African ceremonial building. And they're building a quao, which will be a Maroon museum. Frank Lumsden in Charles Town is putting it together. There is so much going on in Portland so a big part of what I can do is bring people together who don't usually work together."

"That's perfect. I'll call Frank and see if he wants to have a healing ceremony in Charles Town, too," I said.

"Scram, what can I do to help?" Georgia asked. "If you had one thing you could tell me in your wisdom, what do you think I should do?"

"Well, a person dat wan' ta give ta de community, even knowledge, if ya wan' ta give knowledge, it's so easy to appear in the midst of dem and discuss wit' dem and when ya speak wit' dem, dey will love ya. Dey love ya fe de love dat ya 'ave and if ya come wit' de true love, people love ya and if you doan't come wit did true love, people will know."

"If I may say this now," Kris said turning to face Georgia. "Georgia Berland has already done more than any other human being I could think of. In the 10 days you have already helped so much. You may not see the effect of it before you leave but you planted some very beautiful seeds of goodwill, fellowship and love in the minds of many, many people."

After Georgia and Kris left, Scram suggested we go visit, JAH Priest's son, JAH LandSea. We had met JAH LandSea a few days earlier in front of Scram's. After our brief talk with him, we felt drawn to see him again. The three of us drove about 20 minutes up in the hills directly behind Port Antonio, past small subdivisions with half-built houses, with breathtaking views of the ocean. On the way up the road crossed a small, shallow stream. Several people had parked their cars in the middle of the stream and were washing them—a roots car wash. We parked where the road petered out and walked a hundred yards or so to a hilltop opening surrounded by trees with one large shade tree in the center. Off to one side was JAH LandSea's small abode, a makeshift one or two room home he shared with his children and wife. I was amazed to learn his teenage daughter was inside hard at work on a computer. Soon they hoped to get phone service so she could connect to the Internet.

Julia, JAH LandSea and I sat on benches under the shade tree and passed a pipe around. Scram sat under another tree and soon fell asleep. He had been up all night on his new job cleaning the downtown marketplace after it closed. Like his father, JAH Priest, JAH LandSea has Indian features. He looks to be in his forties, medium height, slim and well-built like a runner. He had a constant twinkle in his eyes and a mischievous grin on his face. He wore pink drawstring pants and no shirt. His dreads were under a white turban and salt and pepper precepts surrounded his face. He danced around a lot and gestured with graceful hand motions as he spoke—a cross between a playful leprechaun and an Indian holy man.

Julia told him about her vision for the fires and path where people could meet Rastas.

"AHHHH! I 'ave some brethren now in de same energy level and in de circle we doan't 'ave ta talk. We just look at each ot'er and know and understand. We make no sound. Jus' by our eye contact and vibes," he says raising his eyebrows and scrunching up his face a little to give us an illustration.

"You sit around for hours like that?" I asked.

"Yeah. And we no speak. Sometimes we laugh. But we 'ave a conversation wit' de I and if de next brethren come we just look at 'im like dis (he slowly blinks his eyes several times) and if 'e cayn't get inta de vibes, 'e gone because de spirit not active in 'im. 'Ere me now. Dis is what people should understand, too. First, you, like me, as an individual must know de love dat dey need fe 'imself or 'erself. So den 'e or she cayn give it or plant it and it will grow. What would bring peace to all man's minds is jus' ta know de love dat 'e or she needs so dey cayn plant it and share it. So even de love dat you wan' yah wife ta give ya, ya must first plant it in 'er so dat in return she cayn give it ta ya. Den 'er love dat she need, she 'as ta plant it in ya so ya cayn give it ta 'er. Becuz ya might not know exactly what she want and ya doan't wan' ta make a mistake," he said and doubled over laughing.

"So ya seh, 'Tell me. Reason wit' me.' It's like one brudder seh, 'Now dat we found love, what are we gonna do wit' it.' First we must know what I, de first person I, is all about. So no matter 'ow much we try to 'elp someone, even de mon in rags in de street, dere always somet'ing dat will be left ta de individual. Jus' like my Granny used ta seh, 'Ya cayn lead de donkey ta de stream but ya caynnot force 'im ta drink de water' ", he says and breaks up laughing again.

"When my son was a likkle boy, 'e wan' ta play cow. A friend got a rope and tied it around 'is neck and tied it to a tree and den 'e start ta cry and seh, 'I doan't want ta be de cow. I wan' ta be de owner of de cow.' So dat is like Babylon. Dey all want ta be de owner of de cow."

"JAH LandSea, don't you think it is not so much the Babylon system that is enslaving people but rather everyone's enslaved minds are creating the Babylon system?" I asked.

"I really would not look on it dat way becuz I find really and truly ta 'ow people manifest demselves before me. I see dat it really not God jus' dat create de people but de people dat create God. So in a sense, ta what ya seh, I and I believe dat we create de whole Babylon wit'in ourselves. AHHHHH! Even me wit'in myself, I struggle wit' dat. I often seh ta myself ta come out of dat old Babylon t'ing and ta come inta dis One Love wit' all of us. But even like 'ow ya people come now, me got ta show ya 'ow Babylon work, ta stop it. But in myself now, I must take a deliberate step ta change it to One Love becuz I cayn't take dis fire anymore. We cayn't stay in dat water forever, in dat struggle."

"But it's still not going to be easy becuz when God saw dat de people need some saving on eart' and 'E want someone ta go, so 'E called all 'Is angels in 'eaven and 'E seh, 'Who will go down dere and die fe Adam's fallen grace?' and dere was an half an hour of silence in 'eaven. No one wanted ta go," he said, laughing.

"But one voice said, 'I will go.' So dat why I know dat Jesus came and t'ru dat man I learn somet'ing by 'Im coming down and making 'Imself lowly ta men."

"Is it a struggle for you to keep your heart open to us because we are white?" I asked.

"Well, it's not gettin' so big now. It used ta be big, maybe 10 years ago becuz I t'ink like ya might be a traitor. But since I was a child, I was a different yout'. My Granny seh dat spirit used ta come and take me away. When I was a baby dey would find me by a bush and I wanna talk ta myself and now I always 'earing a voice in me telling me 'ow ta balance and maintain a certain peace in myself, or dat fullness, so dat I cayn float and fly. Dere is always somet'ing in me dat wan' ta make me like people and I wan' dat feelings ta flow and it take me now ta wan' ta know God. From when I was a likkle boy, one intention me 'ave, ya know, one aim—to know God and ta get as close ta 'Im or 'Er as possible. So I was always different from o'ter yout's. So if someone bump me or fool me, I no fight. I like ta sit wit' older people and listen ta dem and I find myself gettin' connected ta people and ta 'elp people. Like de old people crossin' de street in town, people jus' pass dem, but I jus' take dem and carry dem across, over ta de post office ta get dere pension and I just a boy but I caynnot resist. Me jus' 'ave ta do it. I feel like I'm jus' responsible fe dese people. I 'ave white friend in Sweden. I 'ave white friend in Germany. I 'ave white friends dat come 'ere. My best brethren is an English surgeon in Ochie," he says, holding two fingers close together. "I know dis brethren over 28 years. It was a struggle ta love de white mon but ya 'ave ta pass it, like an examination. Ya know where ya wan' ta reach so ya 'ave a vision. Dat bond of hate, it 'as ta be broken. I always see myself as a universal figure," he said getting on his feet and gleefully hopping in place. "An if I see myself as a universal figure den I 'ave ta be universal in all respects. So I 'ave ta learn to love de Chinaman, de white man, everyone."

"Iniversal love," Julia said, laughing.

"Yeah. Iniversal love becuz people is people everywhere and love is love

Rasta Heart

everywhere. Dere is no white love, black love, pink love, yellow love. All de same love."

"Is it hard for you to be loving in poverty?" I asked.

"When I was a kid dey tell me story of 'ow Brer Fox went ta a 'ouse and in de yard dere was a fat dog wit' a collar on 'is neck and e' was tied ta a tree and Brer Fox seh, 'Brudder Dog, why ya doan't chew t'ru dat rope and run away?' And de dog seh, 'De master feed me an if I run away, I be skinny like ya.' An Brer Fox look at 'im and seh, 'I rather ta be 'ungry and free dan 'ave a big bellyful and chain on my neck.' Dat 'ow Babylon do it, chain up dat brudder and fatten 'im up," he said, clapping his hands and throwing his head back laughing.

"Well, my grandmudder wasn't an easy lady. She always tellin' me t'ings ta guide me t'ru life. She was a Rasta even though she didn't grow locks. All 'er sehin', all 'er doing, de way she cooks, she eats, she lives, is a Rasta life and she said ta me, she said, "Bwai, t'ree t'ings ta be a mon and ta 'ave power ya must 'ave in dis world. T'ree t'ings. Money, manners and clothes. But if ya cayn't 'ave de t'ree of dem and ya 'ave ta choose, I would advice ya ta take manners becuz by 'aving manners dat will lead ya ta de end of de world. But money might not 'elp ya and clothes might not do becuz clothes will mash up and burn up. But manners, principles, dat dignity, dat Divine t'ing wit'in ya, will take ya wherever becuz dat is what people gwanna wan'. Dat energy."

"Your grandmother was a wise woman," Julia said.

"Yeah, mon. And dat is why I cayn be 'ere wit' ya and laugh and talk and play and when I see de people dat go ta church on Sunday or Saturday, I doan't always see dat joy, dat life, dat fullness. But now dey start ta bring drums, dancing and make a joyful noise and start ta dance," he said as he jumped up and danced around, swinging his arms out, his head back, laughing. "You must feel de energy, de life, joyful. We are nature. We are wind. We are water and when ya touch de water, ya are de water also and when ya touch de wind, ya are de wind also. But becuz of our economics, our domestication, we caynnot find ourselves in that total state of relaxness where we could float and scoot out and get one with the cosmos. But when we get big, we lose dat child inside. But ya must learn 'ow ta be dat child but act as a mon or a lady. An den ya find dat inner peace where ya cayn be comfortable in all situations. Ya cayn go uptown and be comfortable. Ya cayn go downtown and be comfortable. Anywhere ya go, ya comfortable. Becuz 'eaven is not in de sky after ya die. Even in de Pope's 2000 speech, Pope John Paul told de people dat 'eaven is not in no sky. 'E said 'eaven is a state of consciousness, a state of mind, a joy. It is in ya wit' de love dat ya find wit'in yah 'eart."

"Do you see Babylon getting weaker?" I asked.

"Ya, mon. But it may seem like it getting stronger but like my grand-mudder use ta seh, 'When de old cow die, it kick de farmer.' So Babylon just doing it's death kick now but ya got ta watch out fe it or ya will get kicked."

It was now about four-thirty and JAH LandSea had to go help his wife get ready for a sound system party they had every week for the local community. They sold drinks, snacks and even jerk chicken, though he didn't eat any. It was one of their ways of earning money. We drove to another larger concrete block house a little farther down the hill where his wife was setting up a small sound system while a few children played around. We met his wife and kids and thanked him before heading back to Port Antonio. I gave him some recompense and as I was leaving he said, "Thanks. I cayn use it. Ya know 'ow expensive raisin' teenage girls cayn be." Some things are the same all over.

"I'm beginning to see that there are different tribes," Julia said as we drove down the hill. "There is a teacher tribe, a builder tribe, a child-rearing tribe, a trader tribe, a protector tribe, a money-handling tribe, a food-raising and cooking tribe, everything needed for a complete village life. And we're at our best, our most natural, when we're doing our tribal work. Robert, you and Scram are from the leader/teacher tribe. You both like to communicate wisdom to people. I'm from the priestess/priest tribe. That's why I don't seem to fit in the States where they're under the influence of the trader and money-handling tribes. I love to talk about the love of God and humanity. All of us are capable of being in all the tribes but there is one tribe that we naturally radiate to because our enthusiasm comes out when we talk about that one tribe. I can remember conversations as a child when I was talking passionately about love and philosophy and I knew I had wisdom beyond my years. That's your tribal expression."

As Luciano sings, "I'm claiming my position in creation."

"I have a lot of builder tribe in me too and keep wanting to build things,"

Rasta Heart

Julia continued. "I began to think about Bucky's bamboo geodesic dome. You could build it entirely from native materials with a bamboo support structure and a thatch covering. It could be built for free. In fact, I'll call it the 'Freedome'," she said laughing. "People here could have a large, round dwelling that would be uplifting to be in. A dome is so strong, if you secured it right, when a hurricane came through, you'd just have to repair the thatch."

The geodesic dome is not just another type of building design. It was invented by futurist F. Buckminster Fuller, affectionately referred to as "Bucky" by his friends and admirers. Being the simplest, strongest and cheapest way to enclose space, he designed it "to solve the world's housing problems." Through his many books and teachings, Bucky promoted the concepts of sustainable lifestyles and "small is beautiful." Born in 1895, he was a philosopher, visionary, inventor, architect, engineer, mathematician, poet, cosmologist, and futurist. As a global thinker, he coined the term "Spaceship Earth" and illustrated the concept with his Dymaxion Map. This map shows the continents on a flat surface without visible distortion and shows the earth as essentially one island in one ocean.

Bucky also coined the term "Synergy," defined as a combined or cooperative action of parts whose cumulative effect is greater than their effect if taken separately. He believed synergy to be a basic principle of all interactive systems and believed you could anticipate and solve all of humanity's major problems by providing "more and more life support for everybody, with less and less resources."

"We could have other people help like at The Owner Builder Center," I said.

"What's dat?" Scram asked.

"In the late 70s," I said, "I started a school in the San Francisco Bay Area that taught people how to build their own homes. I had about 20 teachers teaching night classes in the area. Every summer we rented a 300-acre campus of a Quaker high school in the Sierra Nevada Mountains. People would live on the campus and learn to build their own home. It was like camp for adults."

"People could come here and stay in the local hotels," Julia said, "and help us build domes for people. They could take their vacation here, meet you and the other Rastas and help the people here at the same time."

Rasta Heart

"It would be like The Owner Builder Center with jerk sauce," I said laughing.

"Dat sound good ta me, too," Scram said. "When ya come back I will 'elp ya. I know 'ow ta do de thatch."

"You know, I've been thinking," I said to Julia as we returned to the San San after dropping Scram off. "I think we should have two book intros. The first would be during Bob Marley's birthday week in February. This would be the 'Healing of the Nation' celebration focusing on Jamaica. We'll talk with the press and go to all the events and ask everyone on the island to join us in making Bob Marley's words a reality by letting go of their past hatreds, as best they can. It's like the idea you had that day at Bath Fountain. And then in June, we'll have the 'Healing of the Nations' ceremony with the tall ships and the Maroons to expand the concept internationally. This could grow and then people who can teach One Love in other countries can organize their own Healing of The Nation ceremonies."

"Sounds great to me," Julia said, smiling.

We ate with Alicia at the San San. After dinner I called Frank Lumsden to talk with him about having a healing ceremony in the saffu yard he was planning to build in Charles Town before the tall ships arrived.

"And by the way, my wife is planning to build a bamboo and thatch dome here sometime," I said.

"I can't believe this," he said, startled. "I went to Southern Illinois University when Bucky taught there 30 years ago. I was one of his students. He was like a hero to me."

The more people have visions, the more people will have visions.

Later we drove back to get Scram to visit Sister P before we left. Ovals was there with Scram so we all decided to go. Ovals was good friends with her, visiting her everytime he was in town. Scram said though he had known her for years, he only ran into her occasionally.

It was now dark and the four of us drove to the other side of Port Antonio where Sister P ran a small shop out of her home that sold crafts and African clothes, which she often wore. She is a powerful, proud woman, articulate and intelligent. She is well known on the island for her interest in Africa, conducting tours to Ghana and appearing often on Mutabaruka's weekly call-in radio show, "The Cutting Edge", which was airing later that night. We all sat on her porch and we began talking about our plans for Moore Town and the tall ship event.

"Maybe we could call Muta tonight on his show and tell him about it?" I said.

"Muta is in Vienna at a human rights conference," Sister P said. "I don't know about this conference. The only time you hear about human rights is in a top level case. Other than that, you're walking down the street and a policeman knocks you down for a spliff. There are plenty of these cases still, plenty of cases where people get arrested wrong, especially for Rastafari. It is an everyday thing here. The human rights cases are only the high profile ones, maybe five out of 5,000."

"When he gets back, we could invite him to join our healing ceremony." I said. "His support would mean a lot on the island."

"You guys are moving too fast," Sister P said. "You don't understand the Maroons or the Jamaican people. Things don't just happen quick here like in the States. Not everyone in Moore Town will be glad to see you come."

"I think there's plenty of time. It's eight months to Bob Marley's birthday and a year until the tall ships come," I said.

"Well, I'm not so sure people will show up," she said. "Maybe the Maroons and tall ship people won't come."

"It really doesn't matter how many show up," I said. "We don't need to be attached to the results. We just extend the invitation to the banquet, to join us in One Love and each individual can chose to or not. If Muta isn't ready, fine. If the tall ship people won't come, it doesn't matter. Gandhi said don't be attached to success or fear failure. If only the five of us show up, it's OK."

"Well, when you see it like that, it's better," Sister P said.

"The important things is to try," I continued. "Like it says on Scram's wall, 'One Love—Let's try.' Otherwise no one would risk it. What if Martin Luther King had stopped because people told him it might not work and he and others might get killed in the process. Julia and Scram and I are not naive idealists. We've all had our hearts broken but we're ready to try again."

"But still I don't see how this is going to help us financially," she said.

Rasta Heart

"That is where all the other problems come from."

"Sister P, we don't claim to be able to solve all the problems here," I said, becoming somewhat impatient. "That's not our job. That's not anyone's job. That's for all the different tribes together to do. We're the teacher tribe. We are just attempting to kick this One Love thing into high gear, to coalesce people behind the idea of forgiving their old hatreds and making Bob Marley's songs a reality."

"It's not going to be so easy to get people to forgive when they have been hurt," Ovals said.

"It's never easy. The only thing that's harder is living with the bitterness, the resentment. We're just inviting everyone to take the next step toward love, even if it's a small one. Maybe invite your brother-in-law over for Christmas if you've been estranged or be nice to a co-worker. Or release your ancient hatred toward Maroons, whites, blacks, Jews or Catholics. If people take the first step, it will feel so good, they'll take the second and the third and the fourth and they won't want to stop. As love permeates the island in greater force, everything will improve. The employer feels more loving so he treats his workers better. The cop feels more loving so he is kinder. The politicians feel the love so they treat the people better. But it has to start with love or it's not going to work. Only change from the inside of a person lasts. Otherwise if it's forced from the outside, they go back to their old behavior as soon as the pressure is off."

"All this may be harder to do in Jamaica than you think," Sister P said.

"I have no idea how hard it will be," I countered. "This is the perfect place to try. The foundation has already been laid. I don't think it's by accident that Bob Marley was born and lived here. People here have been listening to his music for 30 years. A lot of people know the words to every song. They know what he's been saying, what he's trying to teach. The new artists like Bushman and Luciano have been reinforcing this message. For 70 years there have been Rastas that know One Love wandering the island teaching, setting the example no matter how hard Babylon came down on them. Jamaica needs this healing now. The people here are ready for it—ready to claim their power as Elders and to offer this pattern of forgiveness to the planet. And it will be no harder for countries to make peace than for individuals. If President Bush would have a Peace Department and assign people to figure out how to make peace with all the country's enemies, within a few years those countries would be our friends. All it takes is the desire, even if you don't yet believe it's possible. If we just make the first gestures, it will grow from there because it's what everybody really wants. Everyone is looking for love and we've been struggling against our own current. Now we can just relax and float with the flow of the Iniverse."

"Maybe Jamaica is the hundredth monkey that will trigger healing all over the planet," Julia said.

"What's de 'undredth monkey?" Scram asked.

"It's based on a story about these scientist that went to an island inhabited only by monkeys and they took one monkey out of its tribe and taught it how to use a club to open oyster shells," Julia continued. "Before then, all the monkeys were just smashing them against the rocks. After a few days of watching the trained monkey, a few more tried it and then a few more each day. And when the hundredth monkey tried it, the next day every monkey in the tribe was doing it. But what was more amazing is that when the scientists went to neighboring islands, the monkeys on those islands were using clubs even though they had no contact with the trained monkeys."

"Well, if you really want to write a book on Rasta and have it really be about Rasta, you have to visit the Council of Rastafari in Kingston," she said.

"That's fine with me. Do they know One Love?"

Sister P hesitated a long time. I could see her mentally scanning the council looking for love. "Are you writing a book on Rasta or on One Love?" she finally said, a hint of irritation in her voice.

"To me, they're the same," I said, "but if they're not, we're writing a book on One Love. That's what we came here to find."

"Well, I will consult with the ancestors and see if I should be a part of this," she said as we rose to leave.

"Man, that sort of put a damper on things," I said as we drove to the taxi stand so Ovals could get his ride to Moore Town.

"One Love supposed to clarify anything that get's started," Scram said. "Ta get started ta get de positive vibes, ya 'ave ta 'ave de love and Rasta is a mon dat come out speakin' about One Love and fe dat dey get all de bad treatment. She know dat. But everyone t'inks t'ings cayn work and den dey nevah work. So dey cayn't believe now. Dat's why I work alone

Rasta Heart

and dat's why we're not goin' take a big flock ta carry t'rough dis t'ing. We goin' use a small flock. We need people who 'ave faith and de works, brave people. Sister P should be de one ta be so glad someone comin' ta speed it up. Becuz anyone lookin' inta our faith and seh, 'We doan't want ta speed up,' de truth is not in dem. We need it, mon. We need it so fast and we need someone like ya ta seh, 'Dese important guys comin' and we need everyone ta 'elp out'."

"And our works are going to be like a Nyabingi drumming," I said. "If someone's heart is not in the right place, they won't come so there won't be any violence or trouble. In a way, visiting her was perfect. She's just voicing the doubts we're going to hear everywhere, even at times in ourselves. Like her, we're all somewhat disillusioned and fatigued after confronting Babylon for so long. I can't really blame her for getting frustrated. In mythology she'd be a tragic hero, someone who had become embittered and wearied by combating corruption. It is very hard not to. Only a few like Mandela or Gandhi or King engaged the unconsciousness of their societies and stayed in a loving place and even for them it was a struggle."

"Ya. She's a very brave soulJAH. She just getting tired of de battle some days," Scram said.

"I t'ink when she t'ink more about it, she may want ta 'elp," Ovals said.

"I think she's just weary. But she's helped me to see that we're looking for people who want to help when they hear what we are doing," I said. "People like Kris and Georgia who are eager to participate. If they feel in their hearts that they want to improve the world and if they see there might be a way for them to merge their vision with ours, they will be grateful and we will be grateful."

"Do you think Sister P could be right and people up in Moore Town won't support our ideas?" Julia asked.

"No, mon," Scram said. "Ya see, where we are educating dese people now, is goin' ta be one of de most wonderful t'ings dat was ever done in dis region. We're not waiting on a big crowd. We're not waiting until everybody ready. We're goin' push off wit' t'ree people, four people. We already 'ave de consent of de colonel and dis One Love is so wide, people cayn't get around it. It's so low, dey cayn't get under it and it's so high, dey cayn't get over it," and he broke up laughing.

Chapter 20
Under The Reasoning Tree

"When we let freedom ring, when we let it ring from every village and every hamlet, from every state and every city, we will be able to speed up that day when all God's children, black men and white men, Jews and Gentiles, Protestants and Catholics, will be able to join hands and sing in the words of the old Negro spiritual 'Free at last! Thank God Almighty, we are free at last'!"
—Dr. Martin Luther King, Jr.

Julia, Alicia and I spent our last day before returning to the States hanging out at the beach at Dragon Bay. That evening Scram cooked a delicious farewell Ital dinner for the three of us, Bell and Irman. Afterwards, we drove Alicia back to the San San to spend the rest of the evening with her friends there. Julia and I returned to get Scram. Julia had wanted just the three of us to spend the last evening on a piece of land one of Scram's relatives owned. We had gone there to talk several times before and had fallen in love with it.

"I think I know my Rasta name," I said to Julia as we drove to Scram's.

"What is it?" Julia asked.

"Ras Kind," I said.

"Yep. That's it," she said and we both laughed.

We picked up Scram and drove 15 minutes along the coast to the property. Overlooking the Caribbean a few hundred feet below and a half a mile in the distance, it included a hilltop with a high open field. On this hilltop

Rasta Heart

was the most amazing tree. The species was a ficus, also called a "strangler fig." It began as a tiny epiphyte, which, like an orchid, begins life as a small plant growing on the limbs of another tree. Over several hundred years, it slowly drops its roots from the tree's limbs to the ground and eventually "strangles" the host tree.

This particular ficus, more than 200 years old, had dropped its roots around the stone walls of a "great house" that had once sat on the property. Now two intersecting 30-foot long walls were completely covered with a massive system of large and small brown roots, with openings where the doors and windows had once been. It was a huge 60-foot, root-covered "L." The tree's leaf-covered upper branches spread high and broad, like a huge roof over the walls. It was half stone house, half roots—like some botany cloning process gone awry.

We built a fire and roasted corn Scram had harvested from a small garden on the property. It was almost dusk and a light wind was blowing. The tree frogs were chirping and the bats were darting about searching for their nightly catch of insects. We settled down on a low collapsed mound of building stones under the tree and passed a small pipe around. Soon Scram started talking about his vision of our book. It was a vision that we had heard several times before but always inspired us each time we heard it anew.

"De artists put it inta de heart of dem already," he began, his voice powerful yet clear and calm, full of confidence and love. "It's like we are just finishin' dem up, Robbie, Julie. We are just finishin' dem up, ya know."

"What do you mean by 'just finishing them up?" I asked.

"Ya. Wit' de good news, wit' de good news, yaseewhatImean? Becuz Bob wake up de 'eart of dem already. Bob Marley wake up de 'eart of dem and ot'er artist wake de 'eart of dem. See? So right now, we jus' come ta finish all dos little spots in de 'eart, now we jus' come to patch dem up and ta free dem up. Dey 'ave ta get ready fe dat. Dey 'ave ta get ready fe us becuz we just come ta finish up now."

"So Bob Marley's music has been sending out this message of One Love to change people's hearts?" I said.

"Dat's right. Dat's right. We're watchin fe dem now. Becuz now is de time dat if people 'eard about love and dey 'arden dere 'earts, it's not goin' ta be pretty fe dem. If dey 'ear de last angel, we are de last angel now ta

282

seh 'People get ready, get yah 'eart's ready. Get ya 'earts ready ta meet de future—LIVITY.' If dey want ta enjoy de future, LIVITY, people should change de wicked t'oughts and de evils t'oughts wit'in dem. Den ya gettin' ready."

"People are already suffering now," Julia said. "Even now it's not a pretty thing because they're not really happy."

"Babylon now sees dat Rastafari was talkin' about dis true love and dey used ta beat it out of Rastafari. Becuz dey used ta seh dat Rasta should nevah use de word 'love' at any time. So right now dey looking fe it. Dey want crime and violence ta stop. And if dey would 'ave treated de people wit' love from all dese years, den de people would 'ave been educated by dis. De people would be educated by dis love. So when Bob come, it was such a time when 'e start ta reveal dis t'ing as a brave soulJAH. And de stone dat de builder refused, dey try ta grab it up right now."

"What do you mean by 'the stone that the builder refused'?" I asked.

"De stone dat de builder refused in de mornin', dey find out dat is de 'ead cornerstone becuz dey used ta seh, 'Away wit' ya becuz ya speakin' 'bout love. Ya becomes a Rasta now. Come talk 'bout love.' And now dey runnin' fe it. Dey diggin' up fe it. Dey diggin' up fe de true love."

"You know that because the press is saying they're looking for it now?" I asked.

"Ya. Ya. De wurld know dat. And all de people in all parts of de wurld where it is war, dey lookin' fe bettah treatment. Dey lookin' fe dis kind 'earted spirit ta rule dem. So wit'out dis great love, anyone would not 'ave dat great kind 'earted spirit from de 'eart ta deal wit' de masses. Dey all need dis touch, dis love touch wit'in de 'eart, so dat dey cayn know dat dese people need ta enjoy demselves and dey need ta be free. People need ta be free and live 'appy on dis land. Becuz dis earth is big enough fe everyone fe who born already and who doan't born yet. Dis place is 'ere fe all of us. And we need ta be 'appy toget'er, ta enjoy dis earth de right MAXIMUM way. Everyday I pray fe dis system and I cayn see dat my prayer is comin' up. It's comin ta a perfect standstill where people will be able ta jump and shout and seh 'Yes! 'Ere comes de day where we fear no more!'" and with this he busts into a big belly laugh while Julia, almost in tears, joyously, breathlessly says "YES! YES!"

"Yes. Dat's true. I know dat we're goin' ta be on de paradise land toget'er, ya know, ta enjoy all dis," he says, his voice quieter but still confident. He lights the pipe and draws in the ganja. The flame of the lighter illuminates his face in the darkness—his royal, noble features aglow.

His vision was like the strangler fig we were sitting under. Like this tree, Rasta had started out small and had been, slowly over many years, dropping its roots to the ground and it would now soon take over Babylon, something that was once as strong as the stone house had been. One Love would absorb Babylon into itself, until Babylon was gone and there was only Rasta, only One Love.

Shortly before dawn the next morning we stopped at Scram's to say goodbye before driving to MoBay. Irman and Bell were there with him. As we were saying our goodbyes, Alicia started crying, hugging everyone.

"I don't want to leave them," she said, crying profusely, hugging Scram around the waist, her head buried in his chest. "I don't want to go."

"Sweetheart," I said, "you're not saying goodbye to new friends. You're saying hello to family who will be your family your whole life."

"Ain't dat de truth, mon," Scram said, walking us to the car. "Ya be back soon. It just right around de corner."

As we drove off, Alicia settled in the back seat to sleep awhile. "Now that we're going back," she said between sobs, "I realize that all the money and all the cars and all the big houses there just don't mean anything to me anymore. I don't even know if I will be able to relate to my friends."

"It'll be OK, sweetheart," I said reassuringly. "You know when I had my office a few years ago and Harley and Judith and Robert and Anna all worked with me, I knew they didn't always understand me. They weren't always seeing what I was seeing but they were open-hearted people and I had a blast everyday at the office. That's the way it will be for you. When you start high school next month, you're going to have a blast with some open-hearted friends."

"And you'll spread One Love all over that school," Julia said laughing.

With that, she settled down and fell fast asleep. Julia and I looked at each other and smiled and thought chamo, chamo ❟

Epilogue

This was not the end of our journey, just the beginning. When we completed this book in 2001, we decided to introduce it in Jamaica on Bob Marley's 57th birthday and to invite all Jamaicans to help complete Bob's mission of teaching One Love to the world. Mama B, Bob's mother, agreed to let us use his home in Kingston, now a museum, to stage our first public event. Called *The Gathering of the Healers*, it included reggae recording artists Luciano and Abijah, Denroy Morgan, father of reggae group Morgan Heritage, author Dr. Dennis Forsythe, author of *Rastafari:For The Healing of the Nations*, Rasta Elder Mortimo Planno, and then-prime ministerial candidate and conscious talk show host, Antonnette Haughton.

Between 2002 and 2005, we hosted 54 free *One Love Concerts and Events* in Jamaica, taking Abijah and other conscious reggae artists into schools, especially in the ghettos. All carried forward a message of love, equality and forgiveness and donated their time and talent for free. In 2004, our *One Love Leadership Event* took the message to the Jamaican leadership. Every February 6, Bob's birthday, we hosted large public concerts in downtown Kingston.

Our largest concert was on Bob's 60th, when the Jamaican government cordoned off all of the downtown area and over 12,000 people attended live and over 2 million watched on TV or listened on radio. Joining us that night on stage were Bob's daughter, Stephanie, and her children, Governor General Sir Howard Cooke, reggae recording artists Luciano, Abijah, Bunny Wailer, Culture, Ernie Smith, Mackie Conscious, Junior Reid, Warrior King, Prezident Brown, Fanton Mojah, and gospel artists, Janine and Robert Bailey. Alicia gave the opening address.

We then followed this "Bob Marley thread" to two Native American tribes in Arizona who are big Marley and reggae fans, the Havasupai and the Hopi. Between 2005 and 2008, we hosted 20 *One Love Concerts* on their reservations and in other venues in the U.S. These journeys are chronicled in our two sequels, *The Gathering of the Healers:The Healing of the Nations* (2003) and *The Beauty Path:A Native American Journey into One Love* (2006). These connections then led us to our next message of One Love coming from the Mayan Elders in Guatemala. This journey is covered in our latest book *2012:The Transformation from the Love of Power to the Power of Love* (2008).

A year or so after Rasta Heart was released, we started getting letters from Rastafarian inmates and prison groups asking for copies of the books. After reading the books, they would often write us letters—some of the most eloquent, heartfelt responses we have ever received. Julia and I started to make monthly visits to several of the groups at nearby maximum-security and youth facilities.

We have also hosted several prison-wide *One Love Concerts* featuring Laura Reed, a conscious recording artist from Asheville, and her band, Deep Pocket. Our goal is to remind these incarcerated brothers that if you teach and learn love behind prison walls, you are free, freer than you were on the outside, and that you are heading Home—no matter what you did in past or what was done to you. Julia talks to them about going within and finding peace and joy through meditation, a peace that was available to anyone, anywhere—even behind prison walls. The response in the meetings and concerts has been incredible—open-hearted, enthusiastic and healing.

During the warm months, we attend several of the many outdoor reggae and music festivals that spring up every year nationwide. We set up our booth, sell our books and reason with the festival-goers, mostly in their teens and twenties. Sometimes we are invited to speak from the stage. This has led us to host our own festival, *The Gathering of the Peacemakers:Getting Ready for the Changes*.

The Gathering of The Peacemakers
Getting Ready for the Changes
(Our Summer Program in the NC Mountains)

6 Days of Conscious Instruction
6 Nights of Conscious Music

Every summer beginning in 2008, we are holding an event called *The Gathering of the Peacemakers:Getting Ready for the Changes*. The festivals' goal is to prepare ourselves mentally, physically, emotionally, and spiritually for the coming changes so that we might share this peace with others.

The gathering includes six nights of live music and six days of conscious instruction. In the evening, there are live performances from some of the best conscious recording artists in the Southeast, followed by drumming circles. During the day are workshops in solar energy, bio-diesel fuels, living off-the-grid, waste recycling, organic gardening, co-housing and sustainable communities, alternative and holistic healing techniques, wilderness tracking and survival, yoga, meditation, Hopi and Mayan prophecies, building your own house, handling your money, living on less, creating and sustaining loving unions, conscious parenting and finding mission in life.

The festivals are held at Holston Camp in the Blue Ridge Mountains near Banner Elk, NC. The camp includes camping, lodge rooms, dorms and rustic cabins plus a cool mountain climate, swimming lake, climbing wall, dining hall, the Bob Marley Coffee Shop and two meditation tipis. Horseback riding, mountain biking, rafting and tubing are nearby.

Various Native American, Rasta and Mayan Elders join us as "Elders-in-Residence." Attendance is limited to a few hundred and the cost is a few hundred. Care to join us? It is a summer vacation that will change your life! Check it out at www.onelovepress.com.

CONTACT INFO

PEOPLE IN THIS BOOK:

UNITED STATES:
Julia & Robert Roskind
P.O. Box 2142
Blowing Rock, NC 28605
(828) 295-4610
E-mail: roskind@boone.net
Website: www.rastaheart.com
We love hearing from our readers!

PORT ANTONIO:
RAMSCRAM/SCRAM (Thomas Anderson)
9 Nuttall Road
Port Antonio, Jamaica
(876) 887-5918
(Scram is available to take you around to the people and places featured in this book. You can also go by his shop on the main street on the west side of Port Antonio next to the high school.)

MOORE TOWN:
BOOKSON (Major Charles Aarons)
 Moore Town Post Office
 Portland, Jamaica, West Indies
(Seeking assistance to start a Maroon museum in Moore Town and distribute Maroon herbal cures.)

NEGRIL AREA:
BONGO ROACH (Joseph Roach)
(876) 857-8319
Darliston
Westmoreland, Jamaica

RED (Maurice Lynch)
(876) 362-9007
Negril Post Office
Westmoreland
Negril, Jamaica
(Red can act as your guide in the Negril area. Go by and see Errol at the Royal Kitchen.)

HOTELS:
PORT ANTONIO AREA:
SAN SAN TROPEZ
San San Bay P.O.
Portland, Jamaica W.I.
(876) 993-7213/7713
FAX: (876) 993-7399
E-mail: asciuto@bigfoot.com/info@sansantropez.com
WEBSITE:www.sansantropez.com

MONTEGO BAY:
HALF MOON
Box 2560, Half Moon Post Office
Rose Hall, Jamaica
(876) 953-2490
(800) 626-0592 (reservations only)
FAX: (876) 953-2558
Website: www.halfmoon.com.jm

NEGRIL:
ROCK HOUSE
P.O.Box 3024
West End Road
Negril, Jamaica
(876) 957-4373
FAX: (876) 957-0557
E-mail: info@rockhousehotel.com
Website: www.rockhousehotel.com

CAR RENTALS/TAXI:
Chalis Car Rental
Shop 9C
32 Queen's Drive
White Sands P.O.
Montego Bay, Jamaica
(876) 952-9361
FAX: (876)952-3793
E-mail: chaliscarrental@yahoo.com
TAXI: MICHAEL
(He lives in Port Antonio but will take you there from MoBay reasonably and dependably.)
(876) 361-5546

TOURS, ATTRACTIONS & SHOPS:
REACH FALLS
(876) 993-6138
(Check out Renny's craft stall.)

THE ORIGINAL MAYFIELD FALLS
(876) 957-3075 (Negril)
(876) 952-6634 (MoBay)
FAX: (876) 957-3075
E-mail: mayfieldfalls@caribbeanet.com
(Ask for Ras Thomas as a guide.)

TO ORDER BOOKS

For Credit Card Orders:
visit us at www.rastaheart.com

For Money Orders or Check:
Send $14.95 per book plus
$4.95 S&H for 1st book/$2.00 ea. additional book
(International $9.00 S&H 1st book/$3.00 ea. add. book)
Make Checks to: One Love Press

For Wholesale Orders:
Visit us at www.rastaheart.com

One Love Press
P.O. Box 2142
Blowing Rock, NC 28605
(828) 295-4610 FAX: (828) 295-6901
Email: roskind@boone.net
Website: www.rastaheart.com